AMERICAN HISTORY AND NATIONAL SECURITY

Donald A. Ritchie

John J. Patrick

Clair W. Keller

James R. Leutze

Series Editor
Richard C. Remy

▲ Mershon Center, The Ohio State University

▲ Addison-Wesley Publishing Company

Menlo Park, California · Reading, Massachusetts · New York
Don Mills, Ontario · Wokingham, England · Amsterdam · Bonn
Sydney · Singapore · Tokyo · Madrid · San Juan

NATIONAL SECURITY IN A NUCLEAR AGE PROJECT

Project Co-Directors:

James E. Harf, *The Ohio State University*

William H. Kincade, *Georgetown University*

Richard C. Remy, *Mershon Center, The Ohio State University*

B. Thomas Trout, *The University of New Hampshire*

National Advisory Board:

Gordon Cawelti, *Association for Supervision and Curriculum Development*

Maurice East, *George Washington University*

Charles Fox, *Social Studies Supervisors Association*

Alton Frye, *Council on Foreign Relations*

Carole L. Hahn, *Emory University*

Frances Haley, *National Council for the Social Studies*

Gwen Hutchenson, *Council of State Social Studies Specialists*

Effie Jones, *American Association of School Administrators*

William C. Parrish, *National Association of Secondary School Principals*

Robert N. Woerner, *National Congress of Parents and Teachers*

This book is published by the Addison-Wesley Innovative Division.

Cover photo: Library of Congress (facsimile supplied by Independence Hall/ Photographed by Wayland Lee/Addison-Wesley Publishing Company)

This publication was developed at the Mershon Center by the National Security in the Nuclear Age Project with support from the Ford Foundation (International Affairs Program), the W. Alton Jones Foundation, and the Mershon Center. The ideas expressed here do not necessarily reflect the opinions or policies of these organizations.

Copyright (c) 1989 by the Mershon Center. All rights reserved.

ISBN 0-201-26189-8
ABCDEFGHIJKL-ML-89321098

American History and National Security

Contents

ABOUT THE AUTHORS vi

PREFACE vii

INTRODUCTION FOR TEACHERS ix

I. THE AMERICAN NATION IS ESTABLISHED 1

Lesson 1: The Constitution and National Security
Lesson Plan for Teachers 3
Student Material 5

Lesson 2: National Security With Liberty in *The Federalist*, Numbers 4, 23, 41
Lesson Plan for Teachers 13
Student Material 17

Lesson 3: Neutrality and Security: Washington's Proclamation of 1793
Lesson Plan for Teachers 23
Student Material 27

Lesson 4: National Security and Dissent: The Alien and Sedition Acts, 1798
Lesson Plan for Teachers 31
Student Material 33

II. THE AMERICAN NATION DEVELOPS AND EXPANDS BEFORE THE CIVIL WAR 37

Lesson 5: The Louisiana Purchase and National Security, 1803
Lesson Plan for Teachers 39
Student Material 41

Lesson 6: Acquisition of East Florida and National Security, 1819
Lesson Plan for Teachers 45
Student Material 47

Lesson 7: The Debate Over Military Academies
Lesson Plan for Teachers 51
Student Material 55

Lesson 8: The Monroe Doctrine and Security in the Western Hemisphere, 1823
Lesson Plan for Teachers 59
Student Material 65

continued

Lesson 9:   Should I Support President Polk's War?
             Senator John C. Calhoun's Decision, 1846
             Lesson Plan for Teachers 69
             Student Material 71

III. THE CIVIL WAR 75

Lesson 10:   President Lincoln Maintains National Security:
             The Case of Maryland, 1861
             Lesson Plan for Teachers 77
             Student Material 81

Lesson 11:   Press Censorship During the Civil War
             Lesson Plan for Teachers 83
             Student Material 87

Lesson 12:   Operation Crusher, 1864
             Lesson Plan for Teachers 89
             Student Material 93

IV. AMERICA BECOMES A WORLD POWER 97

Lesson 13:   Purchasing Alaska
             Lesson Plan for Teachers 99
             Student Material 101

Lesson 14:   National Security Through Naval Power:
             Ideas of Alfred Thayer Mahan
             Lesson Plan for Teachers 105
             Student Material 107

Lesson 15:   Two Views of Expansionism
             Lesson Plan for Teachers 111
             Student Material 113

Lesson 16:   Shaping the "Open Door Policy"
             Lesson Plan for Teachers 117
             Student Material 119

Lesson 17:   The Ethics of the Panama Canal
             Lesson Plan for Teachers 123
             Student Material 125

Lesson 18:   American Intervention in the Mexican Revolution, 1914
             Lesson Plan for Teachers 129
             Student Material 131

V. AMERICA AND TWO WORLD WARS 135

Lesson 19:   Preparing the Public for the Draft
             Lesson Plan for Teachers 137
             Student Material 139

continued

Lesson 20: Failure of the Treaty of Versailles
　　Lesson Plan for Teachers 141
　　Student Material 145

Lesson 21: National Security Through Air Power:
Ideas of Billy Mitchell
　　Lesson Plan for Teachers 151
　　Student Material 153

Lesson 22: Public Opinion and National Security Before World War II
　　Lesson Plan for Teachers 157
　　Student Material 161

Lesson 23: B-17s: Development and Use of a Weapons System
　　Lesson Plan for Teachers 167
　　Student Material 171

Lesson 24: Deciding to Use the Atomic Bomb, 1945
　　Lesson Plan for Teachers 177
　　Student Material 181

VI. AMERICA IS CHALLENGED BY THE COLD WAR 187

Lesson 25: Mr. X and Containment
　　Lesson Plan for Teachers 189
　　Student Material 191

Lesson 26: The Vandenberg Resolution and NATO
　　Lesson Plan for Teachers 195
　　Student Material 199

Lesson 27: A Network of Alliances
　　Lesson Plan for Teachers 203
　　Student Material 207

Lesson 28: The Domino Theory
　　Lesson Plan for Teachers 211
　　Student Material 215

Lesson 29: Ex Comm and the Cuban Missile Crisis
　　Lesson Plan for Teachers 221
　　Student Material 223

Lesson 30: Why Was the SALT II Treaty Never Ratified?
　　Lesson Plan for Teachers 227
　　Student Material 229

ABOUT THE AUTHORS

Clair W. Keller is a Professor of History and Secondary Education at Iowa State University. Dr. Keller has done research on the teaching of history in secondary schools and has written textbooks and other learning materials for secondary school students of American history, including *Lessons on the Federalist Papers* with co-author John Patrick.

James R. Leutze has recently become President of Hampden Sydney College having been Dowd Professor of History and Chair of the Peace, War and Defense program at University of North Carolina at Chapel Hill. He is author of the award winning *Bargaining for Supremacy: Anglo-American Cooperation, 1937-41* and a biography of Admiral Thomas C. Hart.

John J. Patrick is Director, Social Studies Development Center and ERIC Clearinghouse for Social Studies/Social Science Education at Indiana University, where he is also a Professor of Education. Dr. Patrick has done research and evaluation studies on the teaching of civics, government, and history in secondary schools and has written several widely used textbooks and other learning materials for secondary school students.

Richard C. Remy is Director of the Citizenship Development for a Global Age Program at the Mershon Center, The Ohio State University, where he holds appointments in the Department of Political Science and the College of Education. Dr. Remy has written textbooks for secondary school courses on government and civics and is co-author with John Patrick of *Lessons on the Constitution* for Project '87 of the American Historical Association and the American Political Science Association.

Donald A. Ritchie is Associate Historian, United States Senate Historical Office. Dr. Ritchie has taught at various grades, from Headstart to high school, as well as junior college and university level. He is the author of *James M. Landis: Dean of the Regulators* and *Heritage of Freedom: History of the United States*, a leading high school textbook. He serves as editor of the "Historical Series" of executive session transcripts of the Senate Foreign Relations Committee, and is President of the Oral History Association.

PREFACE

National security is a vital concern increasingly shared by young people and adults alike. In a world of opposing values and interests, armed nations continue to seek control over their own affairs and to influence others. In the American system of government, it is imperative that citizens understand and participate constructively in the debates about our national security. Yet it has been these very issues that many have felt least able to influence, since they thought that only "experts" could understand the complexities of security policy.

The National Security in the Nuclear Age (NSNA) Project has been designed to provide for the systematic inclusion of the subject of national security into American high schools. From its inception in 1983 the NSNA Project has closely collaborated with those responsible for implementing new ideas in the classroom. Secondary school teachers and curriculum specialists, including social studies consultants of state education agencies, have been continuously involved in the planning and development of NSNA activities. In June 1983, representatives from 43 state education agencies met with the NSNA leadership to assess the state of education about national security and to give advice about school needs. This group of statewide leaders and other social studies educators have continued to provide valuable input into how this project can help schools strengthen instruction about national security.

Three types of books have been developed by the NSNA Project for this Mershon Center *National Security Series*. The first is, *Teaching About National Security*. This book discusses the meaning of national security along with themes for curriculum building. It describes eight strategies for teaching about national security topics complete with sample lessons illustrating each strategy. These strategies include concept learning, decision making, role-playing, and primary sources.

The second is, *Essentials of National Security: A Conceptual Guidebook for Teachers*. This book contains ten chapters written expressly for educators by leading national security scholars. It provides a conceptual overview of the field of security studies for the educator who wants to learn about the field.

The third is a series of five books of lessons of which this book is one. Each book contains approximately 30 lessons, designed to be infused into standard high school social studies courses (American history, American government, economics, world history, and world geography). A full discussion of how these books of lessons can be used is found in the section, "Introduction For Teachers."

Major activities of NSNA have been carried out with the support of the Ford Foundation (International Affairs Program) which funded the meetings with education leaders and the development of six of the books found in the Mershon Center *National Security Series*. Additional support has been received from the W. Alton Jones Foundation to build upon the initial efforts of NSNA by creating a comprehensive and continuing program of support activities for educators across the nation.

We wish to thank a number of individuals who have played an instrumental role in this project. First, we are grateful to Enid Schoettle of the Ford Foundation who offered initial encouragement and continuing guidance, and to her colleague Gary Sick. In addition to the normal kinds of support provided by program officers, they lent their considerable expertise in the field of national security studies to help us design a better strategy for meeting the needs of educators.

Jeffrey Kelleher of the W. Alton Jones Foundation also provided financial support that has sustained the vitality of our commitment to pre-collegiate education about national security.

A note of special thanks is also due Charles F. Hermann, Director of the Mershon Center, who has allowed us to take full advantage of the Center's physical and intellectual capacities.

Mark Denham has served ably as the NSNA Project's Administrative Assistant, a position held originally by Marie Houget. Mark competently managed the day-to-day operations of the Project for the Co-Directors and also made important editorial contributions to the various books in this series.

Saundra Jones served as Editorial Research Assistant to Richard Remy, the editor of this series. In that capacity she made invaluable contributions to the design and editing of the five books of lessons in the series. The books would not have been completed without her hard work and eye for detail.

Patricia Geschwent deserves special recognition for her tireless and creative efforts to make use of a new computer word processing system to design the format for these books and to produce the initial versions of them.

Edith Bivona and Peggy Robinson provided secretarial services in the first stages of the Project. Sherry Thomas and Linda Little competently and cheerfully completed all the word processing for the Project books. Their work was consistently accurate and on time.

The Project owes its gratitude to a multitude of educators who have offered suggestions and inspiration at workshops across the nation. Deserving of special mention is the Council of State Social Studies Supervisors (CS-4) whose members participated in the design of the Project and who offered critical advice on numerous occasions.

Members of our National Advisory Board provided helpful suggestions on the design and format of the lessons.

George Grantham of the U.S. Department of Defense Dependents Schools, Germany Region, provided the opportunity for an in-depth workshop with teachers from high schools throughout the Germany Region. We derived many helpful comments from the participants in that workshop.

Louis Grigar of the Texas Education Agency provided a similar opportunity with social studies supervisors from Texas. Especially to be thanked are the educators who field tested and reviewed all the lessons in this volume:

Dennis Cheek, Bitburg High School, Department of Defense Dependents Schools, Germany Region

James Norris, Linden-McKinley High School, Columbus, Ohio

Sandy White, Beechcroft High School, Columbus, Ohio

Each of the lessons in this volume was also reviewed by at least one national security specialist. The scholars who reviewed lessons include:

Linda P. Brady, Emory University
John L. Gaddis, Ohio University
Robert C. Gray, Franklin & Marshall College
James E. Harf, The Ohio State University
William H. Kincade, Georgetown University
Joseph J. Kruzel, The Ohio State University
Michael Mandelbaum, Council on Foreign Relations
Andrew G. Oldenquist, The Ohio State University
B. Thomas Trout, The University of New Hampshire

Finally, as Senior Consultant on Curriculum Development for the series John Patrick provided invaluable counsel that helped steer the development process to a successful conclusion.

The goal of all associated with the NSNA Project has been to help teachers advance young people's knowledge and intellectual skills in preparation for responsible citizenship. We offer this volume as one contribution to achieving that goal.

James E. Harf
William H. Kincade
Richard C. Remy
B. Thomas Trout

INTRODUCTION FOR TEACHERS

by Richard C. Remy

This is a book for teachers of American history. Teachers of civics or government will also find this book useful. The book contains 30 lessons for teachers to use with their students. Each lesson contains material relating to American history and national security such as a case study, or a set of data, or excerpts from a primary source that can be readily duplicated for student use. Each lesson also contains suggestions for the teacher on how to use the material. *Permission is granted to teachers to make copies of these lessons for use with their students.*

Purpose of the Lessons

The purpose of this book is to help teachers strengthen education about national security concepts and issues in their American history courses. The lessons presented here do not duplicate textbook content. Nor are they presented as a comprehensive survey of the field of national security. Rather, they are designed to introduce national security ideas and concepts into the classroom by:

o filling gaps in textbook coverage,
o enriching current textbook treatment of topics relevant to national security,
o enlivening the curriculum with ideas and information that will help make American history more interesting and understandable to students.

The most basic concern of government is to provide security and safety for people and their property--security and protection against foreign powers which might invade a country or threaten its vital interests in other ways, and security against internal subversion. One former United States Secretary of Defense defines national security as "The ability to preserve the nation's physical integrity and territory; to maintain its economic relations with the rest of the world on reasonable terms; to protect its nature, institutions, and governance from disruption from outside and to control its borders."

In today's world of nuclear weapons, spy satellites, international terrorists and huge armies, the task of providing for national security and the common defense is critically important. A democracy such as ours needs citizens who have an understanding of the problems of national security and an ability to acquire information, form judgments and make thoughtful decisions about national security policies and issues.

Awareness of the societal need for citizen competence with regard to national security issues has been increasing. For many years national security had been considered the narrow preserve of specialists and policymakers. Knowledge and background in the subject were considered too technical even for the most attentive citizens, let alone average students.

This situation has changed. There has been growing recognition among specialists and policymakers that as a democracy the United States cannot successfully plan for its security in today's world without broad citizen support and responsible participation in policy processes by an informed public. This recognition has been paralleled by an increasing awareness among educators that fulfillment of their obligation for citizenship education in our global age requires attention to national security topics. The lessons in this book are designed to help teachers meet this responsibility.

How to Use the Lessons

This book contains 30 **"Lessons."** Each lesson is a complete instructional activity designed to introduce particular content and/or skills. The lessons are not intended to constitute a coherent, separate course or unit of study. Rather, they are intended as a large pool of teaching resources which can be used variously by different teachers to infuse national security topics into their ongoing curriculum. Many teachers will select only a few lessons to supplement given parts of their course. Others may use a large number of lessons.

Different choices about how to use the lessons are possible because each lesson is designed to be used singly, without reference to any other lesson in this volume. Nearly every lesson can be completed in one to three class meetings. A very few lessons might take a little longer to complete.

Fit With Curriculum

The lessons are designed to help teachers deal more effectively with topics relevant to national security that are rooted in American history. They do not call upon you, the teacher, to depart significantly from your course objectives and content. Rather, lessons are organized and presented to help you link them to the content of commonly used textbooks.

The lessons are grouped in six **"Sections"** corresponding to major divisions of subject matter in an American history course. Section I contains four lessons relevant to the creation of the Constitution. Section II has five lessons on topics associated with the expansion of the nation prior to the Civil War. Section III contains three lessons on the Civil War. Section IV presents six lessons dealing with the emergence of America as a world power. Section V includes six lessons related to World War I and World War II. Section VI contains six lessons relevant to events since the end of World War II. Each section contains an **"Overview for Teachers,"** a brief essay on the national security dimensions of the historical period covered by the section.

Format of the Lessons

Each lesson begins with a **"Lesson Plan and Notes for Teachers."** This material includes a description of the main points or themes of the lesson, the American history concepts taught in the lesson, the instructional objectives, and suggested procedures for teaching the lesson. In addition, there are suggestions about connections of each lesson to the content of American history textbooks. These suggestions can provide guidance about how each lesson can be used to supplement the content of standard textbooks.

The teacher material is followed by one or more **Handouts** for students that can be readily duplicated for student use. It is expected that teachers will duplicate and distribute copies of the student materials to each student. The student materials always contain exercises and application activities. Application exercises require students to use information and ideas presented in the Handout in order to indicate achievement of lesson objectives.

A particular lesson may have some exercises that are quite challenging and complex. Some teachers may wish to have all of their students complete all of the application exercises at the end of a lesson. However, other teachers may not want to spend that much time on a given lesson; so they will use the application activities selectively. Another alternative is to assign easier or simpler exercises to the entire class and to assign more challenging or complex activities only to more capable students. Thus, the more challenging activities would serve to enrich and extend the learning experiences of the advanced students.

Steps in Teaching

Little time is needed to prepare to use a lesson. To teach a lesson, follow these steps.

o Read the **Handouts** for students and the **Lesson Plan and Notes for Teachers**.
o Make and distribute copies of the student materials.
o Follow the teaching suggestions for opening, developing, and concluding the lesson.

The lesson plans are presented as suggestions, not as prescriptions. The materials are organized so that you can easily modify or adapt the lessons and lesson plans to make them more useful in a particular situation. Furthermore, you may want to alter lesson plans so that they conform to instructional procedures or strategies with which you are more comfortable or are able to use more effectively with your students.

Main Features of the Lessons

The lessons in this book were developed to meet a set of criteria about instructional design. These criteria describe the distinctive features of the lessons and our approach to developing them. The statements below summarize these criteria.

1. **Each lesson deals with content that complements and fits with courses in American history.** The use of these lessons can be justified in terms of standard curriculum goals and objectives because the lessons connect directly to major topics in the social science curriculum.

2. **Each lesson complements but does not duplicate textbook treatments of American history.** The lessons have been designed to extend and enrich the subject matter found in widely used textbooks through in-depth study, the use of primary sources, and other strategies.

3. **The content of each lesson is accurate.** National security scholars have reviewed each lesson for content validity. Every effort has been made to present factually accurate information on national security concepts and relevant historical topics.

4. **Each lesson presents national security in a balanced way that does not advocate a particular point of view.** The lessons apply concepts and ideas from the academic field of national security studies to the purposes of citizenship education. They do not try to advance explicitly or implicitly one point of view regarding national security topics as superior to all others. Rather, they seek to advance students' knowledge of the national security dimension of American history as well as their intellectual skills in preparation for responsible citizenship.

5. **Each lesson should enhance student understanding of some aspect of national security.** National security is a fundamental concern of any nation. The lessons have been designed to introduce to the curriculum national security topics such as international conflict and cooperation, arms competition and control, military strategy, policy-making for national defense, the relations of the military to society, citizen's responsibilities to their nation, and the like.

6. **Each lesson includes a clear statement of purposes and well-organized content related directly to those purposes.** Effective instructional materials help teachers and learners know what they are expected to do by clearly stating the purposes or objectives of teaching and learning. Further, such materials structure content logically in terms of the objectives to be achieved.

7. **Each lesson encourages active learning by requiring the students to apply knowledge gained to the completion of various cognitive tasks.** Active learning is the meaningful use of knowledge. It involves organization and interpretation of information, the construction of valid generalizations, and appraisal of ideas. To demonstrate achievement, students must be able to apply or use facts, ideas, or skills as indicated by lesson objectives. Each lesson contains some type of application exercise, which is connected to the purpose(s) of the lesson.

8. **Each lesson presents content and learning activities in ways readily usable by students.** Teachers and curriculum supervisors have reviewed the lessons for instructional validity; how well the lessons actually work in the classroom. Every effort has been made to prepare lessons that are practical and usable in typical classroom situations.

Other Books in the Mershon Center National Security Series

This book is one of five books of lessons in a series prepared by the National Security in the Nuclear Age Project (NSNA), an activity of the Mershon Center's Citizenship Development of a Global Age Program. Each of the other four books contains lessons designed to supplement a specific course. The other books of lessons are:

o *American Government and National Security*
o *Economics and National Security*
o *World Geography and National Security*
o *World History and National Security*

Many of the lessons in each of these books would be relevant to courses in American history.

The project has prepared two additional books. *Essentials of National Security: A Conceptual Guidebook for Teachers* consists of ten chapters written expressly for teachers by leading national security scholars. Each chapter presents basic concepts of this academic field related to a particular topic such as arms control. Taken together, the ten chapters provide teachers with a conceptual map of national security subjects and a guide to additional sources of information.

Teaching About National Security: Instructional Strategies and Lessons for Courses in History, Government, Geography, Economics describes eight strategies for teaching about national security topics complete with sample lessons illustrating each strategy. This book discusses the meaning of national security and incorporates key national security elements into themes for curriculum building. These themes illustrate teaching strategies, such as concept learning, decision making, role playing, and primary sources.

A Brief List of Recommended Books for Teachers

Allison, Graham T., Carnesale, Albert, and Nye, Joseph S., Jr., eds. *Hawks, Doves, and Owls: An Agenda for Avoiding Nuclear War.* New York: W.W. Norton, 1986. This edited volume addresses important questions, including how nuclear war might occur, what the dangers are, and how they can be reduced.

Berkowitz, Bruce D. *American Security: Dilemmas for a Modern Democracy.* New Haven, CT: Yale University Press, 1986. Berkowitz discusses the significant limits placed on democratic societies in achieving national security, including the realities of U.S. politics, and intelligence errors.

Blacker, Coit D. and Dufey, Gloria, eds. *International Arms Control: Issues and Agreements*, 2nd ed. Stanford, CA: Stanford University Press, 1984. This is a description and an insightful history of arms control. Especially helpful is its extensive appendix that includes the actual texts of many agreements.

Chaliand, Gerard, and Rageau, Jean-Pierre. *A Strategic Atlas: Comparative Geopolitics of the World's Powers*, 2nd ed. New York: Harper & Row, 1983. This striking multi-colored atlas begins with a quote from Napoleon, "The policy of a state lies in its geography." That sentiment sums up Chaliand and Rageau's volume. The main portion is dedicated to geographical factors relating to the "Security Perception of the U.S., USSR, and Regional and Middle Powers." Also included are sections on historical context of the contemporary world, economic data, and the military balance. An excellent resource for both classroom and teachers preparation.

Gaddis, John L. *Strategies of Containment: A Critical Appraisal of Postwar American National Security Policy.* New York: Oxford University Press, 1982. This thorough history of U.S.-Soviet relations traces the issue of containment through the postwar era. It is a well documented and sometimes technical history that is readable and interesting.

Jordan, Amos A., and Taylor, William J., Jr. *American National Security: Policy and Process*, Revised ed. Johns Hopkins University Press, 1984. One of the most comprehensive yet readable volumes on the entire U.S. national security policy-making process. The first section deals with the evolution of U.S. security policy. There are also chapters on various actors in the policy-making process-- Congress, the Executive, the military, issues, and regions.

Kruzel, Joseph, ed. *American Defense Annual: 1987-1988.* Lexington, MA: Lexington Books, 1987. This annual publication summarizes the present state of national security studies. It includes chapters on the defense budget, arms control, U.S. defense strategy and other timely topics. Many of the issues are presented with more than one competing viewpoint.

Mandelbaum, Michael. *The Nuclear Question: The United States and Nuclear Weapons, 1946-1976.* Cambridge: Cambridge University Press, 1979. Mandelbaum writes about the history of nuclear weapons and the political issues relating to them with specific reference to U.S. policy. This is an excellent and reasonably brief overview that is useful for the advanced as well as the general reader.

Mandelbaum, Michael. *The Nuclear Revolution: International Politics Before and After Hiroshima.* Cambridge: Cambridge University Press, 1981. Mandelbaum concisely overviews how nuclear weapons have reshaped the foreign policy of nations by comparing the nuclear age with other periods of history since the fifth century B.C. An excellent resource for comparing such issues as the British-German rivalry before World War I and modern tariff controversies with U.S.-Soviet relations.

Millett, Allan R., and Maslowski, Peter. *For the Common Defense: A Military History of the United States of America.* New York: The Free Press, 1984. A thorough treatment of the military aspects of U.S. history with a focus on the formulation of military policy and its impact on both domestic and international developments.

Russett, Bruce. *The Prisoners of Insecurity: Nuclear Deterrence, the Arms Race, and Arms Control.* San Francisco: W. H. Freeman and Company, 1983. A clear and concise overview of basic issues relating to nuclear weapons and strategy. Russett does a commendable job of demystifying these issues by clarifying the most relevant issues, the political, while also providing the essential technical information in an understandable manner.

Sivard, Ruth Leger. *World Military and Social Expenditures.* Washington, D.C.: World Priorities, annual. This yearly compilation of charts, graphics and statistics presents in an arresting manner a wide variety of national security issues. Each year the focus is slightly different. For example the 1985 edition contains graphics on wars and war related deaths in the twentieth century, a map locating nuclear weapons and nuclear power plants in the world, and military control and repression in the third world.

Snow, Donald M. *National Security: Enduring Problems of U.S. Defense Policy.* New York: St. Martin's Press, 1987. Snow's first four chapters are particularly helpful. There he discusses national security as a concept and the U.S. historical experience. Each chapter concludes with an extensive listing of additional resources.

Trout, B. Thomas, and Harf, James E., eds. *National Security Affairs: Theoretical Perspectives and Contemporary Issues.* New Brunswick, NJ: Transaction Books, 1982. A reader with chapters by national security specialists touching on the essential issues of national security with an emphasis on teaching. The introduction is entitled "Teaching National Security" and each of the chapters has been written with the teacher in mind. Topics include U.S. and Soviet strategic thought, the military budget process, arms trade, NATO, and others.

Trout, B. Thomas; Harf, James E.; and Kincade, William, eds. *Essentials of National Security: A Conceptual Guide for Teachers.* Addison-Wesley, Menlo Park, CA, 1989. This is part of the Mershon Center National Security Series. Written specifically for teachers by national security specialists, its ten chapters form a balanced perspective on the basic topics of national security. These include the premises of national security, conflict in the modern era, conflict management, strategy, arms control, policy-making, economics, the military and society and morality and national security.

United States Arms Control and Disarmament Agency. *World Military Expenditures and Arms Transfers.* Washington, D.C.: ACDA. Annual. Not only does this reference work include extensive data on arm transfers but each year's issue summarizes a variety of topics related to military expenditures. There are also included several charts and graphs.

Weigley, Russell. *The American Way of War: A History of United States Military Strategy and Policy.* Bloomington: Indiana University Press, 1977. A survey of U.S. military strategy and policy from 1775 to 1973. This is a readable history, not just of U.S. wars but of all the aspects of national security related to the military and to policy-making in general.

SECTION I

THE AMERICAN NATION IS ESTABLISHED

List of Lessons

This chapter has four lessons, which emphasize national security concerns of Americans during the Founding Period of the nation from the 1780s to 1801. The lessons are

1. The Constitution and National Security

2. National Security With Liberty in *The Federalist*, Numbers 4, 23, 41

3. Neutrality and Security: Washington's Proclamation of 1793

4. National Security and Dissent: The Alien and Sedition Acts, 1798

Overview for Teachers

Taking its place among the other nations of the world, the newly formed United States of America had to face an immediate and central issue: how can this nation assure the security of its citizens in an anarchic international environment? That question must be faced by every nation and, so long as the system of self-reliance prevails as the foundation for national security, it must be faced continuously. For the United States, the answer to this question was caught up in the challenges and issues of designing a new form of government. The form of government was established in a formal document--the Constitution of 1787--specifying the powers and limitations of the government and those who would govern.

The United States Constitution therefore became a critical instrument for defining the continuing response of this country to its security requirements. Some Americans were dissatisfied with the Articles of Confederation that initially established a U.S. Government after the Revolution precisely because it was not strong enough to provide for security. The debates surrounding the new Constitution therefore included the question of security. The central issue was how to craft a government sufficiently strong, as the Preamble would say, "to Provide for the Common Defense" while at the same time ensuring the democratic liberties that had been fought for so hard in the Revolution.

As **Lesson 1** demonstrates, the issue was resolved through the broader device of the separation of powers. The Constitution invested great military authority in the President as Commander-in-Chief while reserving for the Congress both fiscal control over appropriations necessary to support a military establishment and the power to declare war. While the Constitution was being formulated during the Constitutional Convention, however, the issue of national security and the protection of liberty was the source of considerable dispute. Few argued against the need for security, but many were concerned that having a standing military force available to a central government would create conditions too close to those of the monarchical system that had just been shed.

Hence, there was significant difference of opinion as to how individual rights and freedoms could be safeguarded while maintaining a force necessary for security. **Lesson 2** traces the extremes of this issue as they were addressed in *The Federalist* papers supporting the Constitution. Out of this debate came the distinctive provisions of the United States Constitution with regard to the military establishment. There would be strict civilian control over the military and federal dominance of all national military power; although the States were allowed to maintain militias, evident today in the National Guard system, these forces would be subject to federal control.

The success of the Constitutional Convention did not, of course, assure success in the competitive world of international politics. The United States faced difficult challenges to its security from the seemingly constant European conflicts that marked the end of the eighteenth and beginning of the nineteenth centuries.

The first test of American national security decision making came almost immediately when the United States was pressured to take a position in the ongoing war between Great Britain and France. There were supporters of both sides. The ties to Britain, despite the Revolutionary War that had established the United States, remained strong. France on the other hand had come to the aid of the new American state in its war for independence, and many felt that there was a reciprocal obligation now to support France. Both France and England possessed naval forces that could put American interests at risk.

Lesson 3 examines how this test was resolved by President George Washington in a Proclamation of Neutrality. The lesson also discusses the arguments favoring alliance with one side or another.

Later in his Farewell Address to the nation Washington set a similar course that would serve as a foundation for American policy well into the twentieth century. He recommended that the United States not participate in any "entangling" political alliances with the non-democratic powers of Europe, but concentrate instead on trade and commerce, demonstrating by example the superiority of our democratic form of government.

Another difficult issue that had been addressed by the Constitution also had to be faced in the real world of politics. This issue was the extent to which criticism and dissent would be tolerated when national security was at stake. The same conflict between Britain and France evoked strong feelings among the new American citizenry. By 1798 the administration of John Adams, representing the Federalist Party, was engaged in a virtual war at sea against France. Critics, representing the opposing party (the Republicans, though not the same party that exists today), openly challenged Administration policy.

Lesson 4 examines how the issue of dissent versus security was joined in the so-called Alien and Sedition Acts. These Acts were efforts to empower the government to control actions that were critical of policy on the grounds of national security. Although the Acts stood during Adams' Presidency, they were firmly opposed and ultimately discarded by his successor, Thomas Jefferson. The right of dissent in issues of national security had been only unsatisfactorily tested. Although shown to be included under the protection of free speech, the requirements of security policy were able to constrain that protection and, some felt, endanger liberty. The issue was one that would recur in American history.

By the beginning of the nineteenth century, the new American nation had begun to set its course in providing for its security. Following Washington's recommendation, based on the unique insulation that distance provided, the United States chose to remain apart from the "power politics" of the prevailing European nations and concern itself with its own national development.

American History - 1   Lesson Plan and Notes for Teachers

The Constitution and National Security

by John J. Patrick

Preview of Main Points

This lesson treats the relationship between the Constitution and national security in the United States. Weaknesses of government under the Articles of Confederation are discussed with reference to two documents written by George Washington. Provisions for national security in the Constitution of 1787 are emphasized in this lesson.

Connection to Textbooks

All American history textbooks have chapters on the writing and ratification of the Constitution and about main principles of government in the Constitution. This lesson can be used to elaborate upon these treatments of the Constitution during the "Founding Period" of the nation.

Objectives

Students are expected to:

1. know the relationships between constitutional government and national security;

2. identify ideas about weaknesses of government and national security under the Articles of Confederation in two documents by George Washington;

3. identify and interpret ideas about national security in Articles I, II, III, IV, and VI of the Constitution of 1787; and

4. use evidence from the Constitution to support or reject statements about how the government of the United States provides national security.

Suggestions for Teaching the Lesson

Opening the Lesson

o Write these words on the chalkboard: national security, government, constitution. Ask students to reveal what they know about the meaning of each of these words. Then ask: How are national security, government, and constitution related? Finally, ask: what do the three ideas have to do with one another?

o Indicate to students that they will examine the meaning and relationships of national security, government, and constitution during the 1780s in the new nation of the United States of America.

(c) *American History and National Security*. Mershon Center, The Ohio State University

Developing the Lesson

o Have students read the introduction and the first part of the lesson, in the Handout, on "Threats to National Security Under the Articles of Confederation."

o After students examine Documents 1 and 2 in the Handout, require them to answer and discuss the four questions about the documents at the end of the first part of the lesson.

o Ask students to read "Provisions for National Security in the Constitution of 1787" in the Handout. Ask students to answer the questions that follow excerpts from Articles I, II, III, IV, and VI of the Constitution. Conduct class discussion of the questions about these parts of the Constitution and what they have to do with national security.

Concluding the Lesson

o Conclude by turning to the two exercises in the last part of the Handout. These two exercises provide a comprehensive summary and review of the main ideas of the lesson. The exercise also challenges students to use evidence in primary sources to support or reject statements about government and national security under the Articles of Confederation and the Constitution of 1787.

o Ask students to complete these two concluding exercises and to participate in a classroom discussion about them. Ask students to support and explain their answers by referring to evidence in the primary sources in the Handout.

Answers to Concluding Exercises

15. Items "c" and "d" can be supported with evidence from Documents 1 and 2.

16. a. No, Article I, Section 8, Clause 11.

   b. No, Article I, Section 8, Clause 12.

   c. Yes, Article I, Section 8, Clause 1.

   d. No, Article II, Section 2.

   e. No, Article II, Section 1.

   f. No, Article III, Section 3.

   g. No, Article I, Section 9.

   h. Yes, Article IV, Section 4.

   i. No, Article I, Section 8, Clause 14.

   j. Yes, Articles I and II.

American History - 1

The Constitution and National Security

Representatives of the United States and The United Kingdom of Great Britain signed the Treaty of Paris on September 3, 1783, which officially ended the American War of Independence. The thirteen United States of America had declared independence in 1776. In 1783, they won recognition of their separation from Britain--the former "Mother Country" and ruler. For more than 150 years, Americans had looked to The United Kingdom for government--law, order, protection and security. After gaining independence, the thirteen American states were on their own--to govern themselves as they might choose.

In 1781, the United States of America approved the Articles of Confederation--a constitution for the union of thirteen states as one nation. A **constitution**, such as the Articles of Confederation, is a plan or framework for government and a supreme law over those who agree to be governed under its terms.

Major purposes of any government are to provide security and safety for people and their property--security and protection against foreign powers, which might invade a country. And protection against anarchy--wild and disorderly behavior by the people within a country that could endanger the life, liberty, and property of individuals. A constitutional government provides security and safety according to law--formal regulations to which the people or their duly appointed representatives have given consent. The supreme law of the constitution not only governs the actions of all the people--it **limits the powers of the government**, of those chosen by the people to be their governors. These constitutional limits on government are supposed to protect the liberties and rights of the people against rulers who might otherwise (without limits of a constitution) try to oppress them.

Threats to National Security Under The Articles of Confederation

During the 1780s, many Americans were satisfied with their constitution--The Articles of Confederation. Many others, however, feared that this government was too limited--too weak to provide security and safety against foreign threats or disorder within the country. George Washington, the great general and hero of the American War of Independence, was a leading critic of The Articles of Confederation. Examine excerpts from two letters written by Washington, which appear below. As you read these two documents, think about these two questions: What were George Washington's criticisms of the Articles of Confederation? What were his recommendations for improving the government of the United States?

Document 1: Washington's Circular Letter to the American People, Sent to Each of the Thirteen State Governments, 1783

There are four things, which I humbly conceive, are essential to the well being, I may even venture to say, to the existence of the United States as an Independent Power.

    1st.   An indissoluble Union of the States under one Federal Head.

    2dly.   A Sacred regard to Public Justice.

    3dly.   The adoption of a proper Peace Establishment, and

4thly. The prevalence of that pacific and friendly Disposition, among the People of the United States, which will induce them to forget their local prejudices and policies, to make those mutual concessions which are requisite to the general prosperity, and in some instances, to sacrifice their individual advantages to the interest of the Community....

... it will be a part of my duty ... to insist upon the following positions:

That unless the States will suffer Congress to exercise those prerogatives they are undoubtedly invested with by the Constitution [the Articles of Confederation], every thing must very rapidly tend to Anarchy and confusion; That it is indispensable to the happiness of the individual States, that there should be lodged somewhere, a Supreme Power to regulate and govern the general concerns of the Confederated Republic . . . ; That there must be a faithful and pointed compliance on the part of every State, with the late proposals and demands of Congress, or the most fatal consequences will ensure; That whatever measures have a tendency to dissolve the Union, or ... lessen the Sovereign Authority, ought to be considered as hostile to the Liberty and Independence of America....

Document 2: Washington's Reply to a Letter from John Jay, August 1, 1786

Your sentiments that our affairs are drawing rapidly to a crisis, accord with my own.... I do not conceive we can exist long as a nation without having lodged somewhere a power, which will pervade the whole Union in as energetic a manner as the authority of the state governments extends over the several states.

What astonishing changes a few years are capable of producing. I am told that even respectable characters speak of a monarchical form of government without horror. ... What a triumph for our enemies to verify their predictions! What a triumph for the advocates of despotism to find, that we are incapable of governing ourselves, and that systems founded on the basis on equal liberty are ... fallacious. Would to God, that wise measures may be taken in time to avert the consequences we have but too much reason to apprehend....

Questions About Documents 1 and 2

1. What were Washington's ideas about the qualities that a government must have in order to maintain the security, safety, and independence of a nation?
2. Did Washington think that government of the United States under the Articles of Confederation possessed the qualities needed to provide security and safety for the nation?
3. What fears did Washington have about the future of the United States?
4. According to Washington, how could the United States avoid the negative consequences that he feared?

Provisions for National Security in the Constitution of 1787

American leaders responded to Washington's warnings about the need to create a stronger national government, which could more effectively provide national security and safety and promote national interests.

American History - 1   Handout

From May 25 to September 17, 1787, a Constitutional Convention met in Philadelphia. Twelve of the thirteen United States of America were represented at the Convention. Only Rhode Island refused to participate.

The delegates to the Constitutional Convention decided to scrap the Articles of Confederation and write a new constitution. They wanted to increase the powers of the national government in order to provide sufficient protection for the nation's security and for the property rights and civil liberties of individuals. At the same time, they wanted to place limits on the power of the national government to protect the rights of individuals against tyranny from government officials. Their goal was a satisfactory balance between power in government needed to maintain order and security and limits on that power to protect the liberties of the people against the threat of tyranny by rulers.

The new Constitution was submitted to the thirteen states for ratification or approval. By the end of July 1788, ratification conventions in 11 states had approved the Constitution of 1787 and this new frame of government was put into operation. (North Carolina finally ratified the Constitution in 1789 and Rhode Island approved it in 1790.)

The Constitution of 1787, with amendments, is still in effect today as the supreme law of the United States. It contains several important provisions that are directly related to national security--that is, to defense of the United States against threats from foreign powers and from internal dangers such as rebellions and unlawful behavior by citizens or other individuals residing in the United States. At the same time, the Constitution includes important limitations on the powers of the national government, so that the people are protected against tyranny.

Examine excerpts from five Articles or parts of the Constitution that pertain to national security and answer the questions that follow each excerpt.

Article I and National Security

Section One:

All legislative powers herein granted shall be vested in a Congress of the United States, which shall consist of a Senate and House of Representatives. . . .

Section Eight:

The Congress shall have power:

1. To lay and collect taxes, duties, imposts and excises, to pay the debts and provide for the common defense and general welfare of the United States; but all duties, imposts and excises shall be uniform throughout the United States;

2. To borrow money on the credit of the United States;

3. To regulate commerce with foreign nations, and among the several States, and with the Indian tribes;

4. To establish an uniform rule of naturalization, and uniform laws on the subject of bankruptcies throughout the United States;

(c) *American History and National Security*. Mershon Center, The Ohio State University

American History - 1   Handout

5. To coin money, regulate the value thereof, and of foreign coin, and fix the standard of weights and measures;

6. To provide for the punishment of counterfeiting the securities and current coin of the United States;

7. To establish post offices and post roads;

8. To promote the progress of science and useful arts, by securing for limited time to authors and inventors the exclusive right to their respective writings and discoveries;

9. To constitute tribunals inferior to the Supreme Court;

10. To define and punish piracies and felonies committed on the high seas, and offenses against the law of nations;

11. To declare war, grant letter of marque and reprisal, and make rules concerning captures on land and water;

12. To raise and support armies, but no appropriation of money to that use shall be for a longer term than two years;

13. To provide and maintain a navy;

14. To make rules for the government and regulation of the land and naval forces;

15. To provide for calling forth the militia to execute the laws of the Union, suppress insurrections and repel invasions;

16. To provide for organizing, arming and disciplining the militia, and for governing such part of them as may be employed in the service of the United States, reserving to the states respectively, the appointment of the officers, and the authority of training the militia according to the discipline prescribed by Congress;

17. To exercise exclusive legislation in all cases whatsoever, over such district (not exceeding ten miles square) as may, by session of particular states, and the acceptance of Congress, become the seat of the government of the United States, and to exercise like authority over all places purchased by the consent of the legislature of the state in which the same shall be, for the erection of forts, magazines, arsenals, dock-yards, and other needful buildings; and

18. To make all laws which shall be necessary and proper for carrying into execution the foregoing powers, and all other powers vested by this Constitution in the Government of the United States, or in any department or officer thereof.

Section Nine:

[This section sets limits on the powers of Congress, such as the following limitation that relates directly to national security.] . . . The privilege of the writ of habeas corpus shall not be suspended, unless when in cases of rebellion or invasion the public safety may require it. . . . [A writ of habeas corpus requires officials to bring a person whom they have arrested and held in custody before a judge in a court of law. If the judge finds the reasons for holding the prisoner unlawful, then the court frees the suspect. The writ of habeas corpus is a great protection of individuals against government officials who might want to jail them only because they belong to unpopular groups or express criticisms of the government.]

Examining Ideas About National Security in Article I

5. Which of the eighteen powers of Congress--listed in Article I, Section 8--pertain directly to national security? Identify the number of each power and explain what it has to do with national security.

6. Which of the powers of Congress that deal directly with national security are most important? (Identify the three powers that are, in your opinion, the most important to the security of the United States. Explain your choices.

7. What is the main idea of the excerpt from Article I, Section 9 that is presented above? What does it have to do with national security?

Article II and National Security

Section One:

The executive power [to carry out laws] shall be vested in a President of the United States of America. . . .

. . . Before he enters the execution of this office, he shall take the following oath or affirmation: "I do solemnly swear [affirm] that I will faithfully execute the office of President of the United States, and will to the best of my ability, preserve, protect and defend the Constitution of the United States."

Section Two:

The President shall be Commander in Chief of the army and navy of the United States, and of the militia of the several states, when called into the actual service of the United States. . . .

. . . He shall have power, by and with the advice and consent of the Senate, to make treaties, provided two-thirds of the Senators present concur, and he shall nominate and by and with the advice and consent of the Senate, shall appoint ambassadors, other public ministers and consuls. . . .

Examining Ideas About National Security in Article II

8. What do the portions of Article II, Section 1, presented above, have to do with national security?

9. What powers of the executive branch of government--in Article II, Section 2--pertain to national security?

10. How does the President share powers pertaining to national security with the Senate?

(c) *American History and National Security*. Mershon Center, The Ohio State University

American History - 1   Handout

11. Look again at the excerpts from Article I, on a preceding page. How does the President share powers pertaining to national security with the Congress (House of Representatives and Senate)?
12. What is the value of having powers pertaining to national security separated between two branches of the government and also shared by these two branches?

Article III and National Security

Section Three:

Treason against the United States, shall consist only in levying war against them, or in adhering to their enemies, giving them aid and comfort. No person shall be convicted of treason unless on the testimony of two witnesses to the same overt act, or on confession in open court.

The Congress shall have power to declare the punishment of treason. . . .

Article IV and National Security

Section Four:

The United States shall guarantee to every state in this Union a republican form of government, and shall protect each of them against invasion; and on application of the legislature, or of the executive (when the legislature cannot be convened) against domestic violence.

Article VI and National Security

The Constitution, and the laws of the United States which shall be made in pursuance thereof; and all treaties made, or which shall be made, under the authority of the United States, shall be the supreme law of the land; and the judges in every state shall be bound thereby, anything in the Constitution or laws of any state to the contrary notwithstanding. . . .

Examining Ideas About National Security in Articles III, IV, VI

13. What is the main idea of each of the preceding excerpts from the Constitution?

   a. Article III
   b. Article IV
   c. Article VI

14. What does the main idea of each of the preceding excerpts from the Constitution have to do with national security?

   a. Article III
   b. Article IV
   c. Article VI

American History - 1   Handout

Concluding Exercises About the Constitution and National Security

15. Which of the following statements accurately describe George Washington's views about government and national security under the Articles of Confederation? Refer to Documents 1 and 2 in this lesson to find evidence to support your responses to each of the items below.

    a. Under the Articles of Confederation the central government had too much power.

    b. The thirteen state governments respected and obeyed the authority of the central government.

    c. Two likely consequences of government under the Articles of Confederation were anarchy or tyranny by a monarch.

    d. The national security of the United States was in danger due to weaknesses of government under the Articles of Confederation.

16. Which of the following statements is an accurate description of how the Constitution provides for national security? If the statement agrees with Articles I, II, III, IV, VI of the Constitution, then answer **YES**. If it does not agree with the Constitution, then answer **NO**. Identify the numbers of the Articles (I, II, III, IV, VI) that support your answers and refer to the excerpts in this lesson to find evidence in support of your answers.

    a. The President alone has power to declare war.

    b. The President has power to raise and support armies.

    c. The Congress has power to provide for the common defense.

    d. The President alone has power to make alliances between the United States and other nations.

    e. The Congress has power to enforce the Constitution as the supreme law of the United States.

    f. The President decides whether or not a person has committed treason and what the punishment for treason shall be.

    g. Neither the Congress nor the President may ever suspend the privilege of the writ of habeas corpus.

    h. The national government has the responsibility of protecting the states against invaders and uprisings by residents.

    i. As Commander in Chief, only the President has power to make rules for land and naval forces of the United States.

    j. The President and Congress share powers having to do with national security.

(c) *American History and National Security.* Mershon Center, The Ohio State University

American History - 2   Lesson Plan and Notes for Teachers

National Security With Liberty in The Federalist, Numbers 4, 23, 41

by John J. Patrick*

Preview of Main Points

The purpose of this lesson is to increase students' knowledge of the treatment of national security with liberty in *The Federalist*, Numbers 4, 23, and 41. Students are challenged to think about the meaning and value of national security and constitutional limitations on the power of military forces in order to protect liberties of the people.

Connection to Textbooks

This lesson can be used with chapters on the introduction of government in civics and government textbooks and with the standard American history textbook chapter on the period of the writing and ratifying of the Constitution. It also fits typical civics and government textbook treatments of issues about civil liberties.

Objectives

Students are expected to:

1. identify and comprehend ideas on national security with liberty;
2. examine, explain, and appraise ideas on national security with liberty;
3. appraise statements about main ideas on national security with liberty in *The Federalist*, Numbers 4, 23, and 41; and
4. state and justify a position on the relationships of national security with liberty and issues of freedom raised by tensions between security and liberty.

Suggestions for Teaching the Lesson

Opening the Lesson

o Place the following diagram on the chalkboard.

Security _____/_____ Liberty
(Point 1)   (Point 2)

Point out to students that this diagram represents a continuum between the extremes of national security and liberty. Both national security and liberty are important ends of a free

---

*This lesson is taken from *Lessons on the Federalist Papers*, published in 1987 by the Social Studies Development Center, the Organization of American Historians, and the ERIC Clearinghouse for Social Studies/Social Science Education. The lesson is used here with permission of the publishers.

(c) *American History and National Security*. Mershon Center, The Ohio State University

government. Indicate that the mark at the midpoint of the continuum represents a balance between the Point 1 and Point 2 on the diagram. Tell students that Federalists and Antifederalists did not argue for extreme emphasis on either national security or liberty. Rather, both sides debated about where to draw the line between the extreme positions represented by Point 1 and Point 2. In order to survive, a free society needs both national security and liberty, but these goals are often in conflict. Ask why. During this discussion, point out that too much emphasis on liberty, for example, could threaten national security and conversely, too much emphasis on national security could destroy liberty and rights of individuals. Ask students to think of examples of negative consequences associated with too much emphasis on either side of the midpoint in the diagram. Indicate that too much emphasis on national security could lead to tyranny by the government over the people with a consequent loss of individual rights and freedoms. Too much emphasis on liberty could lead to disorder and breakdown of society (anarchy), with the consequent loss of security and safety for property, and liberty of individuals. End this discussion by telling students that a free society is always challenged by the need to find a workable balance between the extremes of unlimited liberty of the people and unlimited power by government to provide national security.

o Have students read the introduction in the Handout, to review ideas about national security with liberty and the relationships between these values in a free society. This introduction sets a context for reading about national security with liberty in excerpts from *The Federalist* Numbers 4, 23, and 41.

Developing the Lesson

o Have students read the excerpt from essay 4 in the Handout and respond to the questions at the end of the document. Repeat this procedure with respect to essays 23 and 41. Emphasize general agreement among Jay, Hamilton, and Madison about purposes of a national government with regard to national security. However, the questions at the end of the essays are also designed to draw students' attention to differences between the authors about where to draw the line between extreme emphasis on national security and liberty. Ask: which author's argument would be closer to the national security side of the diagram used in the opening of the lesson? Ask: which author seems to be most concerned with limiting power to provide national security in order to protect the rights and liberties of individuals?

o Check students' comprehension of main ideas in all three essays by requiring them to complete the exercise at the end of the Handout, "What Is Said About National Security With Liberty in *The Federalist* papers--Numbers 4, 23, 41." Following are the numbers of the statements on this list that agree with *The Federalist*: 13, 14, 16, 17, 18, 19, 22, 24, 25, 26. Require students to provide justifications for their answers with references to excerpts from Numbers 4, 23, and 41 in the Handout.

o You might wish to select three or four provocative statements from this exercise as foils for discussion about civic values. For example, you might ask students to agree or disagree with statements from 4, 23, and 41.

o Have students turn to the five exercises on the last page of the Handout. Ask them to complete items 27-31 in preparation for classroom discussion.

NOTE: Students will need access to a copy of the Constitution.

Concluding the Lesson

o Conduct a classroom discussion of items 27-31 in the set of exercises at the end of the Handout. Require students to support or justify answers by referring to pertinent parts of *The Federalist*. In general, ask students to give reasons for their answers and encourage students to question and challenge one another to ask for justification or support for answers.

o Assign item 31 as the final activity of this lesson. Ask students to write a brief essay (no more than 500 words) in response to this item. Tell students to use at least the following sources of information and ideas: *The Federalist*, the Constitution, and their textbooks on American government, civics, and history.

o Use the essays of one or two students to initiate discussion of item 31. In this discussion, highlight the inevitable tension between the concerns for security and liberty in a free society. Identify and discuss issues raised by these tensions. Point out that the tensions and issues associated with civic values are distinguishing characteristics of a free society.

National Security With Liberty In *The Federalist, Numbers 4, 23, 41*

The preamble to the Constitution of the United States says: "We the people of the United States, in order to form a more perfect Union, establish justice, insure domestic tranquility, provide for the common defense, promote the general welfare, and secure the blessings of liberty to ourselves and our posterity, do ordain and establish this Constitution for the United States of America." Framers of the Constitution established national defense, security, justice, liberty, and general welfare of the people as purposes of the federal government.

The framers of the Constitution of 1787 agreed that a national government has the fundamental responsibility of defending the nation and maintaining security. National Security involves the ability of a nation to protect its borders and territory against invasion or control by foreign powers. In 1787, for example, the framers of the Constitution were concerned about the need to defend their new nation from conquest or domination by powerful European nations, such as Britain, France, and Spain, which held territory in the Western Hemisphere. In addition, national security involves a nation's ability to maintain law and order and protect property rights; in other words, the ability to "insure domestic tranquility." Harold Brown, Secretary of Defense under President Carter, defines national security as "the ability to preserve the nation's physical integrity and territory; to maintain its economic relations with the rest of the world on reasonable terms; to protect its nature, institutions, and governance from disruption from outside; and to control its borders."

The authors of *The Federalist* argued that the Constitution of 1787 would be a bulwark of national defense and security by providing for an energetic and effective federal government, which would have enough power to maintain order internally and protect the nation against external threats. They also argued that the Constitution would limit the powers of government sufficiently to protect individual rights and liberties against officials who might otherwise try to undermine them. The authors of *The Federalist* pointed to constitutional limits on powers of the legislative and executive branches of government, which were designed to secure civil liberties and rights and prevent tyranny. In particular, they stressed the civilian control of military forces provided by the Constitution. For example, the President, a civilian, is the commander in chief of the armed forces, and the Congress decides how much money should be provided to support the nation's armed forces. Nonetheless, critics of the Constitution feared basic freedoms might be lost or unduly limited by leaders more concerned with national defense and security than with civil liberties and rights. The critics preferred the more limited government of the Articles of Confederation to the more powerful government of the Constitution of 1787.

Jay, Hamilton and Madison discussed national defense and security with liberty in *The Federalist* Numbers 4, 23, and 41. They argued that the Constitution of 1787 provided government strong enough for national defense and security and limited enough for a free society. Read the excerpts and answer the questions that follow.

The Federalist, No. 4 by John Jay

> . . . the safety of the people of America against dangers from foreign force depends not only on their forbearing to give just causes of war to other nations, but also on their placing and continuing themselves in such a situation as not to invite hostility or insult. . . .
>
> . . . Wisely, therefore, do they consider union and a good national government as necessary to put and keep them in such a situation as, instead of inviting war, will tend to repress and discourage it. That situation consists in the best possible state of defense, and necessarily depends on the government, the arms, and the resources of the country.

But whatever may be our situation, whether firmly united under one national government, or split into a number of confederacies, certain it is that foreign nations will know and view it exactly as it is; and they will act towards us accordingly. If they see that our national government is efficient and well administered, our trade prudently regulated, our militia properly organized and disciplined, our resources and finances discreetly managed, our credit re-established, our people free, contented, and united, they will be much more disposed to cultivate our friendship than provoke our resentment. If, on the other hand, they find us . . . destitute of an effectual government . . . what a poor, pitiful figure will America make in their eyes! How liable would she become not only to their contempt, but to their outrage, and how soon would dear-bought experience proclaim that when a people or family so divide, it never fails to be against themselves.

Publius

Reviewing Main Ideas in *The Federalist* No. 4

1. What is Jay's main point about how America can maintain national security against threats from foreign nations? Write a topic sentence that states this main idea.

2. How does Jay support or justify his main point about maintaining national security against foreign powers? Write two statements in support of your topic sentence.

3. What is your opinion of Jays main point about national security? (Judge his idea with reference to the situation of the United States in 1787. Judge his idea also with reference to the situation of the United States today.) Write one paragraph, in response to this question, that pertains to 1787. Write a second paragraph that pertains to the United States today.

The Federalist No. 23 by Alexander Hamilton

. . . The principal purposes to be answered by union are these--the common defense of the members; the preservation of the public peace, as well against internal convulsions as external attacks; the regulation of commerce with other nations and between the States; the superintendence of our intercourse, political and commercial, with foreign countries.

The authorities essential to the common defense are these: to raise armies; to build and equip fleets; to prescribe rules for the government of both; to direct their operations; to provide for their support. These powers ought to exist without limitation, **because it is impossible to foresee or to define the extent and variety of national exigencies, and the correspondent extent and variety of the means which may be necessary to satisfy them.** The circumstances that endanger the safety of nations are infinite, and for this reason no constitutional shackles can wisely be imposed on the power to which the care of it is committed. This power ought to be coextensive with all the possible combinations of such circumstances; and ought to be under the direction of the same councils [executive branch of the national government] which are appointed to preside over the common defense. . . .

. . . there can be no limitation of that authority which is to provide for the defense and protection of the community in any matter essential to its efficacy--that is, in any matter essential to the formation, direction, or support of the NATIONAL FORCES. . . .

. . . the Union [United States of America] ought to be invested with full power to levy troops; to build and equip fleets; and to raise the revenues which will be required for the formation and support of an army and navy in the customary and ordinary modes practiced by other governments. . . .

Shall the Union be constituted the guardian of the common safety? Are fleets and armies and revenues necessary to this purpose? The government of the Union must be empowered to pass all laws, and to make all regulations which have relation to them. . . .

Publius

Reviewing Main Ideas in *The Federalist* No. 23

4. According to Hamilton, what are the purposes of a national government with regard to national security?

5. What does Hamilton say about limitations on a national government in carrying out its responsibilities for national security?

6. Do Hamilton's ideas on powers needed by government to provide national security pose any dangers to the rights and liberties of individuals?

7. What dangers to rights and liberties of individuals might result from having a national government too weak to exercise powers needed to provide national security?

The Federalist No. 41 by James Madison

. . . Is the aggregate power of the general government greater than ought to have been vested in it? . . .

. . . in every political institution, a power to advance the public happiness involves a discretion which may be misapplied and abused. They will see, therefore, that in all cases where power is to be conferred, the point first to be decided is whether such a power be necessary to the public good; as the next will be, in case of an affirmative decision, to guard as effectually as possible against a perversion of the power to the public detriment.

That we may form a correct judgment on this subject, it will be proper to review the several powers conferred on the government of the Union; and that this may be the more conveniently done they may be reduced into different classes as they relate to the following different objects: 1. Security against foreign danger; 2. Regulation of the intercourse with foreign nations; 3. Maintenance of harmony and proper intercourse among the States; 4. Certain miscellaneous objects of general utility; 5. Restraint of the States from certain injurious acts; 6. Provisions for giving due efficacy to all these powers.

The powers falling within the first class are those of declaring war . . . ; of providing armies and fleets; of regulating and calling forth the militia; of levying and borrowing money.

Security against foreign danger is one of the primitive objects of civil society. It is an avowed and essential object of the American Union. The powers requisite for attaining it must be effectually confided to the federal councils [national government]. . . .

. . . With what color of propriety could the force necessary for defense be limited by those who cannot limit the force of offense? If a federal Constitution could chain the ambition or set bounds to the exertions of all other nations, then indeed might it prudently chain the discretion of its own government and set bounds to the exertions for its own safety.

How could a readiness for war in time of peace be safely prohibited, unless we could prohibit in like manner the preparations and establishments of every hostile nation? The means of security can only be regulated by the means and the danger of attack. They will . . . be ever determined by these rules and by no others. It is in vain to oppose constitutional barriers to the impulse of self-preservation. It is worse than in vain; because it plants in the Constitution itself necessary usurpations of power, every precedent of which is a germ of unnecessary and multiplied repetitions. If one nation maintains constantly a disciplined army, ready for the service of ambition or revenge, it obliges the most pacific nations who may be within the reach of its enterprises to take corresponding precautions. . . .

A standing force . . . is a dangerous, at the same time that it may be a necessary, provision. On an extensive scale its consequences may be fatal. On any scale it is an object of laudable circumspection and precaution. A wise nation will combine all these considerations; and, whilst it does not rashly preclude itself from any resource which may become essential to its safety, will exert all its prudence in diminishing both the necessity and the danger of resorting to one which may be inauspicious to its liberties.

The clearest marks of this prudence are stamped on the proposed Constitution. The Union itself, which it cements and secures, destroys every pretext for a military establishment which could be dangerous. America united, with a handful of troops . . . exhibits a more forbidding posture to foreign ambition than America disunited, with a hundred thousand veterans ready for combat. . . .

Next to the effectual establishment of the Union, the best possible precaution against danger from standing armies is a limitation of the term for which revenue may be appropriated to their support. This precaution the Constitution has prudently added [the provision in Article I that Congress has power, during a two year period, to provide or withhold funds for the army].

. . . the Constitution has provided the most effectual guards against danger from [a standing army of permanent military establishment that might destroy a free government and a free society].

. . . nothing short of a Constitution fully adequate to the national defense and the preservation of the Union can save America from as many standing armies as it may be split into States or Confederacies, and from such a progressive augmentation of these establishments in each as will render them as burdensome to the properties and *ominous to the liberties of the people as any establishment that can become necessary under a united and efficient government must be tolerable to the former and safe to the latter [the liberties of the people]. . . .

Publius

Reviewing Main Ideas in *The Federalist* No. 41

8. According to Madison, what are the responsibilities of a national government in providing national security?

9. Why is national security an inescapable duty of a national government?

10. What does Madison say about limiting the power of government in regard to national security?

American History - 2   Handout

11. What are Madison's ideas about dangers to the rights and liberties of individuals from the exercise of power by government to provide national security?

12. According to Madison, how would government under the Constitution of 1787 provide both national security and protection of the rights and liberties of individuals?

What Is Said About National Security With Liberty in *The Federalist* Papers--Numbers 4, 23, 41?

Which of the following statements agree with ideas presented in *The Federalist*, Numbers 4, 23, and 41? **Place a checkmark in the space next to each statement that agrees with ideas in the excerpts from 4, 23, and 41 on national security with liberty.** Be prepared to support and explain your choices by referring to specific parts of *The Federalist* numbers 4, 23, and 41.

_____ 13. National unity and strength are deterrents to attack by a foreign nation.

_____ 14. A fundamental purpose of any national government is providing security for the nation against threats from foreign powers.

_____ 15. Tyranny is acceptable if it is imposed in order to defend the national and provide national security.

_____ 16. A military establishment is both necessary and dangerous to the protection of civil liberties and rights.

_____ 17. There should be constitutional limits upon power exercised by military leaders.

_____ 18. The Constitution provides for civilian control of military forces as a means to control abuses of power by military leaders.

_____ 19. A nation without an effective military establishment is in danger of losing its security and freedom.

_____ 20. A nation without a standing army will have more freedom than a nation with a strong military establishment.

_____ 21. The more limited a national government is, the freer the people will be who live under the government.

_____ 22. A national government should have sufficient authority to maintain armed forces and regulate them on behalf of the people, in order to achieve goals or interests of the community.

_____ 23. National defense and security are more important than liberty as fundamental purposes of a national government.

_____ 24. The "power of the purse" is an effective means for controlling the power of the military on behalf of the people, which is granted to Congress in the Constitution.

_____ 25. Constitutional government in a free society is designed to balance power needed for national defense and security, with limits on the power needed to protect liberties and rights of the people.

_____ 26. A fundamental purpose of national government in a free society is to seek both security and liberty for the people it serves.

(c) *American History and National Security*. Mershon Center, The Ohio State University

American History - 2   Handout

Examining Ideas About National Security With Liberty

Refer to the preceding excerpts from *The Federalist* 4, 23, and 41 to find ideas and information on which to base answers to the following questions. Be prepared to give reasons for answers with references to specific parts of these excerpts.

27. What are characteristics of a national government and society that are capable of providing national security?

28. Madison says in *The Federalist*, No. 41: "A standing force . . . is a dangerous, at the same time it may be a necessary, provision. On an extensive scale its consequences may be fatal. On any scale it is an object of laudable circumspection and precaution. A wise nation will combine all these considerations; and, whilst it does not rashly preclude itself from any resource which may become essential to its safety, will exert all its prudence in diminishing both the necessity and the danger of resorting to one which may be inauspicious to its liberties."

   a. What is the main idea of this quotation?

   b. What is the relationship of Madison's main idea in this quotation and the main purposes of government stated in the Preamble to the Constitution?

   c. To what extent do you agree with this statement of Madison?

29. Refer to Article I, Sections 7, 8, 9; Article II, Sections 1 and 2; and Amendments II and II of the Constitution.

   a. Identify powers and duties of the national government to provide national defense and security.

   b. Identify limitations on military power that are designed to maintain civilian control of the military and to protect civil liberties and rights against abuses of power by military leaders.

30. Compare and contrast the ideas of Hamilton and Madison on national security as expressed in *The Federalist*, 23 and 41.

   a. To what extent do they agree or disagree?

   b. To what extent do Hamilton and Madison have different ideas about the relationship of national security to liberty?

   c. To what extent do you agree with the positions on national security of Hamilton, Madison, or both of them?

31. a. How are national defense and security related to civil liberty as values of government and citizenship in a free society?

   b. How might strong emphasis on national defense and security threaten civil liberties?

   c. How might lack of concern for national defense and security threaten civil liberties?

   d. What are some characteristics of a constitutional government that is designed to achieve security with liberty?

(c) *American History and National Security*. Mershon Center, The Ohio State University

American History - 3   Lesson Plan and Notes for Teachers

Neutrality and Security: Washington's Proclamation of 1793

by Clair W. Keller

Preview of Main Points

This lesson examines the controversy generated by George Washington's Proclamation of Neutrality issued in 1793. By taking this action, the United States unilaterally nullified a treaty alliance with France that had been in effect since 1778. As President, Washington had to weigh obligations to a former ally with the security interests of the United States. Washington's actions were opposed by many on the ground that the United States had a moral obligation to aid France in its war against England, much as France had come to our aid against the British during the War for Independence. Washington, however, believed that maintaining a policy of neutrality would best serve American security. This lesson illustrates the difficulty of small nations preserving security in a bi-polar world.

Connection to Textbooks

Most American history textbooks examine foreign policy during Washington's Administration, especially relations with France and Great Britain. This lesson treats Washington's Proclamation of Neutrality in terms of the obligations of one state to another.

Objectives

Students are expected to:

1. explain the circumstances that led Washington to issue his Proclamation of Neutrality;

2. list and evaluate arguments made by those who supported and those who opposed Washington's decision;

3. evaluate Washington's actions deciding whether or not the United States had an "obligation" to aid France; and

4. assess the problem that small nations face in maintaining neutrality in a bi-polar world.

Suggestions for Teaching the Lesson

Opening the Lesson

o Ask students to react to the following situation.

   You have promised a friend to do some work in return for a service that the friend has already completed. Before you can fulfill your promise, the friend moves away from town.

Before the friend leaves town, you are asked to do the work for someone else instead. Would you feel obligated to do the work?

o Pursue with students the meaning of obligations. If the United States was obligated to do something for France under Louis XVI, did that obligation still hold when Louis XVI was replaced by the new Revolutionary Government of France?

Developing the Lesson

o Distribute the Handout to students and ask them to read through Washington's Proclamation. Have them develop understanding of the topic by answering questions 1, 2, and 3 on the excerpt from Washington's Proclamation.

o After students have completed examination of the Proclamation, have them read the remainder of the Handout. Then place students in groups and ask each group to discuss the question, "Did the United States have an obligation to come to the aid of France in its war against Great Britain if asked to do so?" Then have each group respond to the questions at the end of the Handout about the clashing ideas of Hamilton and Jefferson.

o Have each group share its decision with the class. To stimulate discussion you could ask:

What reasons were the most persuasive in making your decision?

Should a nation's foreign policy be based on principle or expediency?

Concluding the Lesson

o Compare the situation the United States found itself in as an emerging and newly independent nation in a bi-polar world with that of other nations in the world today.

o Ask students to comment on the view held by a former Secretary of State who declared that neutrality in a world divided between good and evil (Communism and Democracy) was immoral.

Background Information for Teachers

Reasons of Hamilton and Jefferson for Supporting or Opposing the American Treaty with France

Jefferson's arguments supporting aid to France:

1. Treaties are made between people, not governments that may change. Not only France, but the United States has also changed its government.

2. The same moral law that applies to contracts between individuals applies to contracts between peoples.

3. Contracts can be broken but only when the situation warrants it, such as self-preservation. This situation is not one of self-preservation.

4. Jefferson did not state but implied that France aided the United States in our hour of need. France is a friend. We should not turn our back on them at this time.

5. Elsewhere Jefferson argued pragmatically: There is no need for a hasty decision at this time because in fact France hasn't even asked for our aid.

Hamilton's arguments against maintaining the alliance with France:

1. The U.S. had the right to renounce the treaty because France had changed governments.

2. Receiving France's minister (Genet) without qualification would be an acknowledgement of the treaty.

3. If we have no right to renounce our treaty, then we can be dragged into a dangerous situation by a government we may not approve of.

4. Treaties are made by governments, not by people.

5. Now is the time to renounce treaties, or at least suspend them, until we see what happens, otherwise we could get involved in a dangerous situation over which we have no control.

6. Our best interest will be served by neutrality, not involvement on the side of France.

Suggestion for Additional Reading

Flexner, James Thomas. *George Washington: Anguish and Farewell, 1793-1799.* Boston: Little, Brown & Company, 1972, pp. 25-37.

Flexner presents a sympathetic view of the dilemma faced by Washington in arriving at a decision to issue the Proclamation of Neutrality. He describes the opposing views put forth by Hamilton and Jefferson.

Neutrality and Security: Washington's Proclamation of 1793

Origin of Washington's Proclamation of Neutrality

When war broke out between England and France in 1793, Washington feared that the United States might be dragged into it. He realized that he would have to take immediate action because the United States citizens were eager to engage in privateering against British and French shipping. Many in Congress had been upset with the British policy of seizing American ships engaged in trade with the French West Indies. In addition, the British government had not established formal relations with the United States and continually violated the Treaty of Paris that recognized American independence by occupying forts on American soil in the Northwest Territory. Many in Congress clamored for war. But Washington had been able to avoid war, fearing it would be a disaster.

Since Congress was not in session Washington would not be able to consult with the Senate. He would have to take executive action. Because he was the first President, there was no precedent for issuing any order that prohibited privateering. He also feared that Congress might resent his encroachment on their power to make laws. But the urgency of the situation required Washington to act.

Because of France's assistance in achieving independence, as well as the strong anti-British feeling, there was a great deal of pro-French sentiment. In addition, the United States had signed treaties with the French government. One committed the United States to protect the French West Indies if they should be attacked and the French asked for our help. The second allowed French privateers to bring their prizes (captured British ships) to American ports. It also prohibited France's enemies from using American ports for privateering. During the American Revolution it must be remembered, the French had allowed American privateers to operate from French ports.

Washington met with his Cabinet. Alexander Hamilton took a pro-British position and Thomas Jefferson a pro-French position. The Cabinet, however, agreed unanimously that it would be in the best interest of the United States to issue a proclamation. The Cabinet also agreed to receive the new French Ambassador of the French revolutionary government, Edmund Charles Genet, who had already arrived in Charleston. The cabinet bitterly disagreed over the question of whether the treaties with France remained in force. Hamilton argued no, Jefferson yes. With no agreement in sight, Washington stopped the debate and asked everyone to send him written opinions. The Cabinet also agreed not to call Congress into special session.

Here is what the Proclamation stated:

. . . the duty and interest of the United States require that they would with sincerity and good faith adopt and pursue a conduct friendly and impartial toward the belligerent powers:

I have therefore thought fit by these presents to declare the disposition of the United States to observe the conduct aforesaid toward those powers respectively, and to exhort and warn the citizens of the United States carefully to avoid all acts and proceeding whatsoever which may in any manner tend to contravene such disposition.

And I do hereby also make known that whosoever of the citizens of the United States shall render himself liable to punishment or forfeiture under the law of nations by committing, aiding or abetting hostilities against any of the said powers, or by carrying to any of them those articles which are deemed contraband by the modern usage of nations will not receive the protection of the United States against such punishment forfeiture; and further, that I have given instruction to those officers to whom it belongs to cause prosecutions to be instituted against all persons who shall, within the cognizance of the courts of the United States, violate the law of nations with respect to the powers at war. . . .

-- Philadelphia, the 22d of April, 1793, G. Washington.

Examining Ideas in Washington's Proclamation

1. What is the main idea of Washington's Proclamation?

2. What actions of Americans are prohibited by Washsington's Proclamation?

3. Why did Washington make his Proclamation of 1793? What did it have to do with the national security of the United States?

Hamilton and Jefferson Disagree on Foreign Policy

The Proclamation of Neutrality, as it was called (although as you can see, the word neutrality appears nowhere in it), did try to place the United States on a middle course between the great powers of that time. It sparked bitter public controversy between those who were sympathetic to Great Britain and those who favored France.

In his written opinion to Washington on the question of how to receive Genet and deal with the Treaties with France, Alexander Hamilton urged Washington to receive Genet in such a manner that did not obligate the United States to France. He took the view that the present French government was illegitimate and could not rule but through a blood letting "reign of terror" and was not deserving of American support. International law, he continued, did not automatically continue treaties made with one government to another. Reaffirming the treaties could be seen by Great Britain as a course of war. Furthermore, France, not the United States, would determine if the United States were to remain at peace.

Thomas Jefferson on the other hand, argued that treaties were made between peoples that remained constant and not between governments that changed. He saw no need to provoke a confrontation with France over the treaties by stating conditions upon receiving Citizen Genet. France had not requested aid, if France did, that would be the time to face the issue.

Each of the excerpts below give different positions on the obligations of the United States to keep its alliance with France in 1793. The first was written by Alexander Hamilton who argued against the need to keep our agreements with France. The other was written by Jefferson who urged that the United States should keep its obligation to France.

Statements Written by Alexander Hamilton:

France was a monarchy when we entered into treaties with it, but it has now declared itself a Republic, and is preparing a Republican form of government. As it may issue in a Republic, or a Military despotism or in something else which may possibly render our alliance with it dangerous to ourselves, we have a right of election to renounce the treaty altogether, or to declare it suspended till their government shall be settled in the form it is ultimately to take; and then we may judge whether we will call the treaties into operation again, or declare them forever null. Having that right of election now, if we receive their minister without any qualification, it will amount to an act of election to continue the treaties; and if the change they are undergoing should issue in a form which should bring danger on us, we shall not be then free to renounce them. To elect to continue them is equivalent to the making a new treaty at this time . . . To renounce or suspend the treaties therefore is a necessary act of neutrality.

Statements Written by Thomas Jefferson:

. . . The treaties between the United States and France, were not treaties between the United States and Louis Capet [Louis XVI], but between the two nations of America and France; and the nations remaining in existence, though both of them have since changed their forms of government, the treaties are not annulled by these changes.

. . . Compacts then between nation and nation are obligatory on them by the same moral law which obliges individuals to observe their compacts. There are circumstances however which sometimes excuse the non-performance of contracts. . . . When performance, for instance, becomes impossible, non-performance is not immoral. So if self-preservation overrules the laws of obligation to others . . .

Examining Statements by Hamilton and Jefferson

4. What were Hamilton's reasons for opposing the American treaty with France?

5. What were Jefferson's reasons for supporting the American treaty with France?

6. With whom do you agree, Hamilton or Jefferson?

American History - 4   Lesson Plan and Notes for Teachers

National Security and Dissent: The Alien and Sedition Acts, 1798

by Clair W. Keller

Preview of Main Points

Few Presidents like criticism of foreign policy because they want to convey a sense of national unity to other nations. They are also inclined to equate their policies with national security interests and even view criticism of their policies as disloyal. Such criticism undermines what they believe to be in the best interest of the nation. This lesson explores the Federalists' attempt during the administration of John Adams to suppress criticism of his foreign policy in the name of national security.

Connection to Textbooks

This lesson can be used when discussing the so-called "undeclared war with France" during the administration of John Adams. It also can be used as part of discussions about the tensions that exist in a democratic society between freedom of expression and the need for national security.

Objectives

Students are expected to:

1. describe the circumstances that brought about the passage of the Alien and Sedition acts;

2. explain the effect that the Alien and Sedition acts had on political dissent during the last two years of the Adams Administration; and

3. discuss the conflict that exists between freedom of expression and security in a democratic society.

Suggestions for Teaching the Lesson

Opening the Lesson

o Inform students of the main points of the lesson. Distribute Handout 1.

o Have students read Handout 1. First ask students to place a check in the space under Column #1 indicating those activities they believe **should be allowed during peace time**. Then ask them to place a check in Column #2 indicating those activities they believe **should be allowed during war time.**

o Make a retrieval chart on a transparency indicating how many students have checked each statement for each column. Discuss the classes responses. Ask students to give reasons for their choices.

Developing the Lesson

o Have students read Handout 2. Then have students mark which of the actions in Handout 1 would be illegal under the Sedition Act.

Note: All of the above activities would have been **illegal** under the Sedition Act of 1797. Numbers 2, 3, 5 & 7 are actual activities that resulted in arrest, prosecution, and conviction. Number 2 concerns the case of Mathew Lyon, Congressman from Vermont; number 3 was a remark uttered by Luther Baldwin, who in a tipsy mood commented that he hoped some shots would hit the President in the seat of the pants, number 5 was done by a Connecticut editor; number 7 David Brown, a middle-aged New England worker who had placed a liberty pole with a painted sign saying: "No Stamp Tax--No Sedition--No Alien Bills--No Land Tax--Downfall to Tyrants of America--Peace and Retirement to the President--Long Live the Vice President and the Minority--May Moral Virtures be the Basis of Civil Government."

o Make a retrieval chart on a transparency showing which actions students thought were illegal under the Sedition Act.

o Discuss with students the reasons for their answers. The task at this stage is not an evaluation of the activities, but whether or not they were considered illegal. When students have finished their discussion, reveal to them that all of the above activities would have been illegal under the Sedition Act and that numbers 2, 3, 5 & 7 represent actual cases that resulted in conviction. Ask students to speculate what circumstances would prompt a government to pass such legislation. You should attempt to point out the tensions that exist in a democratic society between "freedom and security."

Concluding the Lesson

o Ask students under what circumstances should a government be permitted to suppress the press, assembly and speech?

- What are the appropriate limits on speech and press?

- Do these limits vary according to circumstances?

- Are there occasions when national security interests are so overwhelming that criticizing government policies ought to be forbidden?

If students say no to the third question, ask them if the government should be allowed to keep secrets. How open should government activity be? What if someone wants to disclose a secret that could help an adversary, is that okay?

o Distribute Handout 3. Have students read the short excerpt from Jefferson's inaugural speech. Discuss its meaning and implications in terms of the questions preceding this excerpt.

o Finish the lesson with a discussion of the concluding questions in Handout 3.

Suggestions for Additional Reading

Emery, Edwin, and Smith, Henry Ladd. *The Press & America*. New York: Prentice Hall, 1954, pp. 151-164.

A brief discussion of the results of the Sedition Act on freedom of the press.

Youngs, J. William T. *American Realities: Historical Episodes from the First Settlement to the Civil War*. Boston: Little, Brown, 1981, pp. 121-138.

Excellent summary of circumstances surrounding the origin of and operation of the Alien & Sedition Acts. Could be used for advanced students.

National Security and Dissent: The Alien and Sedition Acts, 1798

Americans are a free people. The Constitution of the United States limits the power of the government and protects liberties of the people, including freedom of speech and the press. However, a major responsibility of any government, including the government of the United States, is to maintain order and security--to protect freedoms and rights of the people against internal disorders and against threats from foreign nations. Should the government ever place limits on freedom of speech and press on behalf of national security? In wartime, for example, should a government restrict freedom to criticize the government or to praise the enemy?

Following is an opinion poll that asks you to think about whether or not certain activities of the people should be restricted in peacetime or wartime.

Opinion Poll on Freedom of Expression

As you read the following statements you are asked to indicate in the space under column #1 whether or not the activity described in the statement should be permitted by the United States government during peacetime. Indicate in the space under column #2 if the activities should be permitted by the United States government during wartime.

Column #1   Column #2

1. Write a letter to a newspaper criticizing the President's handling of a foreign policy issue.

2. Congressman writes a letter to a newspaper accusing the party in power of ridiculous pomp, foolish adulation, and selfish avarice.

3. Make a derogatory comment about the President.

4. Write an editorial against a declaration of war being considered by Congress.

5. Write an editorial criticizing the army and military policies of Congress.

6. Organize a rally opposing the President's foreign policy.

7. Put up a political poster with slogans criticizing the government.

8. Make a speech calling your senator stupid.

9. Make a speech calling the government immoral and corrupt.

10. Write an editorial describing your senator as immoral and corrupt.

American History - 4   Handout 2

The Alien and Sedition Acts, 1798

During the Federalist Party administration of John Adams, 1797-1801, relations between France and the United States had deteriorated so much that an undeclared naval war existed between the two countries. The Republicans blamed this state of affairs on John Adams and engaged in a bitter partisan attack on his presidency. To curb this criticism, the Congress passed several measures to suppress the activities of these Republican critics. The supporters of the administration justified these measures because to them organized opposition to government policy was treasonous and dangerous to the security of the nation.

Two acts, Alien and Naturalization Acts, were aimed at French and pro-French foreigners in the United States. One part established eligibility for citizenship through naturalization at 14 years. Another act authorized the President to deport any alien who he deemed dangerous to the peace and safety of the United States, and in case of war to deport aliens of an enemy country or to subject them to important restraints if they were permitted to remain in this country. The Sedition Act made it a high misdemeanor for any persons to conspire to oppose any measure or to impede the operation of any law of the U.S., but also made it illegal for "any person to write, print, or publish any false, scandalous and malicious writing . . . against the government of the United States [Congress or the President] with intent to defame . . . or bring them or either of them, into contempt or disrepute, or to excite against them or either or any of them the hatred of the good people of the United States."

The Alien and Sedition Acts, as these four measures were called, were immediately attacked by the Republicans as being unconstitutional. But, as discussed in the note above, to no avail.

The Sedition Act, 1798

This is an excerpt from the Sedition Act. As you read it, think of the type of political activity that could be allowed. What kind of criticism could members of the opposition exercise? What criticisms were banned?

Sec. 1: Be it enacted . . . , That if any persons shall unlawfully combine or conspire together, with intent to oppose any measure or measures of the government of the United States, which are or shall be directed by proper authority, or to impede the operation of any law of the United States, or to intimidate or prevent any person holding a place or office in or under the government of the United States, from undertaking, performing or executing his trust or duty; and if said, shall counsel, advise or attempt to procure any insurrection, riot, unlawful assembly, or combination, whether such conspiracy, threatening, counsel, advice, or attempt shall have the proposed effect or not, he or they shall be deemed guilty of a high misdemeanor. . . .

Sec. 2: That if any person shall write, print, utter, or publish, or shall cause or procure to be written, printed, uttered or published . . . any false, scandalous and malicious writing or writings against the government of the United States, or either house of the Congress. . . . President, with intent to defame the said government, or either house of the said Congress or . . . President or to bring them, or either of them, into contempt or disreput; or to excite against them or either or any of them, the hatred of the good people of the United States, or to stir up sedition within the United States. . . . shall be punished. . . .

(c) *American History and National Security*. Mershon Center, The Ohio State University

Jefferson's First Inaugural Address

Below is an excerpt from Jefferson's First Inaugural Address (March 4, 1801). As you read it, think about Jefferson's views on freedom of expression. Where do you think Jefferson would draw the line between freedom and security. Does Jefferson give too much freedom? Why is Jefferson not afraid of free speech and freedom of the press? Do you share his views? Why or why not?

> During the contest of opinion through which we have passed the animation of the discussion and of exertions has sometimes worn an aspect which might impose on strangers unused to think freely and to speak and to write what they think; but they being now decided by the voice of the nation, announced according to rules of the Constitution, all will, of course arrange themselves under the will of the law, and united in common efforts for the common good. All, too, will bear in mind this sacred principle, that though the will of the majority is in all cases to prevail, that will to be rightful must be reasonable; that the minority possess their equal rights, which equal law must protect, and to violate it would be oppression. Let us then, fellow-citizens, united with one heart and one mind. Let us restore to social intercourse that harmony and affection without which liberty and even life itself are but banished from our land that religious intolerance under which mankind so long bled and suffered, we have yet gained little if we countenance a political intolerance as despotic, as wicked, and capable of as bitter and bloody persecutions. . . . But every difference names brethren of the same principle. We are all Republicans, we are all Federalists. If there be any among us who would wish to dissolve this Union or to change its republican form, let them stand undisturbed as monuments of the safety with which error of opinion may be tolerated where reason is left free to combat it.

Note: The Alien and Sedition Acts were repudiated by President Jefferson and the Republican Party majority in Congress.

Concluding Questions About National Security and Dissent

11. Why were the Alien and Sedition Acts passed in 1798?

12. Why did Thomas Jefferson and his Republican Party followers oppose the Alien and Sedition Acts?

13. To what extent do you agree with Jefferson and his followers about the Alien and Sedition Acts?

14. What are the appropriate limits on free speech and press during wartime or other critical threats to national security? (Can you think of examples of actions that might justifiably be banned in the interests of national security?)

SECTION II
THE AMERICAN NATION DEVELOPS AND EXPANDS BEFORE THE CIVIL WAR

List of Lessons

This section includes five lessons that treat national security in relationship to policy decisions and events in the development of the United States. American leaders faced difficult decisions about territorial acquisitions, war and peace, and national defense during this early period of American history. The lessons are

5. The Louisiana Purchase and National Security, 1803

6. Acquisition of East Florida and National Security, 1819

7. The Debate Over Military Academies

8. The Monroe Doctrine and Security in the Western Hemisphere, 1823

9. Should I Support President Polk's War? Senator John C. Calhoun's Decision, 1846

Overview for Teachers

Though professing and practicing "isolationism" from the "power politics" of Europe, which dominated the international system of the time, the United States was not inactive in international affairs as the nineteenth century opened. As the new nation turned its attentions to the expansion of its own territory, continued European interest in the Western Hemisphere--most notably from warring Great Britain and France--was seen to affect America's westward movement. With a growth in the economy and population and an increase in trade, the pressure for expansion grew. And as it did American policy became repeatedly involved with both the European powers and the North American nations that bordered the United States.

Each stage of these developments posed serious questions for American national security. When the French forced Spain to return the huge Louisiana Territory commanded by the busy port of New Orleans at the mouth of the Mississippi River, President Jefferson immediately recognized the change as a potential threat to American security. The ineffectual Spanish had been problem enough, presenting obstacles to the increasing river trade from America's continuing expansion westward. It was feared that the powerful French might choose to impede the expansion itself. **Lesson 5** examines how Jefferson's concern for his growing nation's security motivated him to propose and successfully negotiate the purchase of the Louisiana Territory from France, thereby providing both essential control over a crucial strategic point and room for further expansion. **Lesson 6** shows how similar considerations, though less grand in scope and lengthier in execution, led the United States to press a now even weaker Spain to cede title to East Florida in 1819.

At the same time that its interests and territory were growing, the United States was again embroiled in a domestic dispute over the persistent issue of how to provide the means and manpower to provide for its own defense. In the spirit of its revolutionary beginnings and the growing lore of its frontier culture, the United States had conducted its wars by calling on its citizens to support the cause of the day. The concept of a standing army of professional soldiers was still considered to be contrary to the principles of the new government. However, as the nation grew, many felt that a professional standing army was needed.

Lesson 7 presents the first of long series of debates that would take place over this issue. This lesson examines Congressional debates in 1816 on whether to expand the number of military academies and increase the number of officers trained in the United States. The Military Academy at West Point had been established in 1802, but was still producing only a small number of officers each year. Many still equated development of a professional army with European elitism and therefore opposed the idea.

Regardless of differences on such issues, the security problems of the United States continued to grow more complex. The question of American expansion and continued European interest in the Western Hemisphere faced by Jefferson arose again during the administration of President James Monroe. The United States sought to preserve the opportunities that the North American Continent seemed to present, in part by design and in part because its citizens were simply moving into unclaimed territory. The American leadership also sought to underscore the philosophical foundations for its isolation from the non-democratic politics of the European powers, which many felt lay at the root of the conflicts of that Continent. These concerns were addressed by the President in 1823 in what has become known as the Monroe Doctrine. **Lesson 8** traces the origins of this "doctrine." While it acquired great historic significance, this lesson shows that the Monroe Doctrine was more a self-conscious definition of our own policy than it was a statement of much import beyond the United States. Nonetheless, such a statement both summarized and directed the course of American security policy for the remainder of the century.

Under the protection of self-declared isolation, westward expansion continued to be the primary expression of U.S. policy through the next several decades. Except for sporadic instances, this expansion encountered little resistance from the native Americans who were settled on the land. But as the movement drew further and further west, it began to include territory which was already claimed by other countries--Mexico to the South and Great Britain to the North. In the presidency of James Polk both of these areas had to be confronted. In the case of Britain and the Oregon Territory a peaceful settlement was reached (although some wanted the boundary of that territory to be drawn farther north and were willing to fight for it--"54^0-40' or fight"). In the case of Mexico, however, the U.S. engaged in its first truly territorial war in 1846. The issue was a complex one and occasioned considerable debate and ill feeling as discussed in **Lesson 9**. Ultimately the outcome of this war was to open U.S. territory all the way to the Pacific, paving the way for greater development of America's overseas trade and commerce.

American History - 5 Lesson Plan and Notes for Teachers

The Louisiana Purchase and National Security, 1803

by John J. Patrick

Preview of Main Points

This lesson stresses a single point, that the primary motive for the purchase of the Louisiana territory from France in 1803 was to maintain national security. In addition, Jefferson chose expediency over a concern for strict construction of the Constitution.

Connection to Textbooks

Every textbook explains the purchase of Louisiana, but they usually stress the great land bargain of 4 cents an acre rather than Jefferson's desire for greater national security. This lesson can be used to elaborate upon typical textbook coverage of this topic.

Objectives

Students are expected to:

1. explain the relationship of national security to the purchase of the Louisiana Territory by the United States;

2. explain the constitutional issue faced by Jefferson in deciding to purchase Louisiana;

3. explain how Jefferson resolved the constitutional issue of the Louisiana Purchase;

4. identify and explain all the reasons that Jefferson used to justify the purchase of the Louisiana Territory; and

5. evaluate Jefferson's rationale for the purchase of the Louisiana Territory.

Suggestions for Teaching the Lesson

Opening the Lesson

o Use a political map of North America in 1803 (refer to a textbook or historical atlas to find a suitable map) and identify the boundaries of the United States and the Louisiana Territory and the location of New Orleans. Tell students to study the map and discuss the following question with reference to it: Why was control of the Louisiana Territory by a foreign power a threat to the national security of the United States?

o Turn to the first page of the Handout to find an excerpt from a letter written on April 18, 1802 by President Thomas Jefferson to Robert Livingston, U.S. Minister to France. Distribute copies of this excerpt, either read the letter to the students or have them read it. Discuss

(c) *American History and National Security.* Mershon Center, The Ohio State University

the main ideas of this letter with reference to the overriding idea of national security. You may want to use the questions at the end of the letter to guide your discussion.

Developing the Lesson

o Have students read the case study about the Louisiana Purchase in the Handout. Advise students to pay special attention to Jefferson's consideration of both national security and constitutional questions relevant to his decision about the Louisiana Territory.

o Have students answer the questions at the end of the case study in the Handout. They should prepare for class discussion on these questions.

Concluding the Lesson

o Conduct a class discussion of the six questions at the end of the case study. During this discussion, emphasize the conflict between Jefferson's values about national security and his values about how to interpret the Constitution. Challenge students to examine and appraise Jefferson's reasons for choosing national security over his constitutional principles in this case.

Suggestions for Additional Reading

Morris, Richard B. *Great Presidential Decisions*. Philadelphia: J.B. Lippincott, 1960, pp. 54-65.

   Morris gives an excellent discussion of the issues surrounding the purchase of Louisiana Territory. The book contains commentary and documents.

Malone, Dumas. *Jefferson the President: First Term, 1801-1805*. Boston: Little, Brown, 1970, pp. 263-332.

The Louisiana Purchase and National Security, 1803

Jefferson's Letter to Livingston

Read the following excerpt from a letter by Thomas Jefferson after he learned of the possibility that France might acquire Louisiana. Remember that during Washington's Administration Jefferson favored friendly relations with France. The position of Jefferson in the quote below marks a departure from his previous anti-British, pro-French view.

The letter was written by Jefferson to Robert R. Livingston on April 18, 1802, American minister to France.

> . . . The cession of Louisiana . . . by Spain to France . . . completely reverses all the political relations of the United States, and will form a new epoch in our political course. Of all nations of any consideration, France is the one which, hitherto, has offered the fewest points on which we could have any conflict of right, and the most points of communion of interest. From these causes, we have ever looked into her as our natural friend, as one with which we could never have an occasion of difference. Her growth, therefore we view as our own, her misfortunes our natural and habitual enemy. It is New Orleans, through which the produce of three-eights of our territory must pass to market, and from its fertility it will ere bring yield more than half of our whole produce, and contain more than half of our inhabitants. France, placing herself in that door, assumes to us the attitude of defiance. Spain might have retained it quietly for years. Her pacific dispositions, her feeble state, would induce her to increase our facilities there, so that her possessions of the place would hardly be felt by us, and it would not, perhaps, be very long before some circumstance might arise, which might take the cession of it to us the price of something of more worth to her. Nor so can it ever be in the hands of France . . . The day that France takes possession of New Orleans, . . . we must marry ourselves to the British fleet and nation. We must turn all our attention to a maritime force. . . .

Discuss the following questions about this letter:

1. Why did Jefferson consider France our natural friend?

2. Why was New Orleans so important to the United States?

3. Why was continued possession of New Orleans by Spain not considered a threat to the United States by Jefferson?

4. If France owned New Orleans, why did Jefferson say that our attitude toward Great Britain would have to change? (What does this change in attitude have to do with national security?)

5. How was acquisition of the Louisiana Territory essential to national security?

The Louisiana Purchase and National Security, 1803

The purchase of Louisiana Territory was the most important decision of the presidency of Thomas Jefferson. The Louisiana Territory, owned by France in 1803, was a huge area west of the Mississippi River--extending westward to the Rocky Mountains and southward from the Canadian border to the Gulf of Mexico and the Spanish territories of Texas and New Mexico. This territory of more than 828,000 square miles was larger than all of Western Europe and about as large as the total land area of the United States at the beginning of 1803.

The Question of National Security

Was Louisiana vital to the national security of the United States? Many Americans, including President Thomas Jefferson, thought so. Others, however, disagreed. They pointed out that the port of New Orleans, at the mouth of the Mississippi River, was the only important settlement in the Louisiana Territory, which was mostly a vast wilderness inhabited mainly by various tribes of so-called Indian peoples. But Jefferson and others, especially settlers in the Ohio River Valley to the west of the Appalachian Mountains, believed that their nation was threatened by foreign control of New Orleans. Look at a map of North America and you can see that the Ohio River system flows into the Mississippi River, which flows into the Gulf of Mexico, where New Orleans is located. So whoever controlled New Orleans also controlled river traffic from the interior of North America into the Gulf of Mexico, and from there by sea to South America, the Caribbean islands, the east coast of North America, and Europe.

When Spain controlled Louisiana during the period following the Independence of the United States, the port of New Orleans was sometimes closed to American shipping and at other times unfair taxes were charged for use of the port. American farmers in the Ohio River Valley were often hurt badly by Spanish policies on their use of the port of New Orleans. These farmers loaded their crops onto boats and rafts, which floated down the Mississippi to New Orleans. From there the goods were shipped to American cities along the Atlantic coast or to other countries. These Americans, and those who depended upon their products, wanted free access to the port of New Orleans. So they pressed their national government during the presidential terms of Washington and Adams to help them. However, the new American nation was too weak to force the Spanish to change their policies.

In 1800, however, Americans had a new opportunity to make a deal about New Orleans. France, which had owned Louisiana before 1763, forced Spain to return it. President Thomas Jefferson feared the establishment of powerful French forces in Louisiana. What if the French decided to close the port of New Orleans to Americans? What if they used Louisiana as a military base? Jefferson sent envoys to Napoleon Bonaparte, the ruler of France. The Americans offered to buy the Port of New Orleans, and the surrounding region for $2 million.

President Jefferson was astounded by Napoleon's response to his offer. The French ruler needed money to pay for his ongoing war with Britain. Furthermore, he feared that the British, with the world's strongest navy, might be able to transport military forces to North America and take Louisiana away from him. So he offered to sell the entire Louisiana Territory to the United States. Thus he would get needed funds, prevent Louisiana from falling to the British, and win the good will of the United States.

Napoleon's price for all of the Louisiana Territory was $15 million, which might seem high. However, looked at as a cost per acre, this was a bargain--about 4 cents per acre.

The Question of Constitutional Interpretation

Jefferson wanted to take Napoleon's offer. But he was bothered by a question of constitutional interpretation.

As leader of the Republican party, Jefferson was a strict constructionist, who believed that the national government should be limited strictly to the powers expressed in the Constitution. According to a strict constructionist interpretation of the Constitution, Jefferson could not buy Louisiana; because there was no statement in the Constitution granting power to the President or Congress to buy territory from another country.

According to the broad constructionists, such as Alexander Hamilton, the President could use the "elastic clause" (Article I, Section 8) to justify many actions not expressed specifically in the Constitution. The "elastic clause" says: "The Congress shall have power . . . to make all laws which shall be necessary and proper for carrying into execution the foregoing powers, and all other powers vested by this Constitution in the government of the United States, or in any department or officer thereof."

Jefferson wanted to buy Louisiana, but he was reluctant to stretch the powers of the Federal government, as his Federalist Party rivals had done during the 1790s, when they had established a national bank. Jefferson expressed his dilemma in a letter to John Breckinridge, a Republican leader in the Senate:

> The treaty must of course, be laid before both Houses, because both have important functions to exercise respecting it. They, I presume, will see their duty to their country in ratifying and paying for it, so as to secure a good which would otherwise probably be never again in their power. . . .

On October 17, 1803, the Senate ratified Jefferson's treaty by a vote of 24 to 7. A majority in the House of Representatives voted to appropriate the money needed to make the purchase. The money bill was also passed by the Senate. Jefferson was empowered to conclude the deal with France, which he did.

Jefferson explained his deviation from strict construction of the Constitution:

> A strict observance of the written laws is doubtless **one** of the high duties of a good citizen, but it is not **the highest.** The laws of necessity, of self-preservation of saving our country when in danger, are of higher obligation. To lose our country by a scrupulous adherence to written law, would be to lose the law itself, with life, liberty, property and all those who are enjoying them with us; thus absurdly sacrificing the end to the means.

Later, the President said: "Is it not better that the opposite bank of the Mississippi should be settled by our own brethren and children than by strangers of another family?" Americans responded by moving westward to populate and develop the new territory. Out of it were eventually to be made twelve states: Arkansas, Colorado, Iowa, Kansas, Louisiana, Minnesota, Montana, Nebraska, North Dakota, Oklahoma, South Dakota and Wyoming.

Through the purchase of Louisiana, the United States became one of the largest nations on earth. Later on, Americans learned that the territory included many acres of fertile soil and other valuable natural resources. Louisiana was a richer prize than most people imagined at that time.

In 1828, the Supreme Court affirmed the constitutional basis of Jefferson's decision to purchase Louisiana. In the case of **American Insurance Company v. Canter**, Chief Justice Marshall expressed the majority opinion that the Federal Government could acquire new territory under the treaty-making clause of the Constitution.

American History - 5   Handout

Reviewing and Interpreting Main Ideas

6. Why did President Jefferson and other American leaders think that possession of New Orleans was critical to national security?

7. Why might the entire territory of Louisiana, in addition to New Orleans, be considered important to the security of the United States?

8. What was the constitutional issue about the purchase of the Louisiana Territory?

9. What reasons did President Jefferson give to justify his resolution of the constitutional issue in this case?

10. To what extent do you agree or disagree with each of Jefferson's reasons for purchasing the Louisiana Territory?

American History - 6   Lesson Plan and Notes for Teachers

Acquisition of East Florida and National Security, 1819

by Clair W. Keller

Preview of Main Points

This lesson is designed to show how the acquisition of East Florida was important as a means of securing western trade routes and as a means of maintaining security for the southern part of the United States.

Connection to Textbooks

Most textbooks discuss territorial expansion, including the acquisition of East Florida. This lesson provides a national security perspective to that acquisition.

Objectives

Students are expected to:

1. locate important geographic features related to western trade and acquisition of East Florida;

2. describe how the United States obtained East Florida; and

3. explain the relationship between the acquisition of East Florida and the security of the southern states.

Suggestions for Teaching the Lesson

Opening the Lesson

o Refer students to the outline map of the United States in 1815 in the Handout. Discuss these questions:

- How did farmers who lived in the midwest get products to market in 1815?
- Which route was the fastest? Which the cheapest?
- How did cotton growers in Mississippi, Alabama, Tennessee and Georgia get their cotton to textile mills in the east and Great Britain?

Note: The point to be emphasized here is the importance of trade routes of the Mississippi and other rivers that drained into the Gulf of Mexico.

Developing the Lesson

o Look at the map again. Ask students to locate East Florida.

(c) *American History and National Security.* Mershon Center, The Ohio State University

o Ask students to read the first section of the Handout. Then have them read the list of events, in chronological order, about the acquisition of Florida by the United States.

o Require students to answer the questions at the end of the chronology in the Handout in preparation for class discussion.

Concluding the Lesson

o Conduct a class discussion of the questions 1-4 in the Handout.

o Have students write a brief essay (no more than 250 words) in response to question 5. Ask different students to read their essays to the class and have other students respond to their ideas.

Suggestions for Additional Reading

Pratt, Julius. *A History of U.S. Foreign Policy.* Englewood Cliffs, NJ: Prentice Hall, 1955, pp. 80-82, 128-130, 155-167.

A good summary of events leading to acquisition of East Florida. Treats the acquisition as result of expansionists' policies.

Bailey, Thomas A. *A Diplomatic History of the American People*, 9th edition. Englewood Cliffs, N.J.: Prentice Hall, 1970, pp. 163-175.

A lucidly written discussion that traces the entire history of the acquisition of Florida in a single chapter.

Acquisition of East Florida and National Security, 1819

When the United States declared independence in 1776, Florida belonged to Spain. However, American leaders from the 1780s onward wanted to acquire Florida. They believed that control of Florida by a foreign power was a threat to national security. Why?

We can begin to understand their thinking about Florida and national security by examining the map of Florida at the end of the lesson. Imagine Florida to be the handle of a pistol. It is aimed at the mouth of the Mississippi River. Furthermore, the huge peninsula jutted into the trade routes between New Orleans and the Atlantic seaboard. Finally, most of the navigable rivers of Alabama and Mississippi flowed to the Gulf of Mexico through West and East Florida. Therefore, from the point of view of Americans living in the West, foreign control of Florida was like having a loaded gun pointed at them: What if Spain acted to cut off trade routes needed by settlers of the western territories and states of the United States? This threat haunted Americans.

In addition, pirates operated out of ports in Florida, because the government of Spain did not have sufficient power in Florida to stop piracy. Furthermore, Florida was a haven for runaway slaves from the southern part of the United States. Finally, Indians freely crossed the Florida/USA border to attack American settlers and then retreated into Florida, where they were safe from punishment.

In 1803, President Thomas Jefferson expressed the hopes of Americans to acquire Florida. He wrote: "We have some claims . . . to [West and East Florida]. . . . These claims will be a subject of negotiation with Spain, and if, as soon as she is at war, we push them strongly with one hand, holding out a price in the other, we shall certainly obtain the Floridas, and all in good time."

Spain was soon involved in war with France and after 1810 faced spreading rebellions by the Spanish colonies in Mexico and South America. It seemed that Florida could be acquired by the United States. On May 29, 1819, an article in *Niles' Weekly Register* expressed an opinion held generally in the United States: "[Florida] will just as naturally come into our possession as the waters of the Mississippi seek the sea; and any thing done to obstruct the operation will be as useless, in the end, as an attempt to arrest and turn back the course of that mighty stream."

Niles' Weekly Register was offering an opinion almost after the fact, because in February 1819, the United States signed a treaty with Spain to acquire Florida. However, it was not until 1821, that this treaty was formally approved by both the Spanish government and the Senate of the United States.

Following is a chronological list of events in the acquisition of East Florida by the United States.

Steps Leading to Acquisition of East Florida:

1763   Florida was ceded to Spain as a party to the treaty ending the French and Indian War. The northern border between Spanish and English territory was set at 31 N. latitude, the present northern border of Florida. The line was extended west to the Mississippi River.

1795   Pinckney Treaty confirmed the 31 N. latitude as the southern boundary of the U.S. Spain also agreed to free navigation of the Mississippi River [The west bank of the Mississippi River was part of the Louisiana Territory] giving U.S. shippers the right to land and store goods at New Orleans, at a fair price, for three years.

1803   The U.S. purchased Louisiana and attempted to claim West Florida as part of the Louisiana Territory.

1806   The U.S. attempted to purchase West Florida from Spain, but Spain refused. Jefferson then tried to buy West Florida from France, since the title to the area was not clear, but Napoleon wanted too much money.

1810   Americans in West Florida seized control of the territory, then asked to be annexed to the United States. This pattern would be followed many times in U.S. expansion to the west.

1811   U.S. troops occupied West Florida, moving the border of West Florida east to what is now Mobile, Alabama.

1812   Louisiana was admitted to the USA as a state; part of West Florida was added to Louisiana and included as part of the new state.

1815-1818   There were border problems with East Florida. Slaves fled south. U.S. troops often pursued Indians and ex-slaves across the border.

1818   General Andrew Jackson, Indian fighter and hero of the Battle of New Orleans, invaded Florida after writing a letter to the President requesting permission to invade Florida. He suggested that he could seize the whole of East Florida "without implicating the government. Let it be signified to me through any channel (say Mr. J. Rhea) that the possession of the Floridas would be desirable to the United States and in sixty days it will be accomplished." Jackson stated that he had received an indirect answer to go ahead from President Monroe, later denied by the President who said he never read Jackson's letter until weeks later because of an illness.

Jackson pursued Indians, hung two Englishmen as pirates, and seized Florida. The U.S. was embarrassed. The territory was returned to Spain. While many condemned Jackson's actions, John Q. Adams, Secretary of State, defended him because he believed "Spain must immediately make her election either to place a force in Florida, adequate at once to the protection of her territory, and to the fulfillment of her engagements, or cede to the U.S. a province, of which she retains nothing but the nominal possession, but which is, in fact, a derelict, open to the occupation of every enemy, civilized or savage, of the U.S. and serving no other earthly purpose than as a post of annoyance to them." Adams vigorously pursued the purchase of East Florida.

1819-1821   The Adams-Onis treaty for purchase of Florida was signed on February 22, 1819. The treaty also established the border between U.S. and Spanish territories all the way to the Pacific Ocean. The Senate finally ratified the treaty on February 19, 1821, two years after it was signed.

1821   Jackson was somewhat vindicated by his appointment as territorial governor of Florida.

American History - 6   Handout

Reviewing and Interpreting Main Ideas

1. Why did American leaders, such as Thomas Jefferson and Andrew Jackson, want to acquire West and East Florida?

2. When and how did the United States acquire West Florida?

3. When and how did the United States acquire East Florida?

4. What were the roles of James Monroe, John Quincy Adams, and Andrew Jackson in the acquisition of East Florida?

5. What is your appraisal of the means used by the United States to acquire East Florida? Was the United States, in order to enhance national security, justified in pressuring Spain to give up Florida?

(c) *American History and National Security*. Mershon Center, The Ohio State University

American History - 6   Handout

The United States in 1815

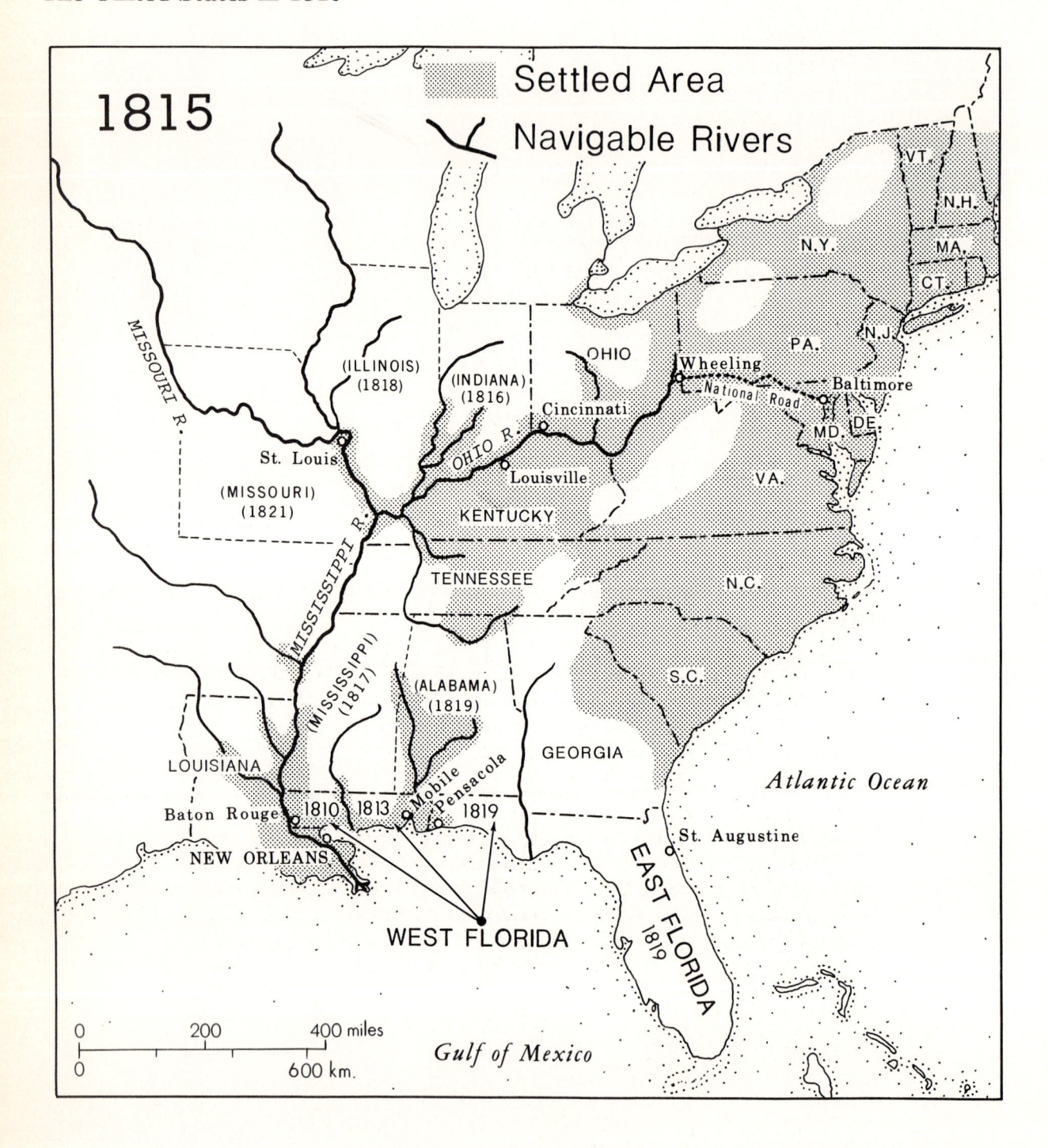

American History - 7   Lesson Plan and Notes for Teachers

The Debate Over Military Academies

by Donald A. Ritchie

Preview of Main Points

This lesson presents excerpts from an actual debate in 1816, which represented a much larger public debate in the pre-Civil War years, over the legitimacy of military academies. The issues were whether such academies were constitutional, whether they were aristocratic, and whether the defense of the nation should not be left to "citizens' armies." The debate ended with a vote in favor of expanding the academies, although not as greatly as their supporters had wished, and in the eventual acceptance of military academies in American life.

Connection to Textbooks

This lesson can be used in connection with chapters covering the War of 1812, early nationalism, and the Jacksonian era. Comparisons between this lesson and the more extensively treated Jacksonian war against the Bank of the United States can easily be made. Many of the opponents of the Bank also opposed the military academies, and for many of the same reasons: they were "monsters" that perpetuated an aristocracy within the American democracy. This lesson adds information usually lacking in textbooks, concerning the debate over a standing army and the early suspicion of military academies. The lesson also highlights a Congressional debate, showing how issues in American history were decided in the legislative arena, and the sharp differences of opinion that often existed.

Objectives

Students are expected to:

1. explain the reasons why Americans were suspicious of a standing army;

2. identify the positions taken by those who supported and those who opposed military academies; and

3. explain the results of the debate in both its immediate and long-term effects.

Suggestions for Teaching the Lesson

Opening the Lesson

o Ask students if they can identify the major military academies (Army: West Point, New York; Navy: Annapolis, Maryland; Air Force: Colorado Springs, Colorado). Ask if any member of their family, or any one they know had attended a military academy. Ask them about what the purposes of these academies are, and what images they have formed of them. Ask why the establishment of these academies might have been considered controversial at one time.

(c) *American History and National Security.* Mershon Center, The Ohio State University

Developing the Lesson

o   Have students read the case study. Then conduct a discussion of the factual review questions, to make certain they have understood the main ideas. Answers to these questions are at the end of this lesson plan.

o   Assign several students to the roles of Cyrus King, John Hulbert, and John C. Calhoun. They can either read or paraphrase the arguments. Note the differences in styles of responses made by Hulbert (mocking) and Calhoun (appealing to patriotism).

Following this reenactment, have the students answer the "Interpreting Primary Sources" questions in the Handout. Answers to these questions are at the end of this lesson plan.

Concluding the Lesson

o   Using the "Decision Making Skills" questions, have the students discuss the goals and values expressed by both sides in this debate. Cyrus King represents the "strict constructionalists" who believe that only those functions specifically provided for in the Constitution are permitted to the government. He was fighting to keep the "rights and property" of the people from being given away piecemeal. King was also contemptuous of academies that educated only the children of the wealthy and seemed aristocratic in nature. Because there was no requirement that these cadets serve in the army after their graduation (since the army was too small in peacetime to need them all), King was afraid that they would become "mere soldiers of fortune" and would use their swords "to carve their way to fortune and to power."

Hulbert and other supporters of the bill adopted a looser interpretation of the Constitution, that the power to raise and support an army implied the ability to train officers in military academies. Their position was that the government should not be stopped from adopting needed programs, unless specifically prohibited by the Constitution. John C. Calhoun's support for this proposal was a reflection of his nationalist position during his early career in Washington. Calhoun wanted to use the power of the federal government to train the future leaders of the community and strengthen the nation's military position. In his later career, Calhoun, because of his fight to support the slave system in the South, became a "strict constructionist" himself.

o   Ask the students whether the House made the right decision. Encourage them to discuss the consequences of votes cast by members of the House on this issue, and to make positive and/or negative appraisals of the two sides of the debate.

Suggestion for Additional Reading

Cunliffe, Marcus. *Soldiers and Civilians: The Martial Spirit in America, 1775-1865*. Boston: Little, Brown and Company, 1968.

Students who are interested in this subject will find Cunliffe to be a highly engaging account of the standing army versus militia debate.

Answers to Handout Questions

1. Because they thought it unnecessary, expensive and dangerous to a democracy; and because it reminded them of the British professionals in the American Revolution.

2. Because there were still very few graduates of the academy.

3. The performance of West Point graduates in the Mexican War and the Civil War.

4. King argued that the Constitution did not have any provision for such academies; that the provision to "raise and support armies" would not apply to this bill because the cadets would not be required to serve in the army; and that if this bill was constitutional, then the government more rightly should educate everyone rather than a privileged few.

5. Their aristocratic nature.

6. Hulbert responded that other laws relating to military academies had been enacted under several administrations, and no one had called them unconstitutional; and that the power to "raise and support armies" was sufficient to permit passage of this bill.

7. That King must have been fooled by schoolboys pretending to be cadets and midshipmen.

8. Because he believed it would provide useful military education and training to men who would go back to become leaders in their communities and their militia, for future service to the nation.

9. That another war with Britain was always possible, and the nation needed to have trained leaders to be prepared.

American History - 7   Handout

The Debate Over Military Academies

Background to the Debate

Americans depend upon their military forces to defend their national security, but what type of military forces? And what role should they play in American society? From colonial times to the Civil War, Americans looked with disfavor on a large, standing army. They identified a professional army with the British redcoats they fought in the War for Independence. They considered such a "regular army" as unnecessary, expensive, and dangerous to their free government. Instead, many preferred a "citizens' army" (militia) made up of citizen-soldiers who could be called into action in time of war or civil disturbance.

Some of this hostility toward professional soldiers was directed toward the military academies. The first military academy was established at West Point, New York, in 1802. In its early years, the academy was small, and it took many years to establish its national reputation. By the time of the War of 1812, only seventy-one cadets had graduated from West Point. They were too few in number to play a commanding role in the war, and Americans hailed the frontier militia under General Andrew Jackson as the real heroes of the day.

After the war, Congress debated improving and expanding military education and training. In January 1816, the House Military Affairs Committee proposed to expand the number of students at West Point and to establish new military academies. This expansion would train more young men than were needed as officers in a peacetime army, and they would not be automatically required to serve. But they would be trained for future emergencies.

What follows are portions of the debate in the House of Representatives on that bill.

The Debate

These excerpts from the debate on January 3, 1816, were published in the *Annals of Congress*, an early version of the *Congressional Record*. Some changes have been made to put the debate consistently in the first-person ("I said") since the reporters sometimes recorded them in the third-person ("he said").

WEDNESDAY, JANUARY 3, 1816

    Mr. [Cyrus] King, of Massachusetts. This bill will turn our military academies into seminaries of learning, and the cadets into students in the various arts and sciences--without any service to be rendered to the public for the expense which must be incurred in their education. And at the end of three or five years, they are thrown back upon society, with nothing but their swords to carve their way to fortune and to power. It is not consistent, sir, with the principles of our institutions, with the genius of our Republican Government, to form and cherish a body of this kind: mere soldiers of fortune.

    In what part of our constitution then, sir, do we find our power to establish academies on the principle contemplated in this bill? It shall probably be pointed to our power "to raise and support armies." But do these cadets form any portion of our Army? Is it even intended, were they capable, that they should do duty as soldiers? Not at all. Sir, I do not like this mode of legislating the people out of their rights and property, by degrees. You first pass a law, organizing a corps of engineers and cadets, provide for their instruction, for an equivalent in duty and service to be rendered by them, and place them in a Military Academy. You now convert this Military Academy into a seminary of learning generally, take away the equivalent, and educate the young men who may be so fortunate as to gain admission there, at the public expense. If you can thus constitutionally educate eight

---

(c) *American History and National Security*. Mershon Center, The Ohio State University   55

hundred young men, why not eight thousand--why not, indeed, all the youth of the country? There would, indeed, be some equality in this latter case, as all the people would then be equally benefited.

The honorable gentleman from the State of New York (Mr. [Erastus] Root) has proved that abuses have crept into the institution at West Point--that none but the sons of the rich and the powerful can gain admittance there. And the most odius partiality is manifested in some of the appointments in the Navy, particularly of midshipmen. Mere children of the favored few, have been appointed, who never were on board a ship of war, and have nothing of the seaman about them except the anchor on their buttons; and this, too, to the exclusion of many brave and deserving sailors.

Mr. [John] Hulbert, of Massachusetts. I wish to reply to some observations which have fallen from my honorable colleague, Mr. King.

I was surprised to hear the objection that Congress has no constitutional right to establish Military Academies. I believe this is the first time that objection has ever been made. If, as my colleague contended, the establishment of Military Academies was unconstitutional, is it not a little surprising that no one has ever before made the discovery? Several laws in relation to the institution at West Point have been passed under Administration of very different political character. But whatever might have been thought of the expediency of those laws, I am confident no one has ever questioned their constitutionality. The Constitution of the United States says, "Congress shall have the power to raise and support armies." This is, I think, a clear and ample authority to pass the bill before us.

As to the story of children strutting in the dress of midshipmen. I strongly suspect that my colleague here has seen another bear, that he has been deceived by some mock military exhibition of the school boys of his city, which I myself have seen here and elsewhere on holidays.

Mr. [John C.] Calhoun, of South Carolina. I oppose the reduction of the number of cadets; because, if the present number were retained, it would afford ample room for a proper selection of officers. I think it materially necessary to retain the proposed number. The whole population of the United States is composed of men active, vigorous, and spirited. With good men to lead them, you may at any time make out of any portion of them active, good soldiers. What is requisite to make our militia efficient? Military knowledge. The cadets will many of them return to the body of the people, and become a part of the militia. Suppose a revival of the struggle between us and the nation with whom we were recently at war; suppose she should put forth her whole strength to crush this young country? We shall then find the use of having men qualified to lead our citizens to meet her invading foe. The whole population of the country becomes an efficient force, because it has among it men properly educated to lead an army into the field.

Result of the Debate

The Annals of Debate reported that: "Some diversity of opinion and some animated debate took place on the number of cadets to be authorized by the bill. It ended in a motion, by Mr. John Taylor, of New York, to strike out eight hundred, the number proposed by the bill. For this motion there were 79 votes; against it, 55. So the motion was passed. Then the members voted 77 to 55 to reduce the number of cadets to six hundred."

American History - 7   Handout

The debate over military academies went on for many years. Such members as Representative Davy Crockett of Tennessee and Senator Thomas Hart Benton of Missouri were among those who loudly complained about the "aristocratic" nature of military academy cadets. Some of these criticisms were stilled during the Mexican War in the 1840s, when West Point graduates performed outstandingly well as engineers and as infantry commanders. During the Civil War, the poor performance of untrained militia in early combat pointed to the need for a well-trained army. Supporters of the academies also pointed out that the leaders of both the North and South, including Jefferson Davis, Ulysses S. Grant, Robert E. Lee, William Tecumseh Sherman, and Stonewall Jackson had all gotten their training as West Point cadets.

Reviewing the Facts and Main Ideas about the Debate

1. Why were Americans suspicious of a professional army?

2. Why did the War of 1812 not help promote the reputations of the military academies?

3. What factors contributed to Americans' eventual acceptance of the military academies?

Interpreting Primary Sources

4. How did Cyrus King use the Constitution to defend his point of view?

5. What did King find most distasteful about military academies?

6. How did John Hulbert respond to King's constitutional objections?

7. How did Hulbert use humor to belittle King's fears?

8. Why did John C. Calhoun support this bill?

(c) *American History and National Security*. Mershon Center, The Ohio State University

American History - 7   Handout

9. In what ways might the recent war with Great Britain have influenced the way members of Congress considered this issue?

Decision Making Skills

10. What were the goals and values of those opposing the military academies?

11. What were the goals and values of those supporting the military academies?

12. Do you think the House made the right decision? Explain.

American History - 8   Lesson Plan and Notes for Teachers

The Monroe Doctrine and Security in the Western Hemisphere, 1823

by Clair W. Keller

Preview of Main Points

This lesson describes reaction to the Monroe Doctrine enunciated by President Monroe in his annual message to Congress on December 2, 1823. The purpose of this lesson is to examine reasons why President Monroe enunciated the doctrine and world reaction to it. This will be accomplished in part through the use of a Simulated Press Conference. It concludes with a discussion examining the relation between the Monroe Doctrine and national security.

Connection to Textbooks

Every textbook describes the main points of the Monroe Doctrine and the reasons for such statements by President Monroe. Textbooks, however, seldom describe reaction by European and South American governments. The Monroe Doctrine has always been viewed as a centerpiece for maintaining American security in the Western Hemisphere.

Objectives

Students are expected to:

1. describe the main points of the Monroe Doctrine;

2. explain the reasons why President Monroe enunciated the doctrine;

3. examine the reaction by other nations to the doctrine;

4. relate the Monroe Doctrine to national security issues; and

5. differentiate between statements of fact or opinion concerning the Monroe Doctrine.

Suggestions for Teaching the Lesson

Opening the Lesson

o Inform students that you plan to hold a Simulated Press Conference the following day. Tell students you will play the role of President Monroe, and they are to be reporters. Describe the circumstances for the Press Conference. Then describe the Press Conference format. Explain that after a few formal remarks by the President, students will be expected to ask questions. Distribute the Handout. They are asked to pick one of the roles on this list and serve as a reporter from that country. You may want to assign students to roles. Those marked by * are the more difficult assignments.

(c) *American History and National Security*. Mershon Center, The Ohio State University

Note: You may provide a list of possible questions for the students and ask them to select a question appropriate for their country. (See Notes for Teacher.)

o Have students read background information in their textbooks on the Monroe Doctrine. In addition, have students read the excerpts from the Monroe Doctrine and the information on the origins and outcomes of the doctrine, which are presented in this lesson.

Developing the Lesson

o You may want a student to serve as your Press Secretary. Have the student introduce you, and describe the setting.

o Begin the Press Conference with some opening remarks. (See outline under Notes for Teacher.)

o Respond to student questions. (See Notes for Teacher for possible questions and answers. These samples might be distributed to students playing certain roles to guide them in performing their roles.)

Concluding the Lesson

o Have students respond to the exercise in the Handout and ask them to match the statements with the appropriate answers. Discuss student responses. See the answers to this exercise below.

o Discuss the importance of the Monroe Doctrine today.

- Was it really a doctrine?

- What purpose did it serve?

- Was the primary purpose of the Monroe Doctrine to promote democracy or secure American interests?

- Is it being violated today (i.e. Cuba, Nicaragua)?

- Whose interest does the Monroe Doctrine serve today?

Notes For Teachers

This Press Conference follows the President's message to Congress on December 2, 1823. The press has been anxious to question the President about the reasons for the declaration and its implications for future American foreign policy. The Conference setting is the new capital of the United States, Washington, D.C., and is being held in one of the large rooms at the President's residence. The interest in the Press Conference has been demonstrated by the large number of representatives from foreign countries. (**Note:** Since this is a simulated Press Conference it might be advisable to make sure that students realize that such conferences did not actually take place and while newspapers from the U.S. and around the world commented on the Monroe Doctrine, few, if any, newspapers would have had reporters in Washington, D.C.)

Your opening remarks could touch on the following points:

1. The main points of the Doctrine.

American History - 8

2. The role played by John Q. Adams.

3. Russian adventures along the west coast.

4. Holy Alliance Congress of Vienna held October, 1823, endorsed French intervention in the Spanish Revolution.

5. Expected reception from other nations.

Possible Questions and Answers

France:

Reporter from the *Etoile*, pro-government newspaper.

(Printed a highly indignant criticism of Monroe. Called him a temporary leader of a country barely independent who had assumed in his message "the tone of a powerful monarch whose armies and fleets are ready to march at the first signal.")

Q. Where, Sir, do you get the power to act so boldly?

Q. Do you have an army or navy ready to enforce such pronouncements?

Reporter from the *Constitutionnel*, a Liberal newspaper.

(Took a favorable position. "Today for the first time the new continent says to the old, 'I am no longer land for occupation.'")

Q. Do you think your policy will deter attempts by Spain to reclaim its colonies?

Great Britain:

London *Times*: Called the Monroe Doctrine a "grave and novel doctrine."

Bell's Weekly--Disapproved, suppose some new land is discovered in the north, would this keep Great Britain from making such claims?

George Canning, British Foreign Secretary, thought Great Britain ought to have been consulted on a matter so directly opposed to its interests.

Q. What if a British expedition, such as that of Captain William Edward Perry, who recently explored the Arctic, had discovered some new land on the continent. Would Great Britain be expected to give up those claims in this previously unknown area?

A. Vague response. Will deal with the issue if it arises. Not going to make statements concerning hypothetical situations.

Q. Will your declaration bring Great Britain and Russia closer together whereas before the declaration the U.S. and Great Britain had been both opposed to Russian actions on the Pacific coasts? Will this hinder settlement of the Oregon question?

A. Perhaps. But British intentions had been leaning in that direction anyway. They seem to have been willing to settle the border between Russia and Great Britain in the Northwest at 55 degrees. The dispute between the U.S. and Great Britain concerns the boundary between the U.S. and Great Britain in the Oregon territory. We have always been willing to settle for 49 degrees. The British have insisted on the Columbia River. This doctrine should have little impact on that impasse.

Q. How do you think the Monroe Doctrine will be received by other nations?

A. The Holy Alliance will undoubtedly condemn it. I suspect the Austrian Chancellor Metternich will condemn our policy (Note: Metternich wrote that . . . "their indecent declarations have cast blame and scorn on the institutions of Europe more worthy of respect." The Russian Tsar said of the Monroe Doctrine that it "merits only our profound contempt . . ." and silence. Some governments may make public statements that disagree with our position while privately assuring us of their acquiescence. But those liberty minded people around the world will hail our position as one based upon the principles of freedom and liberty.

U.S. Newspapers

Reporter--Whig paper

Q. Why did it take so long for the U.S. to recognize the newly independent nations in South America?

A. Perhaps you underestimate the boldness of our actions. We acted alone in this matter. Few nations of the world applaud revolutions. Great Britain, for example, has not yet recognized these newly independent nations.

Q. Does the Monroe Doctrine mark a change in the U.S. attitude toward Great Britain?

A. We have some similar interests. Great Britain has disassociated itself from the designs of the Holy Alliance, especially the French invasion of Spain. It seems that we ought to pursue what we now regard as common interest. Certainly recognition of the new governments in Latin American would be a step in the right direction.

Q. Since it is obvious that the Monroe Doctrine cannot be enforced without cooperation with Great Britain, why didn't the two nations issue a joint declaration? Wouldn't a joint declaration have had greater impact?

A. Although conversation on this matter did take place between British Foreign Secretary George Canning and Ambassador Richard Rush, no agreement was reached. One condition for our agreeing to such joint action was British recognition of Latin American independence.

Q. What are the principles upon which governments we would tolerate in the Western Hemisphere ought to be based?

A. The Secretary of State has outlined these ideas in a dispatch to the Tsar of Russia who had asked the same question. They are as follows, that the institution of government to be lawful must be founded upon consent of the governed and each nation is best suited to make that judgement and should not have a government imposed upon it.

Q. Do you think the American people will support your declarations?

A. The strength of this declaration is that it expresses, not just my feelings or those of the Secretary of State, but also the deep convictions of the American people.

Q. Since your Secretary of State, John Quincy Adams, is a candidate for election next year, would you think this will help in his election?

A. Since the American people agree with our action, it should not be a consideration.

Boston *Advertizer*

Q. Is there anything in the Constitution that makes our government the guarantors of the liberties of the world?

A. You are taking an extreme position. This document expresses our security interest and therefore is fully within the powers granted to the President in the Constitution.

Latin American Reporters

Q. Were any leaders in Latin America consulted?

A. No.

Q. Did any South America countries express concern about European intervention?

A. The Vice President of Columbia did propose to an American agent an alliance with the U.S. to ward off any possible interference from France and Spain.

Q. What do you think will be the reception by such leaders as Simon Bolivar or Jose de San Martin to your declaration?

A. I believe it will be favorably regarded. Vice President of Columbia Santander will undoubtedly greet our declaration with enthusiasm. Only time will tell.

Note: Most Latin American leaders, according to Perkins, saw Great Britain and not the U.S. as having the power to prevent intervention which most doubted would take place anyway.

Q. Will you promote revolution in the Western Hemisphere?

A. Only by our example of freedom that all peoples of the world would find desirable to emulate. We will do nothing else.

Suggestions for Additional Reading

Morris, Richard B. *Great Presidential Decisions*. Philadelphia: Lippincott, 1960, pp. 82-99.

Although it has only a short summary of events leading to the Monroe Doctrine, it contains Monroe's entire message to Congress, enabling one to read the Monroe Doctrine within the context of the annual message.

Perkins, Dexter. *The Monroe Doctrine 1823-1826*. Cambridge: Harvard University Press, 1927.

A most thorough study of Monroe Doctrine. Utilizes many primary sources in text. Especially good on European reaction.

Pratt, Julius. *A History of U.S. Foreign Policy*. Englewood Cliffs: Prentice Hall, 1955, pp. 167-181.

A good summary discussion that, for the most part, accepts Dexter Perkins' assessment.

Answers to Handout Questions

1. **False.** Passages inserted in his annual address to Congress. This was done instead of sending separate messages to nations involved.

2. **True**

3. **True**

4. **Opinion.** Some might argue U.S. has right to do whatever is needed to preserve its own security. Others argue that U.S. has no right to tell other nations what they can or can't do.

5. **False.** No formal protests were made. Although many statesmen condemn it, it was officially ignored.

6. **False.** Most Latin American leaders thought Great Britain's opposition to French and Spanish interference, not U.S. pronouncements, was most important factor.

7. **False.** Pledged not to get involved in wars not a threat to U.S. security.

8. **False.** Might argue that alien philosophies exist today--not just Communism but military regimes.

9. **False.** Great Britain also wanted to prevent re-establishment of French and Spanish power in the Western Hemisphere.

10. **Opinion.** Although U.S. was not particularly formidable. Some critics pointed out the dismal showing of the U.S. against Great Britain in the War of 1812.

11. **False.** Much of the language was written by the Secretary of State, although President Monroe was not manipulated by Adams. In fact, according to Dexter Perkins, no one was more sympathetic to Latin America independence than Adams.

12. **Opinion.** Certainly U.S. sympathy for independence in Latin America played an important role. But the Monroe Doctrine also protected U.S. interests by opening trading opportunities with newly independent Latin American countries and stopping Russia's advances along the Pacific Coast.

American History - 8   Handout

The Monroe Doctrine and Security in the Western Hemisphere, 1823

Roles for a Simulated Press Conference

Newspaper Reporters From the U.S.

      Pro-administration

  * Anti-administration

Newspaper Reporters from Europe especially

  * Great Britain

      Austria

      France

      Prussia

      Spain

      Russia

  * Portugal

Latin America -- especially

  * Argentina

  * Chile

  * Mexico

  * Peru

  * Columbia

The Monroe Doctrine

On December 2, 1823, President James Monroe presented his annual message to Congress. He emphatically commented on the seeming designs of certain European powers on territory in the Western Hemisphere. The former colonies of Spain in Latin America had recently acquired their independence, and leaders of the United States were anxious that these new nations of the Western Hemisphere maintain their freedom from European domination.

Following are excerpts from the President's message, which was called "The Monroe Doctrine."

    . . . the occasion has been judged proper for asserting, as a principle in which the rights and interests of the United States are involved that the American continents, by the free and independent conditions which they have assumed and maintain,

(c) *American History and National Security.* Mershon Center, The Ohio State University

are henceforth not to be considered as subjects for the future colonization by any European powers. . . .

The political system of the Allied Powers [Holy Alliance] is essentially different . . . from that of America. This difference proceeds from that which exists in their respective [monarchical] governments; and to the defense of our own . . . this whole nation is devoted. We owe it, therefore, to candor and to the amicable relations existing between the United States and those powers to declare that we should consider any attempt on their part to extend their system to any portion of this hemisphere as dangerous to our peace and safety.

With the existing colonies or dependencies of any European power, we have not interfered and shall not interfere. But with the governments [of Spanish America] who have declared their independence and maintained it, and whose independence we have, on great consideration and on just principles, acknowledged, we could not view any interposition for the purpose of oppressing them, or controlling in any other manner their destiny, by any European power in any other light than as the manifestation of an unfriendly disposition toward the United States. . . .

Our policy in regard to Europe . . . is not to interfere in the internal concerns of any of its powers. . . .

But in regard to those [American] continents, circumstances are eminently and conspicuously different. It is impossible that the Allied Powers should extend their political system to any portion of either continent without endangering our peace and happiness. Nor can anyone believe that our southern brethren [the new nations of Latin America], if left to themselves, would adopt it of their own accord. It is equally impossible, therefore, that we should behold such interposition in any form with indifference. . . .

Origins and Outcomes of the Monroe Doctrine

The Monroe Doctrine was neither a doctrine nor was it written by Monroe. The statements were written by the then Secretary of State John Q. Adams, son of the still living second President John Adams. The statements were not even placed together in President Monroe's December 2, 1823 message to Congress. Nevertheless the Monroe Doctrine has served as a guide for American foreign policy for more than a century and a half. While the doctrine's influence on American foreign policy is clear, its impact abroad is not so clear.

The Monroe Doctrine consisted of four separate parts: Two of the parts were directed at other nations indicating what type of actions the United States would no longer tolerate in the Western Hemisphere.

The first of these two parts directed at other nations stated: ". . . the American continents, by the free and independent condition which they have assumed and maintained, are henceforth not to be considered as subjects for future colonization by any European power."

This statement was directed specifically at Russian actions on the Pacific Coast, and according to Dexter Perkins was destined to have the greatest impact as time went on. From it were deduced many of the corollaries of the Monroe Doctrine. Remember that in 1823 the U.S. did not own Alaska or California and claimed the Oregon Territory as far north as the present Alaskan border, 54-40. These claims had been transferred to the U.S. by Spain in a treaty signed in 1819.

These were vigorously disputed for two more decades by Great Britain, when both countries agreed to the 49th parallel.

The second type of action by foreign powers declared by Monroe to be unacceptable was any attempt to re-establish colonial governments in the Western Hemisphere. "With the governments (that is, of the Spanish American Republics) who have declared independence, and maintained it and whose independence we have, on great consideration and just principles, acknowledged, we could not view any interposition for the purpose of oppressing them, or controlling in any other manner their destiny, by any European power . . . as . . . an unfriendly disposition toward the United States."

This declaration was aimed at the menace of the Holy Alliance to the independence of the newly independent states in South America. Fortunately for the U.S. position, Great Britain also favored a policy of non-intervention in the Western Hemisphere by the Alliance. This policy had its origin in the U.S. political sympathy for the newly created nations. The Monroe Administration, however, had acted slowly in recognizing these newly independent nations. Monroe, although personally favoring recognition, seemed to follow the lead of his Secretary of State who followed a policy of caution and prudence.

Even though Henry Clay, Speaker of the House and a long-time advocate of recognition, had pushed through resolutions urging U.S. recognition in 1821, it was not until 1822 that the U.S. recognized these new nations. Still, in light of the anti-liberation view of most nations in the world, specifically the Holy Alliance, recognition when it finally came must be viewed as a bold step.

Part of the Declaration also emphasized that the "non-interference" principle was a two-way street, that having declared no European country should try to reimpose its system in the Western Hemisphere, we have not interfered and shall not interfere "with the existing colonies or dependencies of any European power." This pronouncement was undoubtedly directed at Portugal's colonies, especially Brazil, Spain's Cuba and colonies still belonging to Great Britain, France and the Netherlands.

Finally Monroe assured Europe that the U.S. had no intention of taking part "in the wars of the European powers in matters relating to themselves." This last phase left the door open for U.S. involvement in European wars that might affect American security. Hence World Wars I and II did not violate the U.S. pledge not to interfere in European wars.

Reaction to the Monroe Doctrine was generally muted. European statesmen condemned it as boisterous, and as an exaggerated form of American pomposity. Such terms as blustering, monotonous, arrogant, haughty, unmeasured in ambition, consecrating the principles of disruption were used to describe it. But for the most part the declaration was greeted with official silence. In Latin America it received only minimal attention. Most Latin American leaders saw the power of Great Britain, not U.S. pronouncements, as providing a protective shield from European intervention.

What of the short term and long term consequences of the Monroe Doctrine? For one, there were no effective interventions of European powers in the Western Hemisphere--which violated the Monroe Doctrine--during the 19th century. However, in the short run the enhanced security of the Americas was due more to the naval power of the British, who agreed in principle with the Monroe Doctrine. Later on, as the United States developed great military power of its own, Americans were able to assert their own power in defense of security in the Western Hemisphere.

American History - 8   Handout

Judging Statements About the Monroe Doctrine

Mark each of the following statements about the Monroe Doctrine as True (T), False (F), or Opinion (O). If false, explain why.

_____ 1. President Monroe signed the Monroe Doctrine at a Pan-American Conference being held in Washington, D.C.

_____ 2. The "non-interference" principle in the Declaration pledge that neither the U.S. or Europe should interfere with existing governments.

_____ 3. The non-colonization principle was aimed primarily at Russia.

_____ 4. The U.S. has every right to decide what type of governments ought to exist in the Western Hemisphere.

_____ 5. All European nations vigorously protested Monroe's doctrine.

_____ 6. All leaders from newly independent Latin American nations welcomed Monroe's doctrine as an important impediment for European aggression in Latin America.

_____ 7. The U.S. pledged never to get involved in European wars.

_____ 8. The Monroe Doctrine has been responsible for keeping the Western Hemisphere free from philosophies alien to the democratic principle of "government by consent."

_____ 9. The Monroe Doctrine was viewed by Great Britain as a threat to its policies in Latin America.

_____ 10. Without the support of the British fleet the U.S. would not have been able to enforce the Monroe Doctrine.

_____ 11. President Monroe developed the Monroe Doctrine despite opposition by his Secretary of State John Quincy Adams and his cabinet.

_____ 12. The Monroe Doctrine was motivated primarily by our concern to preserve democracy in the Western Hemisphere.

American History - 9   Lesson Plan and Notes for Teachers

Should I Support President Polk's War?
Senator John C. Calhoun's Decision, 1846

by Clair W. Keller

Preview of Main Points

This lesson is about the dilemma faced by John C. Calhoun, Senator from South Carolina, when asked to vote for the war with Mexico. The lesson points out the issues posed by the war for many Americans.

Connection to Textbooks

Textbooks always describe the issues surrounding the war with Mexico. This lesson personalizes the dilemma faced by many Americans during the conflict.

Objectives

Students are expected to:

1. explain the circumstances that brought about the war with Mexico;
2. identify the alternatives faced by John C. Calhoun;
3. identify the reasons for and against supporting the war with Mexico;
4. explain the reasons for John C. Calhoun's final decision; and
5. explain the consequences of John C. Calhoun's decision.

Suggestions For Teaching The Lesson

Opening The Lesson

o Ask students if they know why the United States went to war with Mexico in 1846.

o Have students review the material in their textbook on the origins of the War with Mexico.

Developing the Lesson

o Discuss the questions in the Handout. Some historians have called the war one of imperialism.

   - Why would they do that?

   - Why did many people at the time call it Mr. Polk's War?

o Have students read the case in the Handout about the circumstances surrounding John C. Calhoun's dilemma on the War with Mexico.

o Tell students to read the Handout and then fill in the blanks in the decision tree. They should include what they would do if they were in Senator Calhoun's place.

(c) *American History and National Security.* Mershon Center, The Ohio State University

Note: If the Decision Tree has not been used before, then you should make sure they have a clear understanding of their task.

o Discuss students' responses on the Decision Tree. Ask students to verify their responses with data from the Handout. Resolve differences. Require students to make and defend a decision on the issue in this case.

o After the class discussion of the Decision Tree, have students meet in small groups. Ask each group to decide what decision they think John C. Calhoun made: voted in favor of the war, voted against the war, abstained. List the reasons for their choice.

Concluding the Lesson

o Have each group report. Make a retrieval chart on the board or transparency.

o List reasons for each group's choice.

o Reveal what decision John C. Calhoun made and the reasons for that decision. (See the background notes on the next page.)

o John F. Kennedy wrote a book titled, *Profiles in Courage*. He defined courage in political terms: those rare individuals willing to risk the wrath of their constituents or community in order to stand firm on a principle.

- Does John C. Calhoun's decision in this case fit John F. Kennedy's definition of courage for his action in opposing President Polk's war message?

Notes For Teachers

Several votes to weaken Polk's demand were taken before the final vote. The first was an attempt to restrict the reinforcements to repelling the apparent invasion. This motion lost 26-20. Then an attempt was made to delete the preamble, declaring a state of war existed by Mexico's actions, from the Bill. This also lost, 28-18. Most of the votes were on party lines, with Whigs voting in opposition. Only John C. Calhoun deserted his party and voted with the opposition on these two amendments.

When the bill came to a final vote, it passed forty to two. John C. Calhoun and two Whig senators **abstained**.

Calhoun defended his action. The war question had been forced on the Congress by Polk's decision to move troops. He feared that hostilities with Mexico would hurt a peaceful settlement of the Oregon dispute. (They had settled before receiving knowledge of the war.) He stated that putting the raising of an army and war declaration together put the opposition in an untenable position. He blamed the President for mismanaging the situation.

Suggestions for Additional Reading

Lander, Ernest McPherson, Jr. *Reluctant Imperialists: Calhoun, the South Carolina, and the Mexican War.* Baton Rouge: Louisiana State University Press, 1980, pp. 1-39.

Shows Calhoun's dilemma. Describes the debate in the Senate and in the South Carolina press on the war issue.

Schroeder, John H. *Mr. Polk's War: American Opposition and Dissent, 1846-1848.* Madison: University of Wisconsin Press, 1973. Especially pp. 1-50.

Good summary of events leading to war and the dissent of the war by Whigs and Democrats.

American History - 9   Handout

Should I Support President Polk's War?
Senator John C. Calhoun's Decision, 1846

Senator John C. Calhoun was a top leader of the southern wing of the Democratic Party. In 1846, he represented South Carolina in the U.S. Senate. Conflict between the United States and Mexico led to a difficult decision faced by Senator Calhoun. He had to decide whether or not to vote in favor of war with Mexico.

Background to the Dilemma

President Polk received word on May 9, 1846, of an attack on American troops by Mexican troops who had crossed the Rio Grande and ambushed the Americans who were led by General Taylor. Polk, who had been expecting this news for several days, seized the moment. He called his Cabinet together and asked them to support his decision to ask Congress to declare war. Although some had misgivings, the Cabinet unanimously agreed.

The Democratic party (President Polk's party) held a large majority in the House 144-77. In the Senate, the majority was less, 30-24. While this should have provided enough support from Polk's party to carry the day against the Whigs, his party was split. Among those who were antagonistic to Polk was John C. Calhoun, a Democrat from South Carolina.

Polk's war message depicted the U.S. as a nation suffering a long series of insults and injuries at the hands of Mexico. According to Polk, Mexico had consistently refused to pay several million dollars in damage claims owed to U.S. citizens. Mexico had been unwilling to recognize annexation of Texas by the U.S. or to concede the legitimate border of Texas. Mexico had refused our offer to negotiate these disputes and had even refused to receive the American envoy John Slidell. Mexico had also threatened to invade Texas after the U.S. had annexed it.

Troops had been sent to Texas for defensive purposes only and were instructed to take no aggressive steps. But Mexican troops had attacked American troops. "As war exists, and not withstanding all our efforts to avoid it, it exists by the Act of Mexico itself. We are called upon by every consideration of duty and patriotism to indicate with decision the honor, the rights, and the interests of our country," said President Polk in his war message.

Polk requested Congress not to declare war but to recognize that it already existed. The House took up Polk's request first. The House passed it with limited debate and without reading the documents the President had sent to support his position. Rather than declaring war, the preamble of the resolution stated: "War exists by an act of Mexico herself." This was combined with money for troops and supplies. Attempts to separate the two issues by the opposition failed. The bill was now sent to the Senate. Senator John C. Calhoun thought about reasons for opposing or supporting war with Mexico.

Reasons Against the War

John C. Calhoun was a Democrat from South Carolina but he belonged to one of the factions opposed to President Polk. He was upset at having not been offered the position of Secretary of State by Polk, a position he had held earlier. He believed that Polk's aggressive policies toward Oregon and Mexico, as symbolized in the campaign slogan, "54-40 or fight" would bring about a war with both Mexico and Great Britain. Calhoun hoped that preventing war against Mexico and Great Britain would enhance his own presidential ambitions in 1848.

(c) *American History and National Security*. Mershon Center, The Ohio State University

Calhoun was concerned about rushing into war. He wanted the Senate to delay consideration of Polk's declaration of war until all the facts concerning the border clash were available. He was not convinced that a state of war existed between Mexico and the United States. He believed that a state of hostilities did not necessarily mean war.

He was concerned that a war with Mexico would jeopardize a peaceful settlement of the Oregon dispute. Great Britain would take advantage of U.S. involvement in Mexico to press the claims for a settlement at the Columbia River.

Calhoun had felt Polk's ordering General Taylor into the disputed territory had been a provocative act.

Public opinion in South Carolina seemed divided. Newspapers argued both for and against the declaration of war. The Charleston *Mercury* claimed that Polk had committed an enormous folly by placing an army of 25,000 in a vulnerable position against a Mexican force of 10,000. The Charleston *Patriot* argued the problems the U.S. would face in invading and conquering a nation so different in race, customs, political institutions and religion. The Mercury asked if the U.S. conquered Mexico, what would it do with seven million Indians who were "bigoted, ignorant, idle, lawless, slavish, and yet free."

Reasons Supporting the War

Most Southerners had favored the annexation of Texas. As Secretary of State under President John Tyler, Calhoun had played an important role in the successful passage of the annexation resolution during the last days of Tyler's presidency.

Rejection of the Slidell mission by the government of Mexico on April 6, 1846 had placed much of the blame for failure to resolve the disputes on Mexico. The U.S. had sent Slidell to Mexico to negotiate the disputes, refusal to accept our envoy was an insult. Mexico seemed the aggressor. The Peredes government had overthrown the previous government because it had tried to settle the dispute. The new government allowed Santa Ana, the butcher at the Alamo to return from exile.

The Senate had tied the Declaration of War with the funds needed to support troops in Texas. Voting against the war resolution meant that war supplies would be denied American soldiers. Efforts to separate the two measures in the Senate had failed. Voting no would be seen as unpatriotic. Constituents might not understand.

The Abolitionists were against the war. Voting against the war would put a Southern Senator in the same camp as the hated Abolitionists. Not a very good position for a Southern Senator. The entire South Carolina delegation in the House of Representatives, when faced with a similar dilemma (although opposed to the war), had voted for the war resolution. Many undoubtedly remembered the fate of the Federalists who opposed the War of 1812. Their refusal to support the war effort resulted in the demise of the Federalist Party. It never again could erase the stigma of being a peace party when the country was at war.

The Charleston *Courier* wrote a scathing editorial about Mexican insults, atrocities, and invasion of "our territory". The U.S. should invade Mexico up to the gates of her capital--this was the message of the editorial from the most important newspaper in South Carolina.

American History - 9

Handout

Senator Calhoun's Vote

What would Senator Calhoun, Democrat from South Carolina, do when called upon to vote in the Senate on going to war with Mexico? What would you do, if you were in his place? Why?

Calhoun's alternatives were:

    a. vote in favor of war;

    b. vote against war;

    c. abstain.

Using a Decision Tree

Use the Decision Tree on the next page to help you respond to the decision that faced Senator John C. Calhoun in 1846.

1. What was the issue or occasion for the decision facing Calhoun?

2. What alternatives or options did Calhoun have?

3. What were likely positive consequences of each of Calhoun's options?

4. What were the likely negative consequences of each of Calhoun's alternative choices?

5. What were the goals (or overriding values) that Calhoun had or (in your opinion) should have had in this case?

6. Use your views about goals and values in this occasion for decision to guide your choice of one alternative as better than the others. Given your goals and values in this case, what choice would you have made, if you had been in the place of John C. Calhoun in 1846? Why?

7. What choice do you think Calhoun made in 1846?

(c) *American History and National Security.* Mershon Center, The Ohio State University

American History - 9   Handout

DECISION TREE

GOALS/VALUES

CONSEQUENCES

GOOD

BAD

ALTERNATIVES

OCCASION FOR DECISION

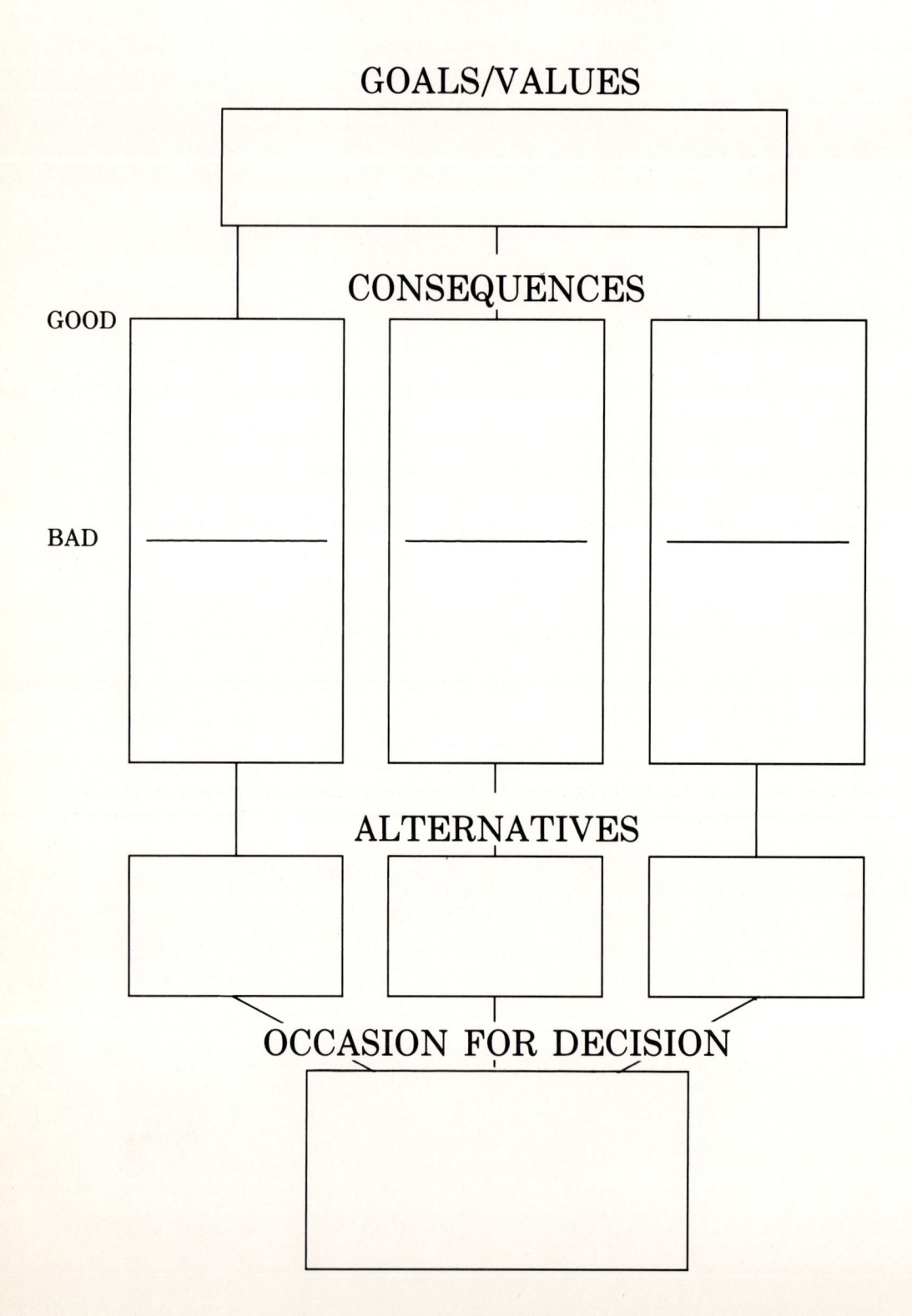

The decision-tree device was developed by Roger LaRaus and Richard C. Remy and is used with their permission.

(c) *American History and National Security*. Mershon Center, The Ohio State University

SECTION III
THE CIVIL WAR

List of Lessons

This section contains three lessons stressing national government decisions and military strategies during the Civil War that had a significant bearing on the national security of the United States. The problem of maintaining national security and liberty during a national crisis is highlighted. This is a perennial issue in a free society. The lessons are

10. President Lincoln Maintains National Security: The Case of Maryland, 1861

11. Press Censorship During the Civil War

12. Operation Crusher, 1864

Overview for Teachers

As the United States entered the second half of the nineteenth century, the greatest threat to its security proved to come not from overseas but from within the country itself. That threat was the Civil War--a cruel and divisive conflict that was to have an unalterable long-term effect on our notions of the conduct of war. The application of American ingenuity and technology introduced a number of concepts that changed the character of warfare. Among these changes were the mass production of weapons, the development of armor clad and a new strategic understanding of the relationship between military objectives and civilian casualties.

Amidst the multiple issues that gave rise to the Civil War, President Lincoln fought principally to maintain the integrity of the Union. Of special importance in facing the division of the South from the North was how to preserve security within the nation itself. **Lesson 10** chronicles how Lincoln faced the issue in the state of Maryland which surrounded Washington on three sides and which was sympathetic to the secessionist states of the Confederacy.

The Civil War resurfaced the continuing question of the preservation of Constitutionally guaranteed rights, such as the First Amendment guarantee of free speech, when national security is considered to be at risk. **Lesson 11** examines the problem of maintaining national security and liberty by examining efforts by Union generals to impose press censorship.

The Civil War introduced another aspect of national security that was perhaps to have even more profound impact. The conduct of this war proved to be bitter and bloody. The Civil War produced enormous casualties and struck hard against the population and economy, especially in the South. In the final campaign of the war, the question of casualties among non-combatants and strikes against civilian centers became a matter of overt strategy. **Lesson 12** describes "Operation Crusher," a drive through the South by General Grant designed to end the war by inflicting maximum casualties against forces he knew to be inferior. The execution of this strategy included the march through Georgia by General Sherman who destroyed everything in his path. This operation introduced the concept of total war, war against the entire population, in order to reduce not only the capacity to fight but also the will to fight. It was an approach that was to leave a grave legacy for the future of national security strategy.

American History - 10   Lesson Plan and Notes for Teachers

President Lincoln Maintains National Security: The Case of Maryland, 1861

by Clair W. Keller

Preview of Main Points

This lesson explores the problem faced by President Lincoln in maintaining national security during the early stages of the Civil War while surrounded by a potentially hostile environment, the state of Maryland. Lincoln's tactics utilized methods in the name of national security that some people believed were illegal. This lesson presents two case studies focusing on the dilemma governments faced between freedom and security. The essential question is how much freedom can democracies allow during a crisis of national security.

Connection to Textbooks

Most textbooks have one or two chapters on the Civil War but devote little attention to internal security except to describe the copperhead problem and *ex parte Milligan*, the celebrated *habeus corpus* case. No mention is made of the tactics used by Lincoln to diffuse dissent and insure a Union government in Maryland during April-November 1861.

Objectives

Students are expected to:

1. explain the dilemma governments face between the need for national security and the exercise of constitutional liberties;

2. describe the problem President Lincoln faced concerning the state of Maryland;

3. explain the constitutional issues raised by the tactics Lincoln employed to deal with this problem; and

4. assess whether or not Lincoln had viable alternatives for solving the problem of national security.

Suggestions for Teaching the Lesson

Opening the Lesson

o Ask students to imagine if they lived in a border state when the Civil War began, how would they decide whether to fight on the side of the Union or Confederacy. Make a list of the attributes that might influence a person one way or the other. The point to be made here is that border states had economic and cultural ties to both sides. Individuals faced a dilemma and were tugged in both directions. Maryland presented a special case of divided loyalties because it surrounded three sides of Washington, D.C., the nation's capital. Maryland consequently posed a special problem for President Lincoln.

o   Put the following list of presidential actions on the chalkboard or overhead transparency.

Column 1	Column 2	Action
_____	_____	1. Arrest and detain people without charging them with a crime.
_____	_____	2. Declare martial law in a city over objections of city officials.
_____	_____	3. Suspend meeting of state legislature.
_____	_____	4. Arrest members of the state legislatures.
_____	_____	5. Arrest city officials.
_____	_____	6. Arrest newspaper editors.

o   Have students decide either individually or in groups which of the actions the President ought to take for all occasions (column 1) and those which the President ought to take only when national security is threatened (column 2). (**Note:** Make sure students understand the actions before ranking them.

o   Make a retrieval chart on the board or on a transparency summarizing student views. Discuss the results.

Developing the Lesson

o   Give students Case Study #1 in the Handout. Divide students into groups. Ask each group to decide what the President should do.

Note: Taney's arguments were based on the idea that the writ of *habeas corpus* appears in that part of the Constitution which pertains to Congressional powers. You may want students to look it up in the Constitution (Article I, Section 9, Clause 2). Congress, not the President, has that power. Those suspected of treason should be reported to the district attorney and dealt with through the regular judicial process.

o   After groups have reached a decision have them share conclusions with the class. Make a retrieval chart. Ask each group to provide reasons for their conclusions.

o   Reveal what Lincoln did. He refused the judge's order. He defended his actions in a speech to Congress on July 4. His reasons were as follows. He reminded Congress that he had acted very sparingly. He did not act without considering whether or not he had the power. Lincoln stated:

> Are all the laws but one to go unexecuted and the government itself go to pieces, lest that one be violated? I acted because we have a rebellion and consequently the privilege may be suspended.

o   Congress took no action, which was tantamount to agreeing with the President. Congress did authorize the President power to suspend writ when he deemed the public safety required it in 1863.

o   Divide the students into groups and assign them to read Case Study #2. Have them decide what actions federal authorities should take.

o   Make a retrieval chart of student results.

   -   Why do you think such actions ought to be taken?

   -   Which of these actions would you believe to be constitutional?

   -   Does it make any difference whether or not actions were constitutional?

Note: The Federal authorities did numbers 2 through 6. The government did not interfere in the November election. Unionist sentiment was increasing. A Unionist party was organized and it defeated the State's Rights Party. Federal authorities aided the election, however, by granting leave to soldiers from Maryland so they could vote in the election and used Federal troops to protect union voters. Those Marylanders who had gone to Virginia were arrested if they returned to vote. The government did not give loyalty oaths as some Unionists wanted. The Unionists won the governor's office 2-1, the House of Delegates 68-6, and the Senate 13-8.

Concluding the Lesson

o   Do the election results indicate Lincoln's actions prevented a minority from usurping power in Maryland and leading it against the will of the majority who wanted to remain in the Union? Thus it could be concluded that Lincoln preserved democracy in Maryland rather than usurping it.

o   Focus on the general question. Did the needs of national security justify Lincoln's actions? When would similar action be justified today? Have students make a list. Discuss their examples.

o   What limits should be placed on government actions in a democratic society.

Suggestions for Additional Reading

Duncan, Richard R. "The Era of the Civil War: the Crisis of Loyalty" Chapter V-2. in *Maryland, a History*, pp. 333-360. Edited by Richard Walsh and William Fox, Baltimore: Maryland Historical Society, 1974.

   A thorough summary of the actions taken by Federal authorities during the Secessionist crisis, April to November, 1861.

Randall, James B. *Constitutional Problems Under Lincoln*. New York: Appleton and Company, 1926, pp. 118-136.

   An excellent discussion of the *habeas corpus* controversy.

American History - 10

Mr. Lincoln Maintains National Security: The Case of Maryland, 1861

Case Study #1: The Activities of John Merryman

John Merryman lived near Cockeysville, Maryland. He was an avowed secesssionist. He was arrested for acts of treason stemming out of burning of the bridges leading to Baltimore, Maryland. These bridges had been burned on orders from the governor and from city authorities. They were burned, authorities argued, to prevent Federal troops from passing through the city. When troops had passed through the city before, rioting had taken place. Thus the authorities in Baltimore believed they were trying to prevent further rioting and bloodshed. Lincoln believed officials were obstructing the legitimate passage of Federal troops needed for the defense of Washington, D.C. Merryman also held a commission as a lieutenant in a company of men with hostile intentions toward the government. After his arrest his lawyers asked the Supreme Court for a writ of *Habeas Corpus*. Such a writ requires the authorities to show cause why the person should be held in jail or to release the person.

Judge Roger B. Taney, Chief Justice of the Supreme Court, ordered the military commander, General George Cadwalder, to appear at the judge's hearing and make known the reasons for Merryman's arrest. General Cadwalder refused to appear, informing the judge that Merryman was charged with acts of treason and that his arrest had been made by virtue of the authority of the President of the United States to suspend writ of *habeas corpus* in the interest of public safety. Judge Taney questioned the constitutionality of the military's position. Persons should not be arrested on vague and indefinite charges and jailed without right to determine the legality of the charge. He further declared that the President "cannot suspend the privilege of the writ of *habeas corpus*, nor authorize a military officer to do it. Only Congress has that power."

What do you think President Lincoln should have done when he received Judge Taney's order?

1. Obey the Chief Justice of the Supreme Court.

2. Refuse to obey the judge's order.

3. Refuse to obey the judge's order, but ask to impeach the Chief Justice.

4. Refuse the judge's order and ask Congress to impeach the Chief Justice.

5. Appoint another Chief Justice more in turn with his views.

6. Appeal the judge's ruling to the entire Supreme Court.

American History - 10   Handout

Case Study #2: Acting to Maintain National Security

Read the case study and decide what action(s) Federal authorities ought to take.

The Maryland legislature was called into special session on April 19, 1861 by Governor Thomas Hicks. Lincoln was concerned that the legislature might adopt a resolution to secede from the Union. If this happened Lincoln had directed General Winfield Scott "to adopt the most prompt and efficient means to counteract, even, if necessary, to the bombardment of their cities--and in the extremest necessity, the suspension of the writ of *habeas corpus.*" In other words, the President was prepared to take extreme actions to prevent Maryland from seceding from the Union.

The Maryland legislature met and denied it had the power to pass a secession resolution. This action, the legislature decided, could only be accomplished by a state convention. The legislature refused to call for a state convention. The legislature, however, was antagonistic to Federal policy and protested many of Lincoln's actions, and described Maryland as a conquered state. The Maryland legislators denounced the war and called for recognition of the Confederacy. They also protested the growing number of military arrests in their state, including the police commissioners of Baltimore. The legislature then adjourned until September 1861.

When the legislature met again in September, the Union had suffered a defeat at Bull Run. Federal authorities were concerned that the Maryland legislature might do more damage and undermine Union morale. They didn't want the legislature passing any more pro-southern resolutions or issuing a call for a state convention on the issue of secession.

Which one or more of the following actions do you believe the Federal authorities should have taken to control the Maryland legislature? Be prepared to explain your choice.

____ 1. Do nothing but be prepared to suspend the legislature, if they took pro-southern actions.

____ 2. Arrest legislators who were Southern sympathizers.

____ 3. Prevent the legislature from meeting by proclaiming martial law in the city where they were to meet.

____ 4. Seal off the city where the legislature was to meet and prohibit anyone from leaving.

____ 5. Arrest city officials sympathetic to the Confederacy.

____ 6. Arrest editors of newspapers sympathetic to the Confederacy.

____ 7. Suspend forthcoming legislative election.

____ 8. Supervise forthcoming legislative elections to insure a Unionist victory.

(c) *American History and National Security.* Mershon Center, The Ohio State University

American History - 11   Lesson Plan and Notes for Teachers

Press Censorship During the Civil War

by Donald A. Ritchie

Preview of Main Points

This lesson describes some of the means by which military authorities imposed censorship on the press during the Civil War. The lesson contrasts the early rules covering what correspondents could and could not report, against later orders that barred them completely from certain armies. It raises issues of both military secrecy and sensitivity to criticism, and it poses questions about how a fundamental constitutional right, freedom of the press, could be limited for reasons of national security.

Connection to Textbooks

Most textbooks cover the major battles of the Civil War, and discuss civil liberties on the homefront. But rarely do they connect civil liberties to the battlefield. This lesson can build on textbook accounts of Lincoln's suspension of *habeas corpus* and his "stretching" of the Constitution to preserve the Union, for a general discussion of rights and liberties during wartime. The lesson also provides supplementary information on censorship and a case study of one General and the press.

Objectives

Students are expected to:

1. understand the basic conflict between reporters seeking news to satisfy the growing readership of their papers, and military authorities trying to keep valuable information from falling into enemy hands;

2. identify the types of news that was permissible or forbidden to send under General Scott's orders;

3. recognize the differences between this type of limited press censorship and General Sherman's more sweeping orders barring reporters from his lines;

4. interpret and appraise General Sherman's decision to court marshall the reporter; and

5. recognize the complexity and ambiguities in the clash between freedom of the press and national security.

Suggestions for Teaching the Lesson

Opening the Lesson

o Suggest the following scenario to the students: a reporter for the high school paper discovers that the star player for the school's football team has been injured and may be unable to play in the upcoming game against a rival school. Absence of the player would cause a major revision in the team's strategy, and they have held back the news to avoid alerting the rival team. The student paper is due for publication on the day before the big game. Should the reporter publish the "scoop?"

o Poll the students for their reaction. If sentiment is largely in favor of suppressing the story, ask what the difference would be if the reporter had discovered that a key player on the rival team had been injured. What is the basic responsibility of the reporter? Discuss the conflicting loyalties between reporting for the paper and protecting the school.

Developing the Lesson

o Have the students read the first part of the Handout, "General Scott's Telegraph Orders," and answer questions 1. through 6. Ask them to justify their answers. Answers are:

1. Could be published, since it violates none of the three stipulations.

2. Could not be published, reveals troops movements.

3. Could not be published, predicts troop movements.

4. Could be published.

5. Could not be published, reveals mutiny among the soldiers.

6. Could be published.

o Ask the students to identify which of the three stories that **were** publishable (i.e., 1, 4, 6) might raise additional objections from the military for reasons not specified in General Scott's orders. Answers are stories 1 and 4 because:

1. Reports of major defeats were sometimes censored or delayed because they might demoralize the public. Thus the government held back news of the Union army's defeat at Bull Run in July 1861.

4. Criticism of individual officers damaged their reputations and wounded their pride.

o Conclude the discussion of General Scott's orders by informing students that in addition to controlling the telegraph, many military officers tried to censor the letters that war correspondents sent to their papers from the military camps. The generals feared that such news would give valuable information to the Confederates. Some officers also objected to unflattering accounts and criticism they received in some papers. Officers held up newspaper dispatches until the correspondents agreed to make certain changes, such as substituting the word "withdrawal" for "retreat."

Concluding the Lesson

o Have the students read the remainder of the Handout, "General Sherman Bars the Press." Then ask them to respond to the review questions at the end of the Handout.

o Conduct a discussion of the review questions to be sure they understand the main ideas and motivations involved.

o Use questions 12-15 to determine whether the students recognize the differences between the first portion of the lesson, concerning General Scott's specific prohibitions, and the second portion, concerning General Sherman's blanket prohibition. These are open-ended questions, designed to stimulate debate but not to elicit definite answers. Discuss the ambiguities in knowing what are legitimate and illegitimate restrictions on a free press and the public's right to know.

Further Discussion

You might want to compare the situations of the Civil War to recent times. Ask the students if television reporters should be barred from battlefields. Class discussion might be related to the media's role in changing public opinion during the Vietnam War. Or comparison could be made to the government's prohibition against reporters during the sending of American troops to Grenada in the Caribbean in 1983. Press criticism of their exclusion led to a government proposal that a small pool of reporters be available to accompany such emergency missions, as a means of preventing news from leaking prematurely.

Or students could be asked to construct their own scenarios in which the desire of the press to cover a story would be pitted against security considerations.

Suggestions for Additional Reading

Students who wish to explore this subject further can be directed to J. Cutler Andrews, *The North Reports the Civil War* (Pittsburgh: University of Pittsburgh Press, 1985 [1955]); Bernard A. Weisberger, *Reporters for the Union* (Westport, CT: Greenwood Press, 1977 [1953]). These books describe censorship and other hazards facing the Civil War reporters.

Students might also want to read Knox's account, published in the New York *Herald*, on January 18, 1863, and other Civil War era reporting in newspapers available on microfilm.

For a more recent historical event, see Daniel C. Hallin, *The "Uncensored War": The Media and Vietnam*, (New York, 1986). Students could compare press censorship of the Civil War with the relative lack of censorship in Vietnam, and its effect on government-press relations.

Press Censorship During the Civil War

The First Amendment to the Constitution protects the freedom of the press. However, there is often uncertainty about what limitations on the press are legitimate to protect national security. This problem becomes even more difficult during wartime.

When the Civil War began in 1861, the public clamored for news of the latest battles, strategies, and casualties. The sales of newspapers increased dramatically throughout the North. As their circulation increased, newspapers could afford to send out many correspondents to cover the battlefronts. These reporters risked their lives to follow the troops, observe the battles, and send back reports to their papers.

The Union government did not want news reports to interfere with the war effort. In this lesson you will read how two Union generals acted to control the war news.

General Scott's Telegraph Orders

Because of the demand for quick news, Civil War correspondents sent stories over the telegraph whenever they could. But early in the war the federal government took control of telegraph lines out of Washington, and set certain conditions under which stories could go out.

In July 1861, General Winfield Scott, commander of the Union armies, set the following conditions for reporting military activities over the telegraph, based on an agreement with the correspondents: Reporters could not telegraph anything about 1) troop movements, 2) mutinies among the soldiers; and 3) predictions of future military movements.

Under these conditions, which of the following stories could be telegraphed, and which would be censored?

1. Union troops suffered a crushing loss in battle today. Casualties mounted to over 500 men killed and a thousand wounded.

2. The 5th Massachusetts Regiment crossed the Potomac into Virginia today, fresh from their recent victories. They will be quartered in Centerville for the next two weeks.

3. General Sherman reports that his forces have completed their mission in Tennessee, having successfully achieved objectives and routed the enemy. It is expected that his troops will move into Georgia within the next week.

4. The failure of our armies at Bull Run can be blamed entirely on the incompetency of General McDowell. He should be removed from command immediately.

5. This reporter has established that the brief rioting among troops from the 1st brigade stemmed from their failure to be paid when promised. Military authorities are at work to solve the problem. Tonight the troops are calm.

6. The 6th Pennsylvania Regiment reports no evidence of the Confederates in the vicinity of Gettysburg.

General Sherman Bars the Press

General William Tecumseh Sherman suffered from especially poor relations with the press. He once complained that newspaper correspondents "come into camp, poke around among the lazy shirk[er]s and pick up their camp rumors and publish them as facts, and the avidity [eagerness] with which these rumors are swallowed by the public makes even some of our officers bow to them. I will not. They are a pest and shall not approach me and I will treat them as spies which in truth they are."

In 1862, Sherman issued orders that barred all civilians from the area occupied by his army. Despite this order, many newspapers correspondents continued to follow his troops and report on their engagements. In December, Confederate forces in Mississippi turned back an offensive by Sherman's troops. Before the correspondents could send out their stories of the defeat, Sherman ordered his staff to seize and open any bulky letters being mailed. This search uncovered a thick envelope containing a story and two maps of the battle being sent by Thomas Wallace Knox to the New York *Herald*. Knox's account criticized General Sherman's leadership, and many of his facts about the battle were wrong. Sherman decided to punish the reporter. As he explained to another officer:

> I am going to have the correspondent of the New York *Herald* tried by court marshall as a spy, not that I want the fellow shot, but because I want to establish the principle that such people cannot attend our armies, in violation of orders, and defy us, publishing their garbled statements and defaming officers who are doing their best.

The *Herald* correspondent was charged with: 1) giving information to the enemy, directly or indirectly, 2) being a spy, and 3) disobeying orders. In February 1863, a military court found Knox innocent of the first two charges, but guilty of the third. He was sentenced to banishment from Sherman's lines and warned that he would be imprisoned if he attempted to return. Other correspondents also moved away from Sherman's armies.

Reviewing Main Facts and Ideas

7. What reasons made military officers uneasy about newspaper correspondents accompanying their armies?

8. What were General Sherman's objections to reporters in his camp?

9. Why did Sherman decide to court marshall Thomas Knox?

10. What orders was Knox found guilty of violating?

11. What was Knox's punishment?

12. In what ways did General Sherman's treatment of the press differ from General Scott's earlier orders on censorship?

13. Why did newspaper correspondents risk offending military officers by reporting on the battles they fought?

14. Should the press be permitted to cover all military engagements?

15. Under what circumstances might the freedom of the press and the public's right to know be restricted to protect military actions?

American History - 12   Lesson Plan and Notes for Teachers

Operation Crusher, 1864

by James R. Leutze

Preview of Main Points

This lesson deals with the military strategy--Operation Crusher--of General Grant that led to the Union victory in the American Civil War. The justification for the strategy is presented and students are stimulated to evaluate the strategy on military and moral grounds.

Connection to Textbooks

All textbooks include a chapter on the Civil War. This lesson can be used to enhance treatments of the Union military strategy in the Civil War.

Objectives

Students are expected to:

1. comprehend Operation Crusher;

2. explain General Grant's justification for Operation Crusher;

3. identify and discuss arguments for and against Operation Crusher; and

4. make value judgments about Operation Crusher.

Suggestions for Teaching the Lesson

Opening the Lesson

o Refer to a map or maps (in a standard textbook) that show the division of the states into contending forces of the Federal Union and the Confederacy in 1861 and the military situation during the period 1861-1863. Use the maps to review the political and military situation facing President Lincoln at the end of 1863.

o Write this term on the chalkboard--"Operation Crusher." Tell them this was the military strategy of General Grant. Indicate that this lesson involves an examination and appraisal of Grant's Operation Crusher.

Developing the Lesson

o Have students read the case study about Operation Crusher in the Handout. Require them to respond to questions 1 and 2 at the end of the case study.

o Divide the class into small groups, from 4 to 7 depending on the size of the class. Challenge each group to respond to the issue about Operation Crusher, which is raised and framed by

---

(c) *American History and National Security.* Mershon Center, The Ohio State University

question 3 at the end of the Handout. Have each group consider the issue about Operation Crusher and to develop a position in response to the issue. Indicate that each group will be responsible for presenting and defending its position in a subsequent class discussion.

Concluding the Lesson

o   Identify a spokesperson for each of the small groups. Call upon one of the spokespersons to present the position of the group on the issue in question 3 at the end of the Handout. Ask other members of the group to elaborate upon or modify the presentation by the group's spokesperson, if necessary.

o   Ask others in the class to listen carefully to the presentation of one group about the issue. Then ask them to make comments, critical or supportive, about the presentation. Call upon the spokespersons for each of the other groups to respond first for their groups. Then involve others in a general class discussion. They should decide about the extent to which they agree or disagree with the position of the reporting group and respond accordingly.

o   The teacher should serve as moderator and facilitator of the discussion about the central issue of this lesson.

Suggestions for Additional Reading

Following is an annotated list of books about the ideas in this lesson. These books are presented as additional sources of information for teachers. However, very able students might be referred to one or more of these books.

Catton, Bruce. *Grant Takes Command.* Boston: Little, Brown and Co., 1969.

Catton describes the rise of U.S. Grant from a man of relative obscurity to commander of the western department, general in chief of all Union forces, and finally orchestrator of the Virginia campaign. The author clearly develops the evolution of Grant's leadership and the Union army's effectiveness.

Foote, Shelby. *The Civil War: A Narrative*, 3 vols. New York: Random House, 1958-1974.

Foote's work is an engrossing three volume narrative capturing the many complexities of war. While Catton and Nevins write from a northern perspective, Foote examines the Civil War from a southern one. With a literary flair, he captures the wide range of human experiences that the long conflict engendered.

Fuller, J.F.C. *Grant and Lee: A Study in Personality and Generalship.* Bloomington: Indiana University Press, 1957.

A controversial assessment of the two great Civil War generals. It surprised and outraged many when originally published because Grant comes out ahead of Lee in some areas. This work is useful for illustrating how personality might influence strategic decisions.

Hattaway, Herman, and Jones, Archer. *How the North Won: A Military History of the Civil War.* Urbana: University of Illinois Press, 1983.

The authors present a broad study of the Civil War including logistical, political, economic, and organizational factors shaping military policy. This revisionist work contradicts the traditional notion that Civil War leaders were obstinately committed to the futile frontal assault.

Liddell-Hart, Basil Henry. *Sherman: Soldier, Realist, American.* New York: Praeger, 1958.

In this study the eminent British military historian finds Sherman to be both a better general than often thought and the father of modern strategic warfare. Well written and provocative.

Nevins, Allan. *The War for the Union*, 4 vols. New York: Scribner's, 1973.

These four volumes constitute the second half of Nevin's masterful study of the turbulent years 1847-1865. Nevins not only analyzes the Civil War from a military standpoint, but he also measures the impact of the long struggle on American society.

Reston, James, Jr. *Sherman's March and Vietnam.* New York: Macmillan, 1984.

This study is an attempt to relate Sherman and his approach to war to the conduct of the war in Vietnam. Many comparisons strain too hard at times to make the connection, but it is a laudable attempt to relate the past to the present.

Sommers, Richard J. *Richard Redeemed: The Siege at Petersburg.* Garden City, N.Y.: Doubleday and Co., 1981.

This is one of the few comprehensive works focusing on the nine and one-half month battle around Petersburg. Sommers combines narrative, analysis, and biographical sketches in this notable study.

Operation Crusher, 1864

The American Civil War erupted in April 1861. This struggle of Americans against their fellow Americans--of the Northern against the Southern states--was the bloodiest and bitterest war in American history. President Abraham Lincoln fought to preserve the Federal Union established in 1787 by the Constitution of the United States. The Confederate States of America, until 1861 loyal members of the Federal Union, fought to create a new American nation. Which side would prevail?

Near the end of 1863, the Confederate forces still held out against the Union armies. Although suffering heavy losses in the Western theater of the war, along the Mississippi River, Confederate leaders still hoped to prolong the war and convince their enemies to stop fighting and allow them to establish their own nation, separate from the United States of America.

Lincoln Turns To General Grant

The Union had suffered very heavy casualties up to this point in the war and the cost in dollars was staggering, more than the United States government had spent on all expenditures between 1776 and 1861. What had been gained? In the Eastern theater of the war, Union armies were only slightly further South than they had been at the start of the war. Six different Generals had failed to lead the Union forces to victory in the East. So President Lincoln turned to General Ulysses S. Grant, the man who had led Union armies to victory in the West. Could General Grant succeed where six others had failed?

Grant was 42 years old in 1864, when he became commanding general of the United States Army. The son of poor parents, he had gone to West Point, the U.S. Military Academy, to escape a life of hard physical labor. In no ways brilliant, Grant had graduated in the middle of his class. After graduation, Grant served honorably in the war against Mexico. But after the war, he got into trouble--heavy drinking and fighting were Grant's undoing. Following a courtmartial, he left the Army, but found little success in civilian life--trying and failing at farming, clerking in a store, and selling wood off the back of a wagon.

When the Civil War began, Grant got a commission because of his West Point education and Mexican War experience. He led Union forces to victories in the West and gained national notice in 1863 by taking the Confederate stronghold of Vicksburg on the Mississippi River. After Vicksburg, Grant took command of a beleaguered Union army at Chattanooga and won a spectacular victory.

The Strategy of Operation Crusher

What had the simple, straightforward, clear-headed man learned about war? "The art of war is very simple," he said, "Find out where your enemy is, hit as hard as you can, as often as you can, and keep moving." Although he never said it in quite these words, he had also learned something else: war is about killing. Once you enter a war you had better be prepared to kill more of the enemy than he killed of your men--or the enemy would win. There was no way of avoiding this simple fact, so there was no reason to delay it. Dragging a war out only increased the cost. Grant didn't like killing--he could hardly stand the sight of blood--but he had a job to do and he intended to do it quickly and get it over with.

His plan was called "Operation Crusher" and he intended to so employ his forces that he took advantage of Northern superiority in transportation, communication, supply and manpower.

He was, in short, going to overwhelm the Confederacy. Against Lee's 62,000 he would move with Meade's army of 120,000. Against Joe Johnson's 57,000, he would send Sherman's 90,000. In addition, he would send General Franz Sigel and an army of 48,000 into the Shenandoah Valley--the Confederate breadbasket--to disrupt the army there and the agricultural process. To round out the plan he would also have General Butler with 36,000 to move against Richmond from the James River. In summary, Grant would send 290,000 men against 160,000 men. He would wage total war.

The most devastating part of Grant's strategy was Sherman's move into Georgia. Obviously the more deeply Union armies moved into Southern territory, the more disruption of civilian life there would be. But among other famous things Sherman would say was his comment that no one needed to tell him how bad war was. He hadn't started this war, but he'd do anything in his power to end it. Until it was ended, he would wage it all out, believing as he did that the quickest way to end the war was to bring its brutal qualities home to everyone.

Grant's Partnership With Sherman

Sherman was a curious man. Although personally very close to Grant, he was unlike him in many ways. Orphaned as a child, Sherman had been adopted by a prominent family. His benefactor had secured his appointment to West Point where, in spite of a rebellious nature, Sherman did well. Much more intelligent than Grant, Sherman graduated sixth out of forty-two at West Point. Much to his distress, he did not get to serve in the Mexican War, instead passing time in a frontier post in Florida. After further frustration he resigned from the army and invested in a business venture in California. Bad luck or poor practice proved his undoing and he lost his own and the money he had borrowed from friends. It took years, but he paid back every cent. After trying other careers he ended up teaching at a military academy in Louisiana. There he learned to love the South and to deepen his friendship with some of his West Point classmates.

When war broke out, however, he returned North and sought a commission. Not because he particularly abhorred slavery or felt strongly about the abstract theory of secession. Sherman hated and feared revolution. He thought that society was held together by the flimsiest of bonds and revolution could lead quickly to anarchy and disaster. His brother, a United States Senator, helped him secure a commission, and in early battles--such as First Manassas--Sherman distinguished himself. Unfortunately, as it turned out, promotion led to pressures of independent command and Sherman suffered an apparent nervous breakdown. Rumors swept the Army that Sherman had lost his mind and only after his wife's intervention was he given the opportunity of another command. It was at this point that the team of Grant and Sherman came on the scene, and together they took Vicksburg and relieved Chattanooga. Later Sherman described the relationship this way: "He stood by me when I was crazy and I stood by him when he was drunk--now we stand by each other always."

The Success of Operation Crusher

So in 1864, it was up to these two men to carry out a program to end the bloodiest and most destructive war in American history. What they did between May 1864 and April 1865 was to make it bloodier and more destructive. In his campaign Grant lost 110,000 men and inflicted 60,000 casualties on Lee's army. In the process Grant introduced the new concept of continuous combat. Instead of pausing after battles he just kept moving on, engaging in one fight after another so as to bleed his enemy to death. Grant knew he had greater manpower reserves and he saw no reason to drag the contest out. In his campaign against Atlanta, Sherman lost 31,600 men and inflicted 35,000 casualties.

But after taking Atlanta Sherman undertook a new venture in modern war--a war against the people of the South. He cut a path of destruction sixty miles wide from Atlanta to Savannah and then north from Savannah to Raleigh, N.C. In his wake he left blackened farms, empty smokehouses, twisted railroad rails, gutted factories, and empty warehouses. Materially it would take the region thirty years to recover. Furthermore, he undertook to break the fighting spirit of the civilian population and imply to them and to their men at the front that no place was safe from Union armies. It was a calculated policy of war against civilian morale. It was the same concept that we later became familiar with in our strategic bombing in World War II and in some operations in Korea and Vietnam.

Reviewing and Interpreting Main Ideas

1. What was Operation Crusher?

2. Why did Grant use the military strategy known as Operation Crusher?

3. Should Operation Crusher have been used? Or was it wrong, for either military or moral reasons, to use this strategy? Following are several questions and statements that stimulate your thinking about the central issue: Was it right or wrong to use Operation Crusher?

   a. Was it better to go all out and win as quickly as possible or should they have fought by the old rules? One argument could be that the older style of warfare had not brought results during the previous three years, the public was getting weary of casualties with no apparent success. If something were not done to end the frustration, public will in the North would falter and all the previous casualties would be for nothing. Moreover, whether Grant and Sherman thought so or not, slavery was a moral evil--so wasn't a higher purpose served by bending the rules a little bit?

   b. Should civilian morale be a legitimate target in modern war? Civilians support the war by their votes, their taxes, and their production. Why shouldn't they share the burden of the war just like the soldier; if they give up, the soldier can't go on, so why not convince them directly to quit?

   c. As Sherman argued, he didn't start the war, he was trying to end it. What was the responsibility of the Southern government? If they couldn't protect their civilians, weren't they obligated to end the war? If you are losing a fight but won't give up, whose fault is it that the other guy keeps hitting you? What if after ten rounds he hits you below the belt? Can he legitimately contend he is trying to convince the enemies that they can't win? However, once you make civilians legitimate targets in modern war, where can you draw the line on what is allowed and what is not allowed?

SECTION IV
AMERICA BECOMES A WORLD POWER

List of Lessons

This section includes six lessons that pertain to entry of the United States into world affairs as a great power, new problems of national security associated with a great power role in international relations, and policies that established the United States as a world power. Global military and geopolitical strategies are examined. Conditions and consequences of new foreign policies associated with national security are also emphasized. Finally, basic ethical issues of foreign policy decisions are raised. The lessons are

13. Purchasing Alaska

14. National Security Through Naval Power: Ideas of Alfred Thayer Mahan

15. Two Views of Expansionism

16. Shaping the "Open Door Policy"

17. The Ethics of the Panama Canal

18. American Intervention in the Mexican Revolution, 1914

Overview for Teachers

After the Civil War the United States began to broaden its vision and expand its involvement in international affairs. Domestically, Americans had determinedly pursued the growth and development of their territory. The West was now won; the Pacific and Atlantic Coasts were soon to be linked by the transcontinental railway. More and more, the U.S. began to see its economic strength and vitality as if it were limitless. This vision of limitless potential became a powerful force accompanying an increasingly self-conscious consideration of America's position in the world and more open concern for U.S. interests beyond its own shores.

Even before the Civil War the U.S. had begun to extend its reach outward into the Pacific. In 1854, Commodore Perry had opened Japan to American trade and commerce, advancing further the thriving trade that already existed with China. But this Pacific presence also brought with it heightened concern for the protection of American interests. The European powers were extending their reach as well (recall that the Russians had put settlements in California, one of the factors contributing to the Monroe Doctrine). By the 1860s, the U.S. began to look more protectively at the areas on its periphery and to consider the opportunities for expansion outward.

The end of the War between the States enabled political leaders like Secretary of State Seward to try to extend America's claims to match its growing interests. Looking south to the Caribbean and outward into the Pacific, many of these efforts met with resistance. But, as **Lesson 13** shows, one successful outcome was the purchase of Alaska from the overextended Russians in 1867.

The pressure for increasing American involvement overseas was to have lingering impact on our sense of ourselves as a nation. Having accepted Washington's concentration on trade and commerce as an appropriate guideline for American overseas interests, now the political and military consequences of that guideline had to be addressed. As the turn of the century approached, the United States had not developed, nor apparently needed, a systematic strategic perspective that expressed its security requirements.

Now it became essential to do so. The orientation for a U.S. strategic perspective developed in the 1880s when a naval Captain named Alfred Thayer Mahan provided an intellectual framework for the growing debate over America's place in the world. Mahan argued for the importance of sea power (including maritime commerce as well as naval force) to the strength of a nation. As **Lesson 14** shows, Mahan was to have a profound impact not only on the emergence of a uniquely American naval posture, but on the American view of its overall security. Mahan's views shaped a significant part of American thinking at a critical juncture in the development of a new national security perspective.

Further context for Mahan's writing was provided by the increasingly venturesome course that American policy was taking. The turn of the century was marked by enthusiastic U.S. entry into the Spanish-American War. Emerging victorious in that War, the United States found itself faced with the question of what to do with the former Spanish colonies--Cuba, Puerto Rico and the Philippine Islands. Now the political debate over the issue of overseas expansion was joined full force.

Lesson 15 outlines the main arguments in this debate. The Expansionists, professing a new spirit of American vitality, argued that U.S. security, strength and economic growth dictated overseas expansion. The Anti-expansionists, stressing traditional American principles in international affairs, argued that overseas expansion would reduce the United States to the level of the imperialist powers of Europe. In the end the United States kept Puerto Rico and the Philippines, but debate over the question of the proprietary and extent of U.S. involvement in international politics was to continue.

Indeed the issue arose again almost immediately as the United States sought to define its role--based on its long-standing interest--in the increasing commercial competition among the European powers in Asia. Because it focused principally on economic concerns the issue was resolved more easily within the United States. The "Open Door Policy," described in **Lesson 16**, stated that, unlike the other powers, the U.S sought only free trade in China and would make no claim on territory. In addition, however, the United States also committed itself to the integrity and independence of China. Once again, the development of policy on a specific issue had produced a general posture that was to endure in American security policy--commitment to an American presence in the Far East and the beginning of a moral position that would later be defined as support for the self-determination of nations.

By this time, in the face of continuing debate, support for the expansion of U.S. interests overseas was advanced on both pragmatic and moral grounds, intensifying the sense of mission and the continuing belief in the limitlessness of America's potential. These notions were evident in the successful U.S. effort led by President Theodore Roosevelt to build a canal across the Isthmus of Panama. The Panama Canal was considered to be essential for U.S commercial and strategic interests. It shortened the sea route between the Atlantic and Pacific Coasts and provided direct support for the growth of American naval power. Once completed, the Canal was to emerge as a central element in United States national security. However, as **Lesson 17** indicates, the manner in which the rights to the Canal were negotiated also became an enduring issue.

Further American attention to its stated security interests in the Western Hemisphere arose in Mexico. After a series of revolutionary changes beginning in 1910, Mexico had entered a period of great political instability. The U.S. had quickly adopted a moral posture condemning the non-democratic forms of government that these changes had produced. But in 1914, as **Lesson 18** describes, the United States determined that its citizens and interests were at risk and intervened directly to establish its position. Once again incident and principle combined to establish enduring policy. The United States had followed a policy of intervention to restore order to unstable governments where the outcome was perceived to affect American interests. That pattern would be applied consistently in the future.

The United States had thus entered the twentieth century with full confidence in its vitality and potential, a confidence upon which it was willing to act. Yet underlying that action was a lingering sense of discomfort about the practical and moral consequences for U.S. interests.

American History - 13   Lesson Plan and Notes for Teachers

Purchasing Alaska

by Donald A. Ritchie

Preview of Main Points

Alaska has become a key part of America's national defense system against the Soviet Union. Ironically, the United States acquired the territory peacefully from Russia in 1867. Secretary of State William Seward, an avid expansionist, fought for the purchase of Alaska despite considerable opposition from the press, the public and Congress. This lesson explores Seward's reasons, as well as the Russian's reasons for selling such a valuable and strategically located territory.

Connection to Textbooks

This lesson expands upon textbook treatment of the Alaska purchase, presenting the motivations involved on both sides of the sale, and calling on the student to develop a position of advocacy regarding the purchase.

Objectives

Students are expected to:

1. recognize the motivations of both Russia and the United States in the purchase of Alaska;

2. understand the nature of the opposition to the purchase; and

3. appreciate the strategic importance of the purchase.

Suggestions for Teaching the Lesson

Opening the Lesson

o Show the students the polar map of the world in the Handout. Ask them to discuss the strategic location of Alaska to the United States. Note from the map how close Alaska lies to the Soviet Union, both across the Pacific and over the North Pole. Without Alaska, the United States would be more heavily dependent on another nation, Canada, for its northern defense.

Developing the Lesson

o Have the students read the material describing the purchase of Alaska.

o Either have them write out assignments A and B in the Handout, or assign students to prepare brief statements for and against the purchase to deliver verbally. Call upon various students to debate the issues as if they were the Congress considering Seward's treaty.

(c) *American History and National Security*. Mershon Center, The Ohio State University

o Be sure the students fully understand both sides, as well as the reasons why the purchase was eventually approved.

Concluding the Lesson

o Historian Walter LaFeber, in his book *The New Empire: An Interpretation of American Expansion, 1860-1898* (Ithaca, 1963), has argued that America did not obtain new territories after the Spanish-American War in 1898 "to fulfill a colonial policy, but to use these holdings as a means to acquire markets for the glut of goods pouring out of highly mechanized factories and farms. The two acquisitions which might be considered exceptions to this statement are Alaska and Hawaii. It is more difficult, however, to understand the purchase of "Seward's Icebox" without comprehending the Secretary of State's magnificent view of the future American commercial empire. This view did not premise a colonial policy, but assumed the necessity of controlling the Asian markets for commerical, not political, expansion. As the chairman of the House Foreign Affairs Committee commented in 1867, Alaska was the "drawbridge" between the North American continent and Asia." (pages 408-409)

o Discuss this economic interpretation of the Alaska purchase with the class, considering the ways in which the lesson does or does not support this interpretation.

Suggestions for Additional Reading

Jensen, Ronald J. *The Alaska Purchase and Russian-American Relations.* Seattle: University of Washington Press, 1975.

   A useful book for students interested in this subject.

Holbo, Paul S. *Tarnished Expansion: The Alaska Scandal, the Press, and Congress, 1867-1871.* Knoxville: University of Tennessee Press, 1983.

   Holbo provides a brief and interesting detective story.

Answers to Questions

1. An America which would spread over the continent of North America and have influence in Asia and the rest of the world.

2. Because of its commercial and strategic value, as well as the nation's destiny to spread over North America.

3. Congress rejected them and the public was hostile to them.

4. Because it was difficult to defend and becoming unprofitable to maintain.

5. Congress, the press and the public were suspicious of the scheme and could not see the advantages of purchasing Alaska.

6. It provided America a strategic command base close to the Soviet Union.

American History - 13   Handout

Purchasing Alaska

Introduction

In the nuclear age, Alaska plays an invaluable role in America's national defense systems. Its position, stretching across the North Pacific to within a few miles of the Soviet coastline, provides the United States with sites for bases both for radar to detect incoming planes and missiles, and for American offensive bombers and intercontinental missiles.

Ironically, the United States purchased the territory of Alaska from Russia. At that time, in 1867, Russian leaders were convinced they had gotten the better of the deal, while many Americans suspected that their government had foolishly bought worthless property. Within Congress there was considerable opposition to the Alaska purchase. There were strong possibilities that either the Senate would fail to ratify the Alaska treaty or the House would not appropriate the money needed to buy this vast northern territory. Even supporters of the treaty, who recognized the potential economic and strategic value of Alaska, never dreamed that it would become such a center for strategic communications, command, and control.

For what reasons and motivations was this monumental purchase made?

Secretary of State William H. Seward

The chief architect of the Alaska purchase was Secretary of State William H. Seward. In 1867 he was 66 years old. During his long political career he had served as New York Governor and Senator and had become a founding member of the new Republican party. In 1860 he narrowly lost the Republican nomination for President to Abraham Lincoln. Seward then became Lincoln's Secretary of State, and he continued in that role after Andrew Johnson became President in 1865.

Always an avid expansionist, Secretary Seward had been unable to pursue his expansionist goals until after the Civil War had ended. Shortly after the war, he said in one speech that if he had thirty to fifty more years of life, he would work to give the United States "possession of the American continent and the control of the world."

Seward's expansion aimed south into the Caribbean, where he negotiated to buy the Virgin Islands, and considered building naval bases on Santo Domingo, Haiti, Cuba, and Puerto Rico. Congress, however, rejected the Virgin Island treaty, and nothing came of his plans for naval bases. Seward also looked west to the Pacific. In 1867 the United States took over the uninhabited Midway Island and negotiated a reciprocal trade treaty with Hawaii, which Seward hoped would serve as a step towards annexation. The Senate failed to ratify the treaty, and for the most part, Seward's expansionist policies were rebuffed by a Congress and a public weary from war and already possessing vast and largely unoccupied territories in the American West.

Then in 1867 the Russian minister to Washington hinted that Russia might be willing to sell its Alaska Territory to the United States. Seward sprang into action.

Pros and Cons of the Alaska Purchase

Why did Russia want to sell its holdings in Alaska? Russia had claimed the territory of Alaska since the 18th century, when Vitrus Bering explored its coast to determine whether Siberia and North America were linked. In the early nineteenth century, the Russian-American

(c) *American History and National Security.* Mershon Center, The Ohio State University

Company was formed to administer Alaska as a colony, and to raise money through such commercial ventures as fishing, fur trading and mining.

In 1861, however, the Russian-American Company was near bankruptcy. Its stock had dropped sharply in value. Its fur trading had declined and was actually losing money. Coal mining, lumbering, and ice operations had failed. The Russians also suffered from competition with the British Hudson Bay Company, based in Canada, and feared that Britain might try to seize control of Alaska. Alaska was too far away for Russia to defend successfully. Then too, some gold discoveries in Alaska raised the possiblity of American miners rushing into the territory. One way or another, Russia seemed destined to lose Alaska. Selling the territory to the United States, therefore, offered several positive solutions to Russian problems: 1) it would raise revenue that Russia badly needed; 2) it would stop British expansion into the North Pacific; and 3) it would maintain Russia's good relations with the United States.

To William Seward, the possibility of purchasing Alaska was tremendously exciting. He firmly believed that the United States would someday spread over all of North America, including Alaska and Canada, but wanted such expansion to come peacefully rather than through warfare. He saw commercial value to the territory and its future fishing, fur and mining operations. Some supporters of the purchase saw it in terms of beating back the competition of the British Hudson Bay Company in Canada, but Seward's vision was more expansive. He saw Alaska as a naval base on the path to Asia. In addition, purchasing Alaska would help strengthen America's relations with Russia.

Against these positive factors, Seward had to weigh the negatives. Not only were the press and public cool to the idea, but many were overtly hostile to spending seven million dollars to purchase a frozen territory they knew almost nothing about. Congress had rejected other expansionist treaties, and Seward had many opponents in his own party. Radical Republicans who were moving to impeach President Andrew Johnson because of his Reconstruction policies, disliked Seward as one of the President's allies. As a result, they were suspicious of anything he proposed. Newspaper headlines were already calling it "Seward's Folly" and "Seward's Icebox," and dismissing Alaska as a barren, worthless land of "short rations and long twilights."

However, Secretary Seward refused to lose this opportunity. He launched a campaign in both the press and the Congress to help win passage of the treaty.

Conclusion

Seward's case was greatly strengthened when he won the support of Senator Charles Sumner, chairman of the Senate Foreign Relations Committee. Because of Sumner's efforts, the Senate quickly passed the Alaska treaty by a vote of 37 to 2. The House of Representatives was more suspicious, and waited over a year before voting 113 to 43 in favor of appropriating money necessary to purchase Alaska. Afterwards, rumors spread through Washington that the Russian ambassador had bribed key members of the House to win the appropriation. The press made much of this scandal, but a Congressional investigation failed to discover any evidence proving the charges true. Nevertheless, because the Alaska purchase was so controversial, from start to finish, no expansionist proposal succeeded in the United States for the next thirty years.

American History - 13   Handout

Questions for Review and Interpretation

1. What was Secretary Seward's vision of the future of America?

2. Why did he want America to acquire Alaska?

3. What was the fate of his other expansionist proposals?

4. Why did the Russians want to sell Alaska?

5. Why did some Americans work against the purchase of Alaska?

6. How has the purchase of Alaska been important to the national security of the United States?

Assignment

Based on your reading of this lesson, and from materials in your textbook and any other source, prepare one of the following items:

A. A newspaper editorial in support of the Alaska purchase.

B. A speech in Congress either in favor of or opposed to the treaty purchasing Alaska.

American History - 13   **Handout**

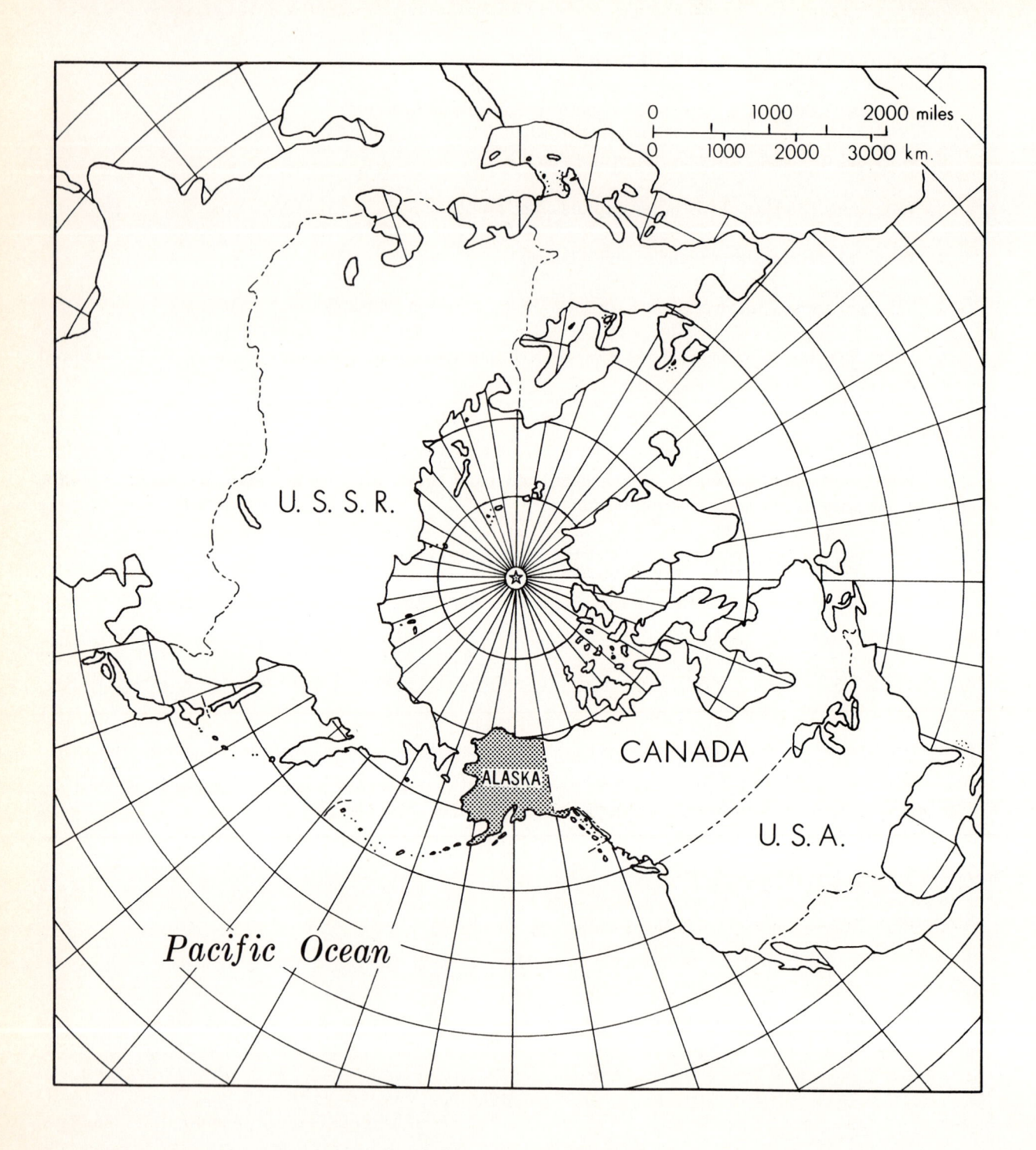

American History - 14   Lesson Plan and Notes for Teachers

National Security Through Naval Power: Ideas of Alfred Thayer Mahan

by James R. Leutze

Preview of Main Points

This lesson treats the ideas and influence of Alfred Thayer Mahan on national security policies of the United States government during the latter part of the nineteenth century and early years of the twentieth century. Mahan's ideas about achieving national security through naval power and about strategies for using naval power are emphasized.

Connection to Textbooks

This lesson is related to textbook treatments of American imperialism during the period from the 1880s to the nation's entry into World War I. The lesson can be used in conjunction with studies of acquisition of overseas territories by the United States and examination of national policies for defense of the Western Hemisphere against threats from European or Asian powers.

Objectives

Students are expected to:

1. know Mahan's ideas about the use of naval power worldwide to achieve national security;
2. identify ideas of Mahan on naval strategy;
3. identify ideas of Mahan on naval strategy in war;
4. assess the influence of Mahan's ideas on national security and foreign policies of the United States; and
5. discuss strengths and weaknesses of Mahan's ideas and their applicability to the contemporary world.

Suggestions for Teaching the Lesson

Opening the Lesson

o   Write the name of Alfred Thayer Mahan on the chalkboard. In addition, write on the chalkboard the name of Mahan's classic book: *The Influence of Sea Power Upon History, 1660-1783.* If possible, obtain a copy of his book from the library or other source and exhibit it to students. Tell students that Mahan, through ideas expressed in his book, became a great influence on American policies on national security. Ask them to speculate on what his ideas about national security were. Also ask them to speculate about how ideas in a book could become a major force on the policy decisions of government officials.

Developing the Lesson

o   Have students read the case study on Alfred Thayer Mahan, in the Handout. Ask them to check their speculations about his ideas, expressed in the opening phase of the lesson, against information in the case study.

o Ask students to answer questions at the end of the case study in the Handout in preparation for classroom discussion.

Concluding the Lesson

o Conduct a classroom discussion about the ideas of Alfred Thayer Mahan in terms of the questions at the end of the case study in the Handout.

o Questions 1-3 require students to identify and comprehend Mahan's ideas about naval power and national security. Require students to justify their answers to items 1-3 by reference to the facts of the case study in the Handout. Check students' answers to items 1-3 directly against information in the case study. In contrast, questions 4-5 require students to express opinions and value judgments about the ideas of Mahan. Require students to ground answers to items 4-5 in the case study in the Handout; however, expect and accept reasonable variations in their answers to these questions.

Suggestions for Additional Reading

Following is an annotated list of books about the ideas in this lesson. These books are presented as additional sources of information for teachers. However, very able students might be referred to one or more of these books.

Livezey, William Edmund. *Mahan on Sea Power*. Norman: University of Oklahoma Press, 1980.

Mahan on Seapower reviews the ideas of this nineteenth century military thinker. Livezey analyzes the strategic thought of Mahan and presents a bibliography of his writings.

Mahan, Alfred Thayer. *The Influence of Sea Power Upon History, 1660-1783*. Englewood Cliffs, N.J.: Prentice Hall, 1980.

This book represents Mahan's prescription for America's rise to greatness. With Great Britain as the primary reference point, Mahan avers that all great world powers achieved pre-- eminence with the inexpendable aid of a powerful navy and merchant marine.

Puleston, Capt. W.D. *Mahan: The Life and Work of Captain Alfred Thayer Mahan, U.S.N.*. New Haven, Conn.: Yale University Press, 1939.

Puleston's book was for many years the standard work on Mahan's life and thought. Although now somewhat dated, this sympathetic account conveys a first-hand feeling for the times about which he writes.

Seager, Robert. *Alfred Thayer Mahan: The Man and His Letters*. Annapolis, MD: Naval Institute Press, 1977.

This is perhaps the best book to date on Mahan. Seager presents a more critical look at Mahan than does Puleston. If he emphasizes the shortcomings of this nineteenth century strategist, Seager also notes his intellectual contributions.

Seager, Robert and Maguire, Doris D., eds. *The Letters and Papers of Alfred Thayer Mahan*. Annapolis, Md.: Naval Institute Press, 1975.

Seager and Maguire claim to have found only a quarter of Mahan's writings. Nevertheless, this is the most comprehensive collection available to scholars.

American History - 14   Handout

National Security Through Naval Power: Ideas of Alfred Thayer Mahan

Captain (later Admiral) Alfred Thayer Mahan had great influence on the national security policies of the United States from the 1880s through the early years of the twentieth century. Today, many experts believe that Mahan's ideas are out-of-date. However, in his own time, Mahan's views prevailed. Furthermore, Captain Mahan has been judged to be one of the most influential thinkers on national security affairs in the last one hundred years. Who was Alfred Thayer Mahan? What were his ideas on how to achieve national security? How did these ideas affect policies of the United States government? What were the value of these ideas?

Background Information About Alfred Thayer Mahan

Alfred Thayer Mahan was born in 1840 the son of another important military intellectual, Dennis Hart Mahan, who was teaching at West Point at the time. The younger Mahan decided upon a naval career and entered the Naval Academy at the age of sixteen. Three years later he graduated near the top of his class--second out of twenty. The next twenty-four years were not particularly exciting ones for Mahan although he served at sea in many places around the world. He participated in the Civil War, but did not actually see combat since most of his service was in the blockading fleet off the Southern coast. After the war he went back to foreign duty and was finishing a tour in South American waters, when, in 1884, Mahan was called to teach at the new Naval War College in Newport, Rhode Island.

While European navies were turning increasingly to metal hulls, steam propulsion and modern gunnery, the United States was still maintaining wooden ships, relying on sail power and firing guns forged twenty-five years before. Not that everything in the U.S. Navy was old-fashioned. There were some steam propelled, metal vessels, but there is no question that the U.S. Navy was being left behind in what we now know was the beginning of a technological revolution. By the late 1870s this fact was recognized by some influential, forward-looking people in the United States. Generally, they saw the U.S. as a country with great potential and believed that a modern navy was essential if the U.S. was to realize its destiny. The War College, where professional officers could go back to school to learn more about naval strategy, was part of the campaign to reinvigorate the U.S. Navy.

Within two years after he arrived in Newport, Mahan was named president of the College; four years later he put his lectures on military history together in his greatest intellectual accomplishment *The Influence of Seapower Upon History, 1660-1783*. As the title implies, this was a study of how nations had either profited or suffered from the possession or lack of naval power. Relying particularly on the history of England, Mahan showed how that country had prospered and gained an empire through the proper utilization of their naval arm. Just having a large navy was not enough, Mahan claimed, you must also use it in the right way. This principle was related to another guiding concept the Captain had: history, studied properly, revealed a set of rules or guidelines which if followed led to a similar result. On the other hand, if you violated these rules you were lost in the unexplored, the unknown. The lesson was obvious: find the historical actions that had led to success, pattern your conduct on those actions and success would follow. It was a way of using the past as a guide to the future and it provided a very satisfying way of avoiding the uncertainty that had always attended dealing with the years ahead. Satisfying it no doubt was, but we also now know that it was over-simplified. But Mahan was not alone in trying to discover "laws" that governed human success or failure, this search was very popular toward the end of the nineteenth century.

Mahan's Ideas on National Strategy

He did not always make it explicit, but Mahan implied that if the United States intended to be a great power it should pattern its national strategy on Great Britain's strategy. In Mahan's view, much of Britain's success resulted from possession of a large, powerful navy. In writing about the national strategy for this navy, Mahan relied heavily on the ideas of the famed military (land) strategist, Baron de Antoine Henri Jomini. Mahan suggested that the seas were similar to "commons" or public lands across which there were highways; as in land warfare, nations had to control those highways--hence he argued for control of the seas. Clearly Mahan was also arguing for his own service, he wanted to see the U.S. enlarge its naval arm and he was willing to provide historical examples of why it needed to do so. Constantly referring to the British example, Mahan "proved" that a nation to be prosperous needed not only a large navy but also a large merchant fleet to compete for the world's trade.

There was an unbreakable bond between a merchant fleet and a fighting navy. The navy needed the resources, both materiel and human, maintained by a peacetime fleet, to adequately arm itself in war. The ship building capacity and the men trained by sea service could be used in a time of crisis, while the merchant fleet needed the navy for protection. This led to one of Mahan's most basic principles: the ability of nations to get and maintain lines of communication across the seas was their single most important goal. These lines were needed in peace and war. In war, if denied to the enemy, the enemy could not approach your coast; and conversely, they provided you a route to your enemy. In peace, they allowed you access to the world's resources and a way to transport your products abroad.

By following these principles Mahan very logically could support an imperialistic position. To maintain world-wide lines of communications you needed bases where your navy could assemble to protect your merchant fleet, moreover you needed coaling stations where both fleets could refuel. Since you could not run the risk of relying on other countries to provide you with these outposts, each nation that aspired to world power should control its own far-flung ports and coaling stations. The U.S. also needed a quick route from the Atlantic to the Pacific for trade as well as defensive reasons, in other words, it needed a canal through Central America. These arguments were very appealing to many who were convinced that the United States should join the rush for colonies presently dominated by the European powers; unless we did so, they said, all the prime locations would be taken and the U.S. would be doomed to second class status.

Mahan's Views on Naval Strategy in War

Mahan also had views on naval combat strategy. Here, too, he borrowed from Jomini arguing that the "laws" of naval warfare were very similar to the "laws" of land war. In Mahan's view the primary objective for a navy was the opponent's navy just as in land warfare it was the army. Therefore, all efforts should be directed toward bringing the enemies' organized force into a climactic battle. Mahan was not very subtle, he didn't put a lot of emphasis on maneuver or surprise, he sought a decisive clash of arms. The primary instrument in this fight would be the big guns of the big ships, the battleships. Emphasis in his view should be given to building these big ships and little effort should be wasted on constructing small, fast ships suitable for commerce raiding. The battle, the war, and the future would be determined by the nation with the most and the best big ships.

Influence of Mahan's Ideas

Although the foregoing is a very simplified and very short version of Mahan's thoughts, you probably can see why it would appeal to many people. For one thing, it would obviously appeal to the Navy who wanted justification for building more ships. His theories would also appeal to businesspeople and others who wanted to see the country's markets and sources of supply increased. There also were missionaries and other well meaning people who wanted to see the "civilized" world have more influence over the "backward" or "uncivilized" world. Then there were the politicians who either believed in these things themselves or wanted to appeal for the support of those who did. There were also nationalists, many of whom belonged to one or more of the groups noted above. They wanted the U.S. to be strong and expand because it was our destiny and our obligation to lead the world. For all of these people, having historical laws to use in justifying their arguments for expansion was very useful. Mahan quickly became very popular with people like Theodore Roosevelt, Henry Cabot Lodge, and later Franklin D. Roosevelt.

One problem though was that Mahan's books could be read by other people in other countries and they could apply his lessons also. Specifically, Mahan became popular in Germany and Japan, two countries that could be seen as competing with the U.S. for colonies and for markets. Moreover, if everyone believed that the important thing to do was to prepare to fight and win a climactic battle, then everyone would try to win the battle before the first gun was fired by building the biggest and the best. These competing desires could and did lead to costly arms races. Obviously Mahan was not solely responsible for the arms race before World War I or the arms competition in the 1930s, but his ideas gave support to those who argued for larger fleets.

Ironically, in planning for actually fighting a war in the Pacific, both the American Navy and the Imperial Japanese Navy based their strategy on Mahan's principles. Both tended to concentrate their attention on building battleships and both anticipated that a titanic surface battle would decide the war. Indeed considerable effort was expended both before the war and in the early years of the conflict to prepare for this war-winning stroke. However, as we know there never was this great surface battle (unless you consider Leyte Gulf to have been the culmination of these plans, but it didn't occur until late 1944 when the war had already been decided). Instead, the most important developments in the naval war were amphibious assault and two weapons Mahan had hardly considered, the submarine and carrier-based aircraft. This brings us to the issue of technological change. Mahan was not very good at anticipating how new developments would influence warfare. To his credit, he realized that he was living at a time of revolutionary change, but still the finality with which he proclaimed his laws and principles made it appear that they applied across time despite technological change. This sense of finality and ultimate truth was very appealing to some of those who became the most enthusiastic supporters of Mahan.

So, Mahan was very influential, but he also made some serious errors. For instance, he failed to adequately consider that the geographic position of the U.S. was very different from the geographic position of Great Britain. There also are real questions about whether there are any "laws" that govern events. Many historians would say that you are misusing history when you try to learn specific lessons from it.

Reviewing and Interpreting Main Ideas

1. What were Mahan's ideas about national strategy?

2. What were Mahan's ideas about naval strategy in war?

3. How did Mahan's ideas influence national security policies or foreign policies of the United States?

4. What were strengths and weaknesses of Mahan's ideas?

5. To what extent are Mahan's ideas applicable to national security policies in today's world?

American History - 15   Lesson Plan and Notes for Teachers

Two Views of Expansionism

by Donald A. Ritchie

Preview of Main Points

This lesson highlights two speeches by United States Senators during the debate over overseas expansion after the Spanish-American War. Although both Republicans, George Hoar and Albert Beveridge represented entirely different views. The older Hoar cautioned against abandoning American principles of self-determination and imposing U.S. will on smaller countries. The young Beveridge, starting his political career, pictured a bright future of strength, security, and economic growth resulting from overseas expansion. Their contrasting views explain the alternatives facing the United States at that juncture.

Connection to Textbooks

This lesson fits history textbook chapters covering the Spanish-American war and imperialism. It supplements these materials with the use of historical documents, in the form of speeches delivered at the time.

Objectives

Students are expected to:

1. identify and explain the conflicting views over American overseas expansion;
2. identify and explain the motives behind the arguments of Senator Hoar and other Anti-expansionists;
3. identify and explain the motives behind the arguments of Senator Beveridge and other Expansionists;
4. analyze the decision made as a result of this debate; and
5. practice skills in using evidence in documents to answer questions about the debate.

Suggestions for Teaching the Lesson

Opening the Lesson

o Review with the class the events of the Spanish-American war covered in previous lessons and assignments. Using a map, have the students locate the Spanish possessions which the United States occupied at the end of the war. How should the United States deal with these territories? Point out that the United States had previously taken territory only on the North American continent, including Alaska, which was not connected to the other states and territories. Also remind them that the Census of 1890 officially declared the American frontier closed. Discuss with the students the reasons why some Americans might look for overseas expansion.

Developing the Lesson

o Have the students read the materials in this lesson found in the Handout. Focus their attention on the two documents.

(c) *American History and National Security*. Mershon Center, The Ohio State University

- o Have the students respond to the questions and complete the Decision Tree at the end of the Handout.

- o Possibly have two students give dramatic readings of the two speeches in a reconstructed debate; or have them paraphrase the remarks in their own words.

Concluding the Lesson

- o Discuss with the students the decision Americans made after the debate over expansionism. How do they evaluate that decision now? Were the consequences as negative as Hoar predicted? Or as optimistic as Beveridge predicted? Looking at the map, in what areas have imperialist nations lost territories they once occupied? What territories are still occupied? What role does morality play in the relationships between larger and smaller nations?

Suggestions for Additional Reading

Beisner, Robert L. *Twelve Against Empire: The Anti-Imperialists, 1898-1900*. New York: McGraw-Hill, 1968.

Beisner gives profiles of Senator Hoar and other Anti-expansionists.

Braeman, John. *Albert J. Beveridge: American Nationalist*. Chicago: University of Chicago Press, 1971.

This is a useful book for students interested in this debate.

Answers to Handout Questions

1. a. A world of tyranny and despotism.

    b. The doctrine that people have a right to self-determination and to overthrow governments they disapproved of.

    c. Because it is tyrannical to impose a government on another people against their will.

    d. Self-government.

    e. It was a birth-right belonging to all people.

2. a. Toward commercial supremacy of the world.

    b. By finding new markets for farm and industrial products, and for what our ships carry.

    c. That the United States already imposed government on American Indians and on American territories without their consent.

    d. A "just, humane, civilizing government," free from "savage, bloody rule."

    e. That the American flag, and American settlements, would continue to march northwards and southwards across the oceans just as it had marched across the continent during nineteenth century expansion.

3. a. The United States had gained several of Spain's colonial territories, and debated what to do with them.

    b. The Anti-expansionists wanted to make these territories free and independent; the Expansionists wanted to make them American territories.

    c. The Anti-expansionists saw tyranny and despotism as the alternative to self-determination; the Expansionists saw weakness and economic stagnation as the alternative to territorial growth.

    d. They chose the Expansionist side, seeing it as a way of achieving strength, security and economic growth.

Two Views of Expansionism

As a result of the Spanish-American war in 1898, Spain lost its colonial possessions of Cuba, Puerto Rico and the Philippine Islands. A great national debate began in the United States whether it should hold these former Spanish colonies as its own colonies or make them independent. Some argued that America had always been a colonial power, taking new territories constantly as it moved westward across the continent, and that overseas expansion was the natural continuation of American expansion. Such expansion would add to the prosperity and the security of the United States, they insisted. Opponents charged that the taking of overseas colonies was no different from European imperialism, and that it would violate a fundamental principle of America: the right of all people to self-government.

Two views of what America should do about overseas expansion were expressed by two prominent Republican Senators. George Frisbe Hoar was seventy-four years old, and had represented Massachusetts in the United States Senate for twenty-three years when he made the following address on April 17, 1900:

> There lies at the bottom of . . . imperialism a doctrine which, if adopted, is to revolutionize the world in favor of despotism. It directly conflicts with and contradicts the doctrine on which our own Revolution was founded. . . . It is the doctrine that when, in the judgment of any one nation or any combination of nations, the institutions which a people set up and maintain for themselves are disapproved, they have a right to overthrow that government and to enter upon and possess it themselves. . . .
>
> Our imperialistic friends seem to have forgotten the use of the vocabulary of liberty. They talk about giving good government. 'We shall give them such a government as we think they are fitted for.' 'We shall give them a better government than they had before.' Why, . . . that one phrase conveys to . . . a free people the most stinging of insults. In that little phrase, as in a seed, is contained the germ of all despotism and of all tyranny.
>
> Government is not a gift. Free government is not to be given by all the blended powers of earth and heaven. It is a birthright. It belongs--as our [ancestors] said and as their children said, as Jefferson said and as President McKinley said--to human nature itself. There can be no good government but self-government.

Albert J. Beveridge was thirty-six years old and at the very beginning of his political career, when he attracted national attention during his successful race for a Senate seat in Indiana. He delivered this speech during that campaign, on September 16, 1898.

> In this campaign, the question is larger than a party question. It is an American question. It is a world question. Shall the American people continue their march toward the commercial supremacy of the world? Shall free institutions broaden their blessed reign as the children of liberty [increase] in strength, until the empire of our principles is established over the hearts of all mankind?
>
> Have we no mission to perform, no duty to discharge to our fellow men? Has God endowed us with gifts . . . and marked us as the people of His peculiar favor, merely to [have us] rot in our own selfishness . . . ?
>
> . . . Shall we reap the reward that waits on our discharge of our high duty? Shall

we occupy new markets for what our farmers raise, our factories make, our merchants sell--aye, and, please God, new markets for what our ships shall carry?

Hawaii is ours. Puerto Rico is to be ours. At the prayer of her people, Cuba finally will be ours. In the islands of the East, even to the gates of Asia, coaling stations are to be ours, at the very least. The flag of a liberal government is to float over the Philippines....

The opposition tells us that we ought not to govern a people without their consent. I answer: The rule of liberty--that all just government derives its authority from the consent of the governed--applies only to those who are capable of self-government. We govern the Indians without their consent. We govern our territories without their consent. How do they know that our government would be without their consent? Would not the people of the Philippines prefer the just, humane, civilizing government of this Republic to the savage, bloody rule . . . from which we have rescued them?

Will you say by your vote that American ability to govern has decayed? . . . Will you affirm by your vote that you are an infidel to American power and practical sense? . . . Will you remember that we do but what our fathers did? We but pitch the tents of liberty farther westward, farther southward. We only continue the march of the flag.

In this debate, the Expansionists captured the public's imagination and support. The youthful Senator Beveridge represented a new and ambitious generation; the older Senator Hoar represented a more guarded and cautious generation that was passing from the scene. Those opposed to expansion had emphasized justice and morality in international relations. They called on the nation not to abandon the principle on which it was founded, and warned of the consequences of its actions. The Expansionists, however, presented a more compelling argument of American strength, security, and economic growth through overseas expansion. When the debate was over, the United States had granted Cuba its independence, but imposed certain conditions--written into the Cuban constitution--that kept Cuba as an American protectorate for the next thirty years. The United States governed the Philippine Islands until making them independent in 1946. Puerto Rico remains an American Commonwealth, or territory.

Interpreting Evidence in Documents

1. Review Senator Hoar's speech to find the answers to these questions.

    a. What kind of a world did Senator Hoar see growing out of imperialism?

    b. What American doctrine did he believe imperialism violated?

    c. Why did he interpret the statement "We shall give them a better government than they had before" as an insult?

    d. What was Hoar's definition of "good government?"

    e. How was such government achieved?

2. Review Senator Beveridge's speech to find the answers to these questions.

    a. Towards what did Senator Beveridge believe the American people were marching?

American History - 15 **Handout**

    b. How was America going to reap its rewards?

    c. How did Beveridge answer the argument that the United States should not govern a people without their consent?

    d. What kind of a government did he think the Philippines preferred?

    e. What did Beveridge mean by "the march of the flag?"

3. Use the Decision Tree to help you answer the following questions.

    a. What was the situation facing the United States that stimulated this debate?

    b. What were the goals of each side in the debate?

    c. What alternatives were identified by each side?

    d. What were the likely consequences of each alternative?

    e. Which alternative did the American people choose? Why?

    f. What is your judgment of this choice? Was it a good or bad decision? Why?

(c) *American History and National Security*. Mershon Center, The Ohio State University

American History - 15   Handout

DECISION TREE

GOALS/VALUES

CONSEQUENCES

GOOD

BAD

ALTERNATIVES

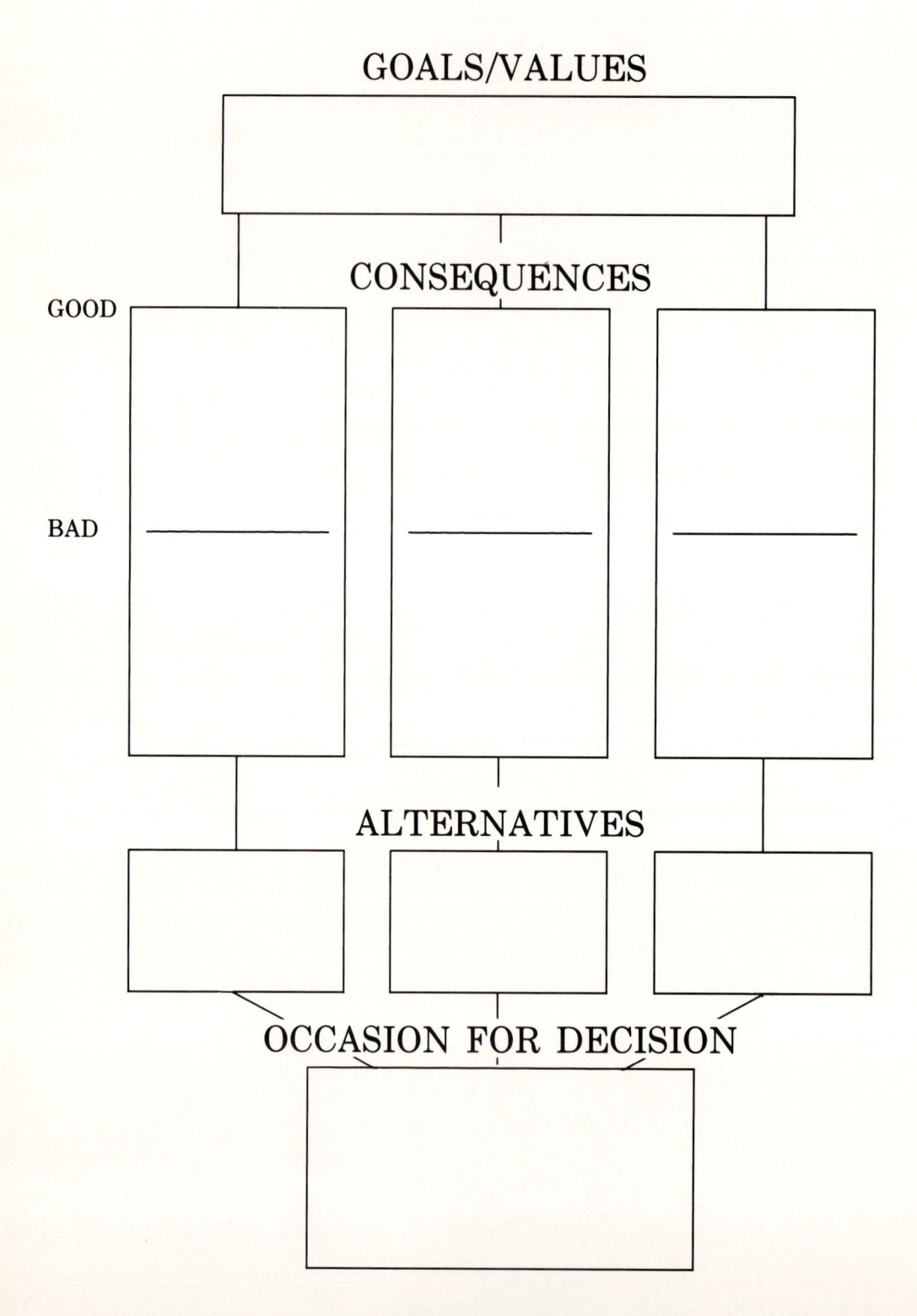

OCCASION FOR DECISION

The decision-tree device was developed by Roger LaRaus and Richard C. Remy and is used with their permission.

(c) *American History and National Security.* Mershon Center, The Ohio State University

American History - 16　　　　　　　　　　　　　　　　Lesson Plan and Notes for Teachers

Shaping the "Open Door Policy"

by Donald A. Ritchie

Preview of Main Points

This lesson uses a humorous poem to demonstrate British influence on the American Open Door policy, and encourages closer examination of a fundamental policy of the United States that long defined American national security policy in the Far East.

Connection to Textbooks

All American history textbooks devote considerable attention to the Open Door notes. This lesson is designed to supplement that coverage and to present some of the issue's complexity in an entertaining but meaningful format.

Objectives

Students are expected to:

1. interpret the objectives of the Open Door policy;

2. understand British influences on the Open Door policy, and the larger issue of mutuality of interests among nations; and

3. understand the consequences of the Open Door policy on American national security interests.

Suggestions for Teaching the Lesson

Opening the Lesson

o Require students to read sections in their textbook relating to the Open Door policy before beginning this lesson.

o Then have the students read the introduction in the Handout and discuss with them-- drawing from both their textbooks and the introduction--the reasons behind the Open Door policy: American economic expansion, concern over colonialism, belief in self-determination, etc. List the reasons that the students suggest on the board.

Developing the Lesson

o Have the students read the poem to themselves. Then pick two students to read it aloud, one taking John Bull's part and the other Uncle Sam's.

o Discuss the students' reaction to the poem, and have them answer the accompanying questions, either orally or in writing.

(c) *American History and National Security.* Mershon Center, The Ohio State University

o Ask the students to discuss the Open Door policy from the poet's perspective. (You can note that the poet was a Canadian, somewhat of a neutral figure between Britain and the United States.) How does the poet's perception differ from the reasons which the students suggested earlier and which are written on the board?

Concluding the Lesson

o Tell the students that some historians have argued that the Open Door policy shaped American national security interests in the Far East well into the twentieth century. It influenced American policy-making during the Russo-Japanese War in 1905, the Washington Naval Conference of 1921, the Japanese invasion of Manchuria in the 1930s, and the Chinese civil war in the 1940s. Historian William Appleman Williams has argued that the Open Door policy "defines American perspectives and objectives, and hence those who criticize or oppose the policy have been viewed as problems if not enemies. Germany was thus a troublemaker long before Adolph Hitler, Japan long before Hideki Tojo, and Russia long before Josef Stalin." Discuss Williams' argument. Does it suggest that the Open Door policy was an example of an unrealistic or overly ambitious national policy? Did the Open Door policy have implications beyond its original intentions? What lessons should modern-day policymakers learn using the Open Door policy as an historical model?

Suggestions for Additional Reading

Van Alstyne Richard W. "The Open Door Policy," and Williams, William Appleman, "Open Door Interpretation." *Encyclopedia of American Foreign Policy*, Vol. II, ed. Alexander De Conte. New York: Scribner, 1978.

These are two brief but helpful readings which students may find interesting.

Answers to Questions in Handout

1. To win his support for an Open Door in China.

2. Trade walls and other economic barriers.

3. To obtain markets to support his population.

4. As peaceful and benevolent, "to spread the light," and to share his "cake" (or markets) with the world.

5. To come to blows if the United States joined those raising tariff barriers,

6. The other colonial powers.

7. By encouraging him to take a leading role in world affairs, "to show the Path on which world trade must go."

8. He agrees.

9. Sam's dialect makes him sound like a rustic who sees this adventure as a "ruther grand affair."

10. He suggests that the British had most to gain from the Open Door policy, and that the Americans were enticed into it by visions of becoming a global power.

Shaping the "Open Door Policy"

Introduction

Secretary of State John Hay's "Open Door" notes of September, 1899, called on the great powers of the world to maintain free and equal access to Chinese markets. The "Open Door" notes signaled that the United States would not seek to claim territory in China, as other nations were attempting. But the United States did want to increase its share of Chinese trade.

Secretary Hay sent his notes to Great Britain, Germany, France, Italy, Russia, and Japan. He did not consult or inform China. Although the Open Door policy's major objective was to obtain free trading privileges for American enterprise, it also advocated the "territorial integrity and administrative independence" of China. The idealistic tone of Hay's notes was very popular among the American people.

What motivated the "Open Door" notes? At that time, American business had only a tiny share of the Chinese markets. By contrast, Great Britain controlled eighty percent of China's trade. While the United States wanted to enter the market, Britain was worried about losing its advantages to competition from other powers--especially Germany and Japan. The British also advocated an Open Door approach and encouraged the United States to adopt a similar policy.

The Open Door policy in China offered the United States an alternative to the policy that it was pursuing in the Philippines. As a result of the Spanish-American War in 1898, the U.S. gained control of the Philippines, and occupied it with military troops. But it encountered strong resistance from Philippine nationalists. In China, the U.S. was attracted to the British model of securing economic influence without political control.

A Poetic Appeal

On September 3, 1898, the *New York Times* published a poem, "The Open Door," showing how John Bull (Great Britain) appealed to his cousin Sam (The United States).

THE OPEN DOOR

by J.W. Bengough

John Bull spake out in accents clear,
With something of the lion's roar,
(His cousin Sam was standing near)--
"Hello! You there on China's shore,
There's got to be an Open Door!
What say you, Sam?"

Cries Sam, "Encore!"

"This wholesale changing of the map
By the great powers everywhere
May be all right--and I'm the chap
Who takes the cake, they all declare,
But with the world my cake I share,
What say you, Sam?:

Cries Sam, "Ah, there!"

"The 'Open Door' for one and all,
Free trade in every blessed spot
Where I am ruler--at the pole
Or in the tropics; cold or hot--
Fair field for all the blooming lot--
What say you, Sam?"

    Cries Sam, "That's what!"

I've got some millions to be fed,
And markets I must somehow get;
My life depends on my trade:
All round the world I spread my net,
And for free commerce I am set,
What say you, Sam?"

    Cries Sam, "Why sure!"

"My policy all around is Peace,
My mission is to spread the light,
I rule the waves that war may cease,
But in my arm's resistless might,
And for free markets I will fight!
What say you, Sam?"

    Cries Sam, "That's right!"

"Say 'sphere of influence' if the phrase
More diplomatically flows
Than 'Open Door'--but don't you raise,
My friends, lest you become my foes,
Trade barriers: we may come to blows--
What say you, Sam?"

    Cries Sam, "That goes!"

The Gang--Ah, pardon me--the Powers
Retire to think a season, so
John returns to Sam and says; "This ours,
Not mine along, but ours, to show
The Path on which world trade must go,
Hey, Sam?"

    Cries Sam, "It-is-you-know!"

"In fack, I calkilate," says he,
"Twould be a ruther grand affair
If out thar on the Yellow Sea,
With your old flag and mine should appear;
My duty in this thing seems clear,
What say you, John?"

    Cried Bull, "Ear! Ear!"

American History - 16   Handout

Questions for Interpretation and Review

1. Why was John Bull calling Uncle Sam?

2. What did John Bull oppose?

3. Why did John Bull want an Open Door in China?

4. How did John Bull describe his policies?

5. What threat did John Bull make against Uncle Sam?

6. Who were "the Gang?"

7. How did John Bull entice Uncle Sam?

8. What was Sam's decision?

9. What kind of an image of Uncle Sam (the United States) does the poet create?

10. What implications does the poet suggest about the origins of the Open Door policy?

American History - 17   Lesson Plan and Notes for Teachers

The Ethics of the Panama Canal

by Donald A. Ritchie

Preview of Main Points

This lesson describes the events which led to American support for the Panamanian revolution in 1903 and eventually to the building of the Panama Canal. It explores Theodore Roosevelt's frustration with the Colombians, and his belief that they had "no right to block a passageway so vital to the interests of civilization." It also attempts to show the Colombian side of the issue, and raise questions about the ethics of a large state imposing its will on a smaller state through force. The lesson also connects events of 1903 with the Senate debate over the Panama treaties of 1978.

Connection to Textbooks

The Panama Canal is featured in all American history textbooks, generally in the chapters dealing with Theodore Roosevelt or with foreign policy in the early twentieth century. This lesson expands upon textbook material and focuses on events leading up to the revolution, that made it possible for the United States to build the canal. It can also be taught in connection with the 1970s, when a new canal treaty was negotiated and ratified.

Objectives

Students are expected to:

1. know the historical background to American involvement in the Panamanian revolution;

2. understand the motivations of both sides in the dispute;

3. evaluate the ethics of American actions with regard to Colombia and Panama; and

4. assess the results of those actions.

Suggestions for Teaching the Lesson

Opening the Lesson

o Suggest to the students the following scenario: a developer planning a multi-million dollar project has acquired all the land necessary to begin building the project with the exception of one small plot of land with an unassuming house on it. The owner refuses to sell, but the house is so centrally located that no work can begin until the house is demolished. The planned project will benefit the community and will increase the number of jobs in the town, if it can get started. What should the developer do? Open this question for debate among the students. Answers might range from negotiating with the house owner to pay him considerably more for his property, to court actions, to harassment. Draw a parallel between such a situation and the situation in Panama in 1903.

o Preview the main points of the lesson for the students.

Developing the Lesson

o Have the students read the Handout. Then ask them to respond to the review questions at the end of the lesson. The essay question can either be done in class or assigned as a homework project.

o Review the student's answers to the questions.

(c) *American History and National Security*. Mershon Center, The Ohio State University

- Ask the students to evaluate Theodore Roosevelt's actions and his later justifications for his actions. Discuss with the students the long-range implications of Roosevelt's decisions, particularly those expressed by James DuBois.

Concluding the Lesson

- One of the Senate opponents of Roosevelt's policies in Panama, Senator John Tyler Morgan of Alabama, said after the Panamanian revolution: "I fear that we have got too large to be just." Ask the students to evaluate that statement with regard to relations between large nations and small nations in general.

- Ask the students to speculate about situations in the future that might resemble the Panamanian situation. How might the United States respond? How might we learn from history?

Suggestions for Additional Reading

McCullough, David. *The Path Between the Seas: The Creation of the Panama Canal, 1870-1914.* New York: Simon and Schuster, 1977.

This is a well-written and colorful account of the events leading to the completion of the canal. This lesson was drawn from McCullough's account.

LaFeber, Walter. *The Panama Canal: The Crisis in Historical Perspective.* New York: Oxford University Press, 1978.

Answers to Questions for Review and Interpretation

1. To speed passage from the East Coast (Atlantic) to the West Coast (Pacific), which became more desirable after experiences during the Gold Rush.

2. It focused attention on the length of time needed for a warship to round South America during an emergency.

3. He wanted a canal as a military and commercial passage, to help protect American interests in the Philippines, and to make America a dominant power in the Pacific.

4. They wanted to retain sovereignty over the canal zone and to receive a fair share of the U.S. payments to the French for their property and rights in Panama.

5. By threatening to negotiate a canal treaty with Nicaragua and by negotiating with those involved in a Panamanian revolution.

6. Dr. Amador was leader of the Panamanian revolution; while Bunau-Varilla was its spokesman and special negotiator in the United States.

7. Roosevelt felt he had said nothing to encourage a Panamanian revolution; Bunau-Varilla felt Roosevelt would protect a revolutionary government once the revolution occurred. Roosevelt's support may have been implicit rather than explicit.

8. The sending of the *Nashville* to Panama served as a signal to the revolutionaries of American support; the United States also prohibited Colombian troops from landing in Panama, and sent other warships to protect the new government.

9. Roosevelt argued that the U.S. had acted only to protect the railroad and prevent bloodshed; that Colombia had no right to block a canal needed by the rest of the world; and that the United States had acted in a "straight-forewarb" manner.

10. That it disrupted American relations with Colombia, and aroused indignation and distrust of the United States throughout Latin America.

The Ethics of the Panama Canal

Both history and ethics played major roles in the long Senate debate over the Panama Canal in 1978. That emotional debate lasted 38 days, the longest in the sixty years since the debate over the Treaty of Versailles. At stake were two treaties which would turn the U.S.-built and operated Panama Canal over to the Panamanians in the year 2000. They would also provide for the neutrality of the canal and allow U.S. troops, if necessary, to keep it open.

Opponents of the treaty argued that the original treaty that the United States had signed with Panama in 1903 had guaranteed it control of the canal "in perpetuity," that is forever. They believed that only U.S. occupation of the Canal Zone would keep the canal open and safe. Supporters of the treaties believed that passage would heal old wounds dating back to American intervention in the Panamanian revolution of 1903. Panama, they insisted, had a right to control its own territory and to collect revenues produced by ship traffic in the canal.

Both sides cited historical evidence to support their case. The ethics of American treatment of Colombia and Panama also became a central focus of the debate. Had a large and powerful nation intimidated and abused a smaller nation? What events had forced the United States into action? Finally, in April, 1978, the Senate adopted the Panama Canal treaties by just one vote more than the needed two-thirds margin.

How America Became Involved in Panama

The American dream of easy transit from the Atlantic to the Pacific Oceans across the Isthmus of Panama (an isthmus is a narrow strip of land that connects two larger bodies of land), was an old one. In 1846 an American diplomat had signed a treaty with New Granada (later called Colombia), which gave the U.S. rights to free and open transit across Panama. Such transit became especially desirable after gold was discovered in California in 1849. During the Gold Rush, many people made the dangerous journey overland across Panama rather than take the longer and slower voyage around South America. By the 1850s an American-built railroad linked the two oceans.

Ship traffic, however, still had to circle South America. The problems this posed became dramatically clear during the War with Spain in 1898. The battleship *Oregon* was in San Francisco harbor when ordered to the Caribbean at the outbreak of war. The whole nation followed the *Oregon*'s progress as it steamed 12,000 miles around South America, a trip it completed in what seemed an amazingly short 67 days. As one poet wrote:

> When your boys shall ask what the guns are for,
> Then tell them the tale of the Spanish War,
> And the breathless millions that looked upon
> The matchless race of the *Oregon*.

Had there been a water route at the Isthmus of Panama, the *Oregon*'s voyage could have been shortened from 12,000 to 4,000 miles, and the number of days cut proportionately.

Theodore Roosevelt, Assistant Secretary of the Navy and a hero of the Spanish-American war, was one of those who saw the need for a canal, both as a commercial and a military pathway. A canal would help America hold and protect the Philippine Islands, which it had taken in the war, and would help make the United States "the dominant power on the shores of the Pacific Ocean." Three years after the war, Theodore Roosevelt became President of the United States. He used that position to achieve his dream of a Panama Canal.

Negotiating the Panama Treaties

During the 1880s, the French had tried and failed to build a canal across Panama. Tropical diseases rather than engineering difficulties had halted their efforts. As a result of that failure in Panama, some observers thought Nicaragua a more likely place to build a canal. Although longer to cross, it was closer to the United States, and seemed a healthier place than the Panamanian jungles. President Roosevelt, however, was won over to a Panamanian route, and the Congress followed his lead.

Before any work could begin, the United States needed to reach an agreement with Colombia, which controlled the Isthmus of Panama. For the Colombians, a chief issue was their sovereignty over the canal zone--that is, their independent right to govern the area. They had objected, during a recent civil war in Colombia, when Roosevelt sent U.S. Marines to protect the American railroad in Panama, without first consulting them. The Colombians also objected to American moves to purchase French property and rights in Panama. Since they had granted those rights to the French, the Colombians felt that they should receive part of the payment. Tensions ran high, and the Colombian ambassador to Washington resigned rather than follow orders from his own government to sign a treaty. It was only when the United States threatened to build a canal in Nicaragua, that the new Colombian ambassador agreed to a treaty.

Neither the U.S. payments to Colombia, nor the sovereignty rights granted by the treaty, satisfied the Colombians. When the Colombian government delayed ratifying the treaty, Secretary of State John Hay sent a tough message: "If Colombia should now reject the treaty or unduly delay its ratification, the friendly understanding between the two countries would be so seriously compromised that action might be taken by the Congress next winter which every friend of Colombia would regret." Shortly afterwards, newspaper stories appeared indicating that President Roosevelt was outraged over "the greed of the Colombian Government," and that he would be willing to support a revolution of the people of Panama against Colombia as a way to gain rights to build the canal. The President did not deny these stories.

Support for a Panamanian Revolution

Journeying to the United States at this time were several advocates of a revolution to make Panama independent of Colombia. Dr. Manuel Amador represented the Panamanian revolutionaries. A French adventurer, Philippe Bunau-Varilla, who stood to gain financially by an American settlement with France, also supported the Panamanians.

In October 1903, Bunau-Varilla met with President Roosevelt and predicted a revolution in Panama. Roosevelt would not say whether the United States would support such a revolution. He did say that Colombia's refusal to ratify the treaty had forfeited any claim it might have on the United States. Afterwards, Roosevelt insisted that he had made no remark that would encourage the Panamanians to revolt. Bunau-Varilla, to the contrary, was now sure that Roosevelt would support a revolution. He assured Dr. Amador that the United States would protect a revolutionary government in Panama.

Dr. Amador returned to Panama to lead the revolution, and Buna-Varilla returned to Washington to urge American officials to send a warship to Panama. That same day, the gunboat *Nashville* was dispatched from Jamaica to Panama. Its captain later received orders to use troops if necessary to keep the railroad operating, and to prevent "any armed force with hostile intent, either government or insurgent" from landing. Arrival of the *Nashville* served as a signal to the Panamanians of American support. Their revolution was quick, bloodless and successful. Ten other American warships soon arrived to protect the revolutionary government. Dr. Amador told his supporters: "yesterday we were but the slaves of Colombia; today we are free. . . . President Roosevelt has made good. . . . Long live President Roosevelt! Long live the American Government!"

The United States immediately recognized the new Republic of Panama. Bunau-Varilla became its special minister to Washington, where he speedily negotiated a treaty enabling the Americans to purchase French rights in Panama and gave the U.S. perpetual control of the Canal Zone. Then began the hard labor and engineering genius required to cut a canal through Panama. By 1914 ships were sailing through the Isthmus from ocean to ocean.

Criticism and Defense of American Actions in Panama

In his report to Congress that year, President Roosevelt declared that the United States had acted only to prevent the landing of military forces that might have disrupted the American railroad in Panama, and that the presence of American troops had helped prevent bloodshed between the Colombians and the Panamanians. In later years, Roosevelt wrote in his autobiography that "Colombia had no right to block a passageway so vital to the interests of civilization. . . . From the beginning to the end our course was straight-forward and in absolute accord with the highest standards of international morality. Criticism of it can come only from misinformation, or else from a sentimentality which represents both mental weakness and a moral twist." In a speech in 1911, Roosevelt suggested that Congress would still be debating the issue if left to itself. "Fortunately the crisis came at a period when I could act unhampered. Accordingly I took the Isthmus, started the canal and then left Congress not to debate the canal, but to debate me."

The American minister in Colombia, James DuBois, told another side of the story in 1912: "By refusing to allow Colombia to uphold her sovereign rights over a territory where she had held dominion for eighty years, the friendship of nearly a century disappeared, the indignation of every Colombian, and millions of other Latin-Americans, was aroused and is still most intensely active. The confidence and trust in the justice and fairness of the United States, so long manifested, has completely vanished, and the [harmful] influence of this condition is permeating public opinion in all Latin-American countries, a condition which, if remedial measures are not invoked, will work inestimable harm throughout the Western Hemisphere."

Questions for Review and Interpretation

1. Why were Americans interested in a passage through Panama?

2. What impact did the *Oregon*'s voyage have on public opinion?

3. What were Theodore Roosevelt's goals in this case?

4. What did the Colombians want from a treaty with the U.S.?

American History - 17   Handout

5. How did the U.S. Government respond to Colombian objections?

6. What were the roles of Dr. Amador and Bunau-Varilla?

7. In what ways did Theodore Roosevelt and Bunau-Varilla interpret their meeting differently? Could both have been correct?

8. Did the United States support the Panamanian revolution? How?

9. In what ways did Theodore Roosevelt defend his actions in Panama?

10. What did James DuBois see as the results of American intervention in Panama?

Essay Question

11. Drawing from the information in this lesson, and any other sources available, what historical evidence supported the supporters and opponents of the Panama Canal treaties in 1978? What evidence worked against their positions? How did the treaties of 1978 resolve the disputes of 1903?

American History - 18　　　　　　　　　　　　　　Lesson Plan and Notes for Teachers

American Intervention in the Mexican Revolution, 1914

by James R. Leutze

Preview of Main Points

This lesson emphasizes U.S. policy toward Mexico during the early years of the twentieth century. President Wilson's decision to intervene in the internal affairs of Mexico is examined.

Connection to Textbooks

This lesson can be used in conjunction with standard textbook treatments of American imperialism and policies toward Latin American countries during the last part of the nineteenth century and the early years of the twentieth century. Most textbooks include a page or two about Wilson's Latin American policies. This lesson can be used to elaborate upon the brief textbook coverage.

Objectives

Students are expected to:

1. know about American protectionist policies toward Mexico and other Latin American countries during the years before World War I;

2. interpret the Roosevelt Corollary to the Monroe Doctrine in terms of traditional United States policy about Latin America;

3. explain President Wilson's decision to intervene in the internal affairs of Mexico; and

4. appraise President Wilson's foreign policy toward Mexico.

Suggestions for Teaching the Lesson

Opening the Lesson

o Ask students to read the opening paragraph of the Handout. Invite them to speculate about answers to the questions at the end of the paragraph about the conditions and consequences of President Wilson's intervention in the Mexican Revolution.

Developing the Lesson

o Have students read the case study in the Handout of United States policy toward Mexico. Ask them to check their speculations about the opening questions against the information in the case study.

o Require students to answer questions at the end of the Handout in preparation for classroom discussion.

(c) *American History and National Security*. Mershon Center, The Ohio State University

Concluding the Lesson

o Conduct a classroom discussion in terms of the questions at the end of the case study.

o Answers to questions 1-3 involve review of facts and main ideas in the case. Answers should be checked directly against information in the case.

o Answers to questions 4-5 involve opinion and judgment. Thus, variations in responses are acceptable. However, students still should be asked to justify answers with references to the content of the case study.

Suggestions for Additional Reading

Following is an annotated list of books about the ideas in this lesson. These books are presented as additional sources of information for teachers and very able students.

Clendenen, Clarence C. *Blood on the Border: The U.S. Army and the Mexican Irregulars.* London: Macmillan, 1969.

Clendenen covers the series of skirmishes and undeclared wars along the Mexican border from 1848 to 1920, devoting more than half of the pages to the 1900-1916 period. The author attempts to shed light on this neglected aspect of American military history.

Cline, Howard F. *The United States and Mexico.* 3rd ed. Cambridge: Harvard University Press, 1963.

A classic, it is somewhat mistitled because most of the book deals with Mexican history since 1910. Cline's two chapters on the period 1914-1917 provide a sound, if dated, general introduction to the topic.

Gilderhaus, Mark T. *Diplomacy and Revolution: U.S.-Mexican Relations under Wilson and Carranza.* Tucson, Arizona: University of Arizona Press, 1977.

Gilderhaus presents a competent synthesis of Wilson's Mexican policy. Initially hopeful that a free government and free markets would be established in Mexico, Wilson's commitment to self-determination shifted to limited U.S. intervention when limited political reform grew to challenge social and economic tradition.

Haley, P. Edward. *Revolution and Intervention: The Diplomacy of Taft and Wilson with Mexico, 1910-1917.* Cambridge, Massachusetts: MIT Press, 1970.

Haley describes the American reaction to turbulence and "revolution" in Mexico. Taft ignored Mexico due to what he saw as the futility of intervention. Wilson chose to send in the troops until his attention was diverted to war in Europe. With the U.S. looking elsewhere, Mexico promulgated the revolution.

Quirk, Robert E. *An Affair of Honor: Woodrow Wilson and the Occupation of Vera Cruz.* Lexington, Kentucky: University of Kentucky Press, 1962.

An Affair of Honor presents a critical examination of Wilson and U.S. intervention in Mexico. Wilson emerges from the study as inflexible, dictatorial, and uninformed about conditions in Mexico. Quirk argues that there was little public opposition in the United States to military action at Vera Cruz.

American Intervention in the Mexican Revolution, 1914

On April 21, 1914, armed forces of the United States seized the customs port at Vera Cruz, Mexico. There was fighting and several Americans and Mexicans were wounded or killed. U.S. President Woodrow Wilson claimed that important national interests were at stake. Why? What caused this violent intervention into the affairs of a neighboring nation? Was it justified? What were the consequences for the national interests and security of the United States?

Background Information on U.S. Relations with Mexico

The United States had traditionally acted as protector and police power with regard to other countries in the Western Hemisphere. Since proclamation of the Monroe Doctrine in 1823, Americans had acted to keep European powers out of the Western Hemisphere. The U.S. also acted to maintain order and stability in response to numerous internal disorders, including several rebellions or revolutions in Latin American countries. The United States government wanted to protect investments of American businesses and to prevent European countries from using the instability or indebtedness of Latin American countries as an excuse for taking over these countries.

There were periodic crises that led to new policies such as the Roosevelt Corollary to the Monroe Doctrine. This policy was announced in 1904 when a debt crisis in Venezuela threatened to bring German occupation. In a statement describing the policy Theodore Roosevelt declared:

> Chronic wrongdoing, or an impotence which results in a general loosening of the ties of civilized society, may in America as elsewhere, ultimately require intervention by some civilized nation, and in the Western Hemisphere the adherence of the U.S. to the Monroe Doctrine may force the United States, however, reluctantly, in flagrant cases of such wrongdoing or impotence, to the exercise of an international police power.

One of the places where the U.S. had special interest was Mexico. Not only did the two countries share a long border, but by the early twentieth century American investors had poured almost $1 billion into Mexico. Like many other Latin American countries, Mexico had a violent past. Such violence often disrupted American business enterprises and threatened American lives. During the administration of President William Howard Taft, who followed Theodore Roosevelt, the United States had followed a generally non-interventionist policy throughout the Caribbean and Latin American regions, although it strongly supported American investment in the area. Taft's policy has come to be called "Dollar Diplomacy."

In 1910, however, a bloody revolution occurred in Mexico. By 1911, the revolution's leader, Francisco Madero, became president. Madero called foreign financial activity "exploitation" and he expressed an intention to limit investment. Foreign investors did not like that attitude. Madero also announced his intention to crack down on corruption and limit the power of the Catholic Church. These statements irritated many politicians and army officers and made some church officials unhappy. There soon was another revolution. Madero was thrown out of office by General Victorianno Huerta and then, in February 1913, assassinated, no doubt at Huerta's command.

Wilson's Mexican Policy

This was the situation that faced President Woodrow Wilson when he took office in March of 1912. He was appalled at the developing situation in Mexico. Wilson also revered the traditions of free government developed in Britain and practiced in the United States. He quickly decided that he would undertake to teach the Mexicans, as he said, "to elect good men." He also decided that instead of allowing the usual practice of recognizing the existence of the Huerta government diplomatically (the formal policy of exchanging ambassadors and in other ways establishing diplomatic contact with a foreign country), the U.S. would signal its displeasure with Huerta by not diplomatically recognizing his government. In this and other ways, Wilson indicated his unwillingness to deal with a "bloody handed dictator" as he called Huerta.

The problem was that Huerta wouldn't go away, as the U.S. wanted him to. But there were Mexicans who questioned his authority and some took up arms to oppose his government. These included another general, Victorianno Carranza, and the bandit Pancho Villa. Violence brought more violence, and the fragile civil system of law and commerce seemed about to collapse completely.

American citizens and businesses in the country suffered in the general chaos. As reports of attacks on citizens and losses in property mounted, sentiment inside the United States increasingly called for some kind of retaliation or intervention. In Congress, several influential members threatened independent action if the President could do nothing to insure the protection of American lives and property. Other spokesmen implied that the U.S. had a moral obligation to bring a halt to the bloodshed. Obviously, the fact that the U.S. did not have diplomatic ties with Mexico limited our options.

Conflict at Vera Cruz

In April 1914 an unfortunate incident occurred in the harbor at Tampico. A group of sailors from an American warship had gone ashore to purchase supplies, as often had been done in the past. On this occasion, however, they were arrested and held for several hours. When they were released, an informal apology was made for what Mexican authorities described as a misunderstanding. Admiral Mayo, the commander of the U.S. fleet in the area, was not satisfied. He demanded that within 24 hours the Mexican general at Tampico:

> . . . send me, by suitable members of your staff, formal disavowal of and apology for the act, together with your assurance that the officer responsible for it will receive severe punishment. Also that you publicly hoist the American flag in a prominent position on shore and salute it with twenty-one guns, which salute will be duly returned by this ship.

The Huerta government would not meet all of Admiral Mayo's demands. A formal apology was issued, but they would not agree to salute the American flag.

Honor was now at stake, and war sentiment swept the U.S. Wilson seized upon the incident as a way to force Huerta from power. If funds for the government could be cut off, Wilson reasoned, opposition would mount and one of Huerta's opponents, to whom American suppliers were now providing arms, would drive him from office. In pursuit of this goal, on April 20 the President went before Congress to seek the authority to intervene militarily in Mexico. After two days' debate Congress granted him the authority he sought.

The opportunity to intervene actually occurred before the final vote. A German ship loaded with arms was approaching the port of Vera Cruz on the Eastern coast of Mexico. If the ship docked it would provide Huerta with badly needed weapons, which would potentially make it more difficult for the United States to force the solution it sought. Furthermore, Vera Cruz was the main customs port in Mexico. If it were seized by the United States it would deprive the Mexican government of much needed revenue, thus precipitating the economic crisis Wilson sought.

Moving quickly, Wilson ordered the occupation of Vera Cruz by American troops on April 21, 1914. The fighting was intense but brief; by the end of the day Vera Cruz was in American hands. We suffered approximately one hundred casualties, but many more Mexicans were killed and wounded.

Consequences of American Intervention

The Mexicans initially united in opposition to the outside enemy. For a while it looked as though the United States might find itself in a full-scale war that would have pleased many Americans, but would have made a joke of Wilson's highly publicized policy of non-intervention. Finally several Latin American countries got together and proposed international arbitration of the disagreement between the U.S. and Mexico; Wilson, probably greatly relieved, accepted.

Soon after an agreement was proposed, Huerta left office only to be replaced by another dictator. Throughout the rest of Wilson's term in office, Mexico was wracked by violence which sometimes spread across the border. In 1916, with the agreement of the Mexican government, an American military expedition crossed the border between Mexico and New Mexico in pursuit of Pancho Villa who had killed several Americans in a raid into the United States. Wilson's policy toward our immediate Southern neighbor had not been successful, nor had his morality been any more popular with Latin Americans than Roosevelt's "big stick" or Taft's "dollar diplomacy." With the best intentions in the world, Wilson brought the U.S. and Mexico to the brink of war over an incident that today seems trivial.

Reviewing and Interpreting Main Ideas

1. What was the Roosevelt Corollary to the Monroe Doctrine?

2. What did the Roosevelt Corollary indicate about the traditional policies of the U.S. toward Mexico and other Latin American nations?

3. What events prompted President Wilson to intervene in Mexican affairs in 1914?

4. Does the United States have any right or responsibility to intervene in the internal affairs of other countries, such as Mexico in 1914? If so, what should be the limits on intervention?

5. What is your judgement of United States policy toward Mexico, as indicated by the Roosevelt Corollary and by Wilson's actions?

SECTION V
AMERICA AND TWO WORLD WARS

List of Lessons

The six lessons in this section deal with ideas, policies, and events about national security and American history associated with World Wars I and II, and the years between the wars. The lessons are

19. Preparing the Public for the Draft

20. Failure of the Treaty of Versailles

21. National Security Through Air Power: Ideas of Billy Mitchell

22. Public Opinion and National Security Before World War II

23. B-17s: Development and Use of a Weapons System

24. Deciding to Use the Atomic Bomb, 1945

Overview for Teachers

With the onset of World War I in Europe in 1914 U.S. security policy entered a critical period of transition. For all nations, World War I marked a significant turning point in the conduct of modern warfare. For the United States, however, there was a further impact. By entering that war, the U.S. altered forever the nature of its involvement in international affairs. The transition that followed was a long and troubled one that continued until 1941 when the United States entered the Second World War. Although a return to isolationism replaced America's recent activism, the patterns of the past had been irrevocably changed. In the period between the Wars, the debates that developed over policy--foreign and domestic--were often bitter and contentious. Many of those debates revolved around the same issues of security in a democracy that had always concerned America's leaders.

One persistent issue in this regard was how to provide military manpower necessary to provide for the nation's security needs. That issue had arisen when the Constitution was drafted. It arose again during the Civil War, when the imposition of a wartime draft had produced angry, sometimes violent opposition. The problem lay in the contradiction between American distaste both for a large standing force and for conscription (draft) and the need to raise an army in order to fight a war. In anticipation of America's entry into World War I, the same issue had once again to be addressed. As **Lesson 19** shows, President Wilson's answer was a draft to raise the necessary force, but that in turn required a change in public attitude. Wilson was successful, introducing the Selective Service Act in 1917, but the issue would remain.

Entry into the war brought the United States more firmly into the active realm of world politics than ever before. In order to reconcile this conduct with our past disdain for the "power politics" of non-democratic nations, the U.S. approach to the outcome was characteristically moralistic. Woodrow Wilson had declared U.S. participation as a way "to make the world safe for democracy" in a "war to end all wars."

Wilson advanced the League of Nations as an international organization that could achieve such an end. The League, in Wilson's view, was based on institutional principles found in a liberal democracy such as the United States. The League was designed to use "collective security," the commitment of all nations to the security of the others, as a means to ensure that aggression would be stopped and that all nations would be able to live in peace. The League Covenant, contained in the Treaty of Versailles, though accepted by most nations was rejected by the United Sates Senate. As discussed in **Lesson 20**, Wilson tried, and failed twice to have his ideals realized through U.S. participation in the League. The problem was an unwillingness on the part of American Senators to commit the United States in advance to the protection of other nations from aggression.

Another issue of the inter-war period had broader implications. **Lesson 21** presents the case of General Billy Mitchell, an army

135

officer who foresaw the outcome of the technological trends in warfare that had been introduced in World War I. Mitchell was a staunch advocate of air power, drawing effectively upon the creative work of a new generation of strategic thinkers who anticipated the use of long-range bombing behind enemy lines to affect the outcome of a war. Mitchell met resistance as much for his somewhat bombastic style as for the substance of his ideas. Mitchell was one of many military thinkers in the United States and around the world who studied the lessons of World War I in anticipation of the next conflict. This new generation of strategic thinkers would have a profound impact on the conduct of warfare in the Second World War not only in airpower but also in the development of sea and land warfare as well.

The impending war in Europe became a deepening political issue in the United States as the 1930s got underway. For the United States the political and economic aftermath of World War I had been disillusioning in and of itself; now there were the severe effects of the Depression at home to contend with as well. Consequently there was little inclination to move away from the relative safety of isolationism despite the growing evidence that American values and interests were increasingly at stake. The U.S. approached the events that were leading Europe toward war with grave concern, insisting on neutrality. Many leaders, especially President Roosevelt (who had run for re-election opposed to American involvement in the European conflict) were equally concerned that real American interests were at risk. After the outbreak of World War II at the beginning of September 1939, the issue became inescapable for the American people. **Lesson 22** demonstrates the effect of imminent war on U.S. public opinion.

As World War II began it became evident that the kind of warfare that strategists such as Billy Mitchell had envisioned was indeed going to come to pass. From its opening campaigns, it was clear that technology would play a definitive role. Not only did the scope, tempo and destructive power of war increase with introduction of new technology, the rate of increase accelerated as the war advanced. The United States was closely linked to these changes. Through the style of warfare it had introduced in the Civil War and through the creative development of technology having military application, America contributed materially to the transformation in World War II. **Lesson 23** presents one example of technology applied to warfare--the introduction of the B-17, a long-range strategic bomber.

However, technology often carried with it more difficult questions. World War II ended with the most complete expression of the concept of strategic bombing, the detonation of two atomic bombs over the Japanese cities of Hiroshima and Nagasaki. The technology of warfare now entered a new phase and the United States accepted a sense of international responsibility and involvement. America and the world had entered the nuclear age, and the problems of security had acquired a whole new dimension.

American History - 19   Lesson Plan and Notes for Teachers

Preparing the Public for the Draft

by Donald A. Ritchie

Preview of Main Points

This lesson is about the Wilson Administration's efforts to win approval of the American public for a military draft in 1917. It describes efforts of President Wilson and Secretary of War Newton D. Baker to devise and implement programs to discourage the type of violent opposition to the draft that occurred during the Civil War, and to create a more positive and patriotic spirit in favor of conscription. The lesson demonstrates how the federal government may try to shape public opinion to create more favorable attitudes for potentially unpopular programs believed necessary for national security.

Connection to Textbooks

This lesson can be used to supplement standard textbook treatments of the draft and the government's role during World War I. It can also be used in connection to, and comparison with, textbook treatments of the draft during the Civil War and the Vietnam War.

Objectives

Students are expected to:

1. recognize the way government can act to change public opinion;

2. understand and explain how public attitudes on the draft were changed during World War I; and

3. appreciate the need for winning public support for potentially unpopular and disruptive programs.

Suggestions for Teaching the Lesson

Opening the Lesson

o Ask students their opinions of the military draft. Are they in favor or opposed? If people are patriotic, shouldn't they volunteer for military service rather than be drafted? Why do they think people might have opposed the draft in the past, as during the Civil War or the Vietnam War?

o Preview the main points of this lesson.

Developing the Lesson

o Have students read the case study in the Handout. Then conduct a discussion of the review questions at the end of the lesson to make certain they have understood the main ideas of the lesson.

o Was it ethical for government to conduct a campaign to shape and change public opinion? What other instances might they suggest in which government would attempt such a campaign?

Concluding the Lesson

- In what ways do we learn from history? How was the draft handled differently, for example during the Vietnam War? Why was it more controversial than during the First World War?

- Today the United States relies upon an all volunteer military, but young men are required to register when they reach eighteen for a potential draft. Conclude the lesson by asking students to discuss their opinions of mandatory military service. Would it improve the quality of enlisted men and women and officers (bring in better educated people)? Would it be fair? Does every man have a responsibility to serve his country? What about every woman? Should people be forced to serve against their will? Should alternative (non-military) forms of service be offered?

Suggestions for Additional Readings

Anderson, Martin. ed. *The Military Draft: Selected Readongs on Conscription.* Stanford: Hoover Institution Press, 1982.

    Students interested in this subject should consult Anderson's work.

Baskir, Lawrence M. and Strauss, William A. *Chance and Circumstance.* New York: Knopf, 1978.

    Baskir and Strauss provide an informative study on the draft during the Vietnam war.

Sullivan, Mark. "Conscription" in *Our Times: The United Staqtes, 1900-1924*, vol. 5: *Over Here, 1914-1918.* New York, 1933.

    The information in this lesson was drawn from Sullivan's chapter in this book.

Answers to the Questions

1. Because there was deep-rooted opposition to forced conscription in the U.S., dating back to the Civil War; because many people, including Wilson himself for a while, believed armies should be made up of volunteers; and because there was a large number of Americans with German ancestry opposed to war with Germany.

2. By requiring all eligible men to appear at polling places to register, rather than sending out soldiers to compile lists of eligible draftees.

3. To accomplish the draft before any opposition could organize.

4. Sheriffs and other local officials in the communities.

5. They reflected their constituents fears and opposition to forced conscription; they thought it would give too much power to the President; and they were afraid it would cause great domestic unrest.

6. By enlisting Governors, Mayors and Chambers of Commerce to give speeches, hold parades, and treat those registering for the draft as heroes.

7. It made them feel as if the war would be a grand adventure.

8. They were called "slackers" and subject to public abuse, prosecution and imprisonment.

9. Yes, according to a unanimous Supreme Court ruling in 1918.

10. They achieved their goals of winning the approval of the public and the draftees.

American History - 19   Handout

Preparing the Public for the Draft

Background Information

Early in 1917, when it became clear that the United States was moving toward war with Germany, President Wilson and his military advisors realized they would have to establish a military draft. The existing military forces were too small, and modern warfare required too many soldiers for the government to rely on volunteers. But there was a problem: within the country there existed a deep-rooted opposition to forced conscription, otherwise known as the draft.

President Wilson had earlier expressed dislike of a draft. If men did not volunteer to serve their country, he said, then "it is not the America that you and I know; something has happened. If they did not do it, I should be ashamed of America." As an historian, Wilson also knew that there had been riots against the draft during the Civil War. And he was aware that a large percentage--perhaps thirteen percent--of all Americans were of German descent, who might not want to fight in a war against Germany.

Still, if the United States had to enter the war, it had to raise an army. The problem then became: how could the government change public opinion to a more favorable attitude toward the draft?

Secretary Baker Devises a Plan

Wilson's Secretary of War, Newton D. Baker, set about, secretly, to devise a plan to make the draft acceptable to the American people. He began his activities before he was even sure that Congress would pass a draft act. Baker's first concern was to give conscription as much of the appearance of volunteering as possible. He would not send uniformed soldiers out to communities to list all men of draft age. Instead, the government would require these men to come out to register for the draft in the same places where they voted. Instead of having the federal government choose draftees, local officials would make the decision as to who would be drafted and who would be exempt. In this way, the community would assume a large share of the responsibility in the drafting process.

Secretary Baker wanted to put the draft into effect as speedily as possible, before any opposition could be organized. Well before any public announcement was made, Baker ordered millions of draft registration forms printed. He had these forms distributed to local sheriffs throughout the nation. Each sheriff received enough blank forms for his community, and was asked not to reveal their existence until the federal government made a formal announcement. Remarkably, they all kept the secret.

An Angry Debate in Congress

While these activities were going on, Congress was heatedly debating the draft. Many Congressmen reflected the opinions of their constituents when they spoke out against conscription. The Democratic Speaker of the House, Champ Clark, declared: "I protect with all my heart and mind and soul against having the slur of being a conscript placed upon the men of Missouri; in the estimation of Missourians there is precious little difference between a conscript and a convict." Some members of Congress compared the draft to slavery, and said that it would "destroy democracy at home while fighting for it abroad." Senator Robert LaFollette of Wisconsin warned that once the President was granted the power to draft, then that power would be "exercised so long as the Nation shall last, by every successive incumbent, no matter how ambitious or bloody-minded he may be." Senator James A. Reed of Missouri told Secretary Baker that: "You will have the streets of our American cities running red with blood on Registration

---

(c) *American History and National Security.* Mershon Center, The Ohio State University

day." Still, on May 18, 1917 both houses of Congress by wide margins passed the Selective Service Act (the very name avoided the terms "draft" or "conscription").

Implementing the Draft

Now that the draft was the law, Secretary Baker wanted it implemented "under such circumstances as to create a strong patriotic feeling." He enlisted Governors, Mayors, and local Chambers of Commerce to make registration day "a festive and patriotic occasion." This way he hoped to reduce any popular hostility to the draft.

When President Wilson signed the Selective Service Act he also issued a proclamation, "Call to Arms." It was important, Wilson said in the proclamation, that registration day be treated with national honor. "Carried in all our hearts as a great day of patriotic devotion and obligation, when the duty shall lie upon every man to see to it that the name of every male person of the designated ages is written on these lists of honor."

So it was, on June 5, 1917, millions of young men between the ages of 21 and 30 registered for the draft, and were treated as heroes. As the journalist Mark Sullivan wrote, "Speeches from the mayor, the clergyman, and the Chamber of Commerce head, congratulations by starry-eyed committees of women, more intimate attentions from young girls, turned most of the draftees to feeling that the war would be grand adventure." By contrast, those who did not register were called "slackers" and came in for considerable public abuse, as well as being subject to punishment by the government.

One of those who did not register, Joseph Arver, was sentenced to one year in prison. The Supreme Court reviewed his case, and others, in Selective Draft Law Cases (*Arver v. United States*). In 1918 the Court ruled unanimously that the Selective Service Act was constitutional. In the case of the draft, however, this final legal approval was perhaps not as important as the approval President Wilson and Secretary Baker worked so hard to achieve: the approval of the great mass of draft age men, and of the American public as a whole.

Questions for Review and Interpretation

1. Why did President Wilson and his advisors believe it would be difficult to convince Americans to accept the draft in 1917?

2. How did Secretary Baker plan to make conscription appear similar to volunteering?

3. Why did Baker want to put the draft into effect so speedily?

4. Who did Baker want to implement the draft laws?

5. Why were many members of Congress opposed to the draft?

6. In what ways did Baker plan to make draft registration a festive occasion?

7. What was the effect on the draftees?

8. How were those who did not register treated?

9. Was the Selective Service Act constitutional?

10. What were Wilson's and Baker's chief goals? Did they achieve them?

American History - 20   Lesson Plan and Notes for Teachers

Failure of the Treaty of Versailles

by Donald A. Ritchie

Preview of Main Points

This lesson uses editorial cartoons to illustrate the struggle between President Wilson and Congress over the Treaty of Versailles. It also provides a means for examining and discussing how public opinion was shaped and how the public perception of the treaty and the League of Nations changed.

Connection to Textbooks

This lesson goes beyond the standard textbook accounts of the Treaty of Versailles with four visual representations of the fight between the executive and the legislature, in the form of editorial cartoons. This lesson should be used in connection with textbook materials on Woodrow Wilson and the First World War.

Objectives

Students are expected to:

1. analyze editorial cartoons;

2. understand the differences between those for and against the treaty and the League of Nations; and

3. recognize the ways editorial cartoons help shape public perceptions.

Suggestions for Teaching the Lesson

Opening the Lesson

o   Show the class an editorial cartoon from a recent newspaper or news magazine. Discuss with them the ways to interpret such cartoons: how they choose human figures to symbolize political ideas or institutions, how they present those figures in exaggerated situations and expressions, and how they present many visual messages to influence people's opinion. Books by editorial cartoonists such as Herblock or Jeff McNally might be circulated to reinforce these ideas.

o   Preview the main parts of this lesson found in the Handout (the students should already have read appropriate passages from their textbooks concerning the struggle over the Treaty of Versailles, although a summary is provided in their lesson).

Developing the Lesson

o   Discuss with the students the reason why the Senate rejected the Treaty of Versailles, and the fears about the League of Nations. America's absence weakened the League, which proved ineffective in preventing the rise of aggressive nations during the 1930s and the eventual outbreak of World War II. Discuss with the class the more favorable attitude in the United States and in Congress toward the United Nations after World War II, contrasting it to earlier fears. Do we learn by our mistakes?

Concluding the Lesson

o Conclude by giving students one or the other (or a choice) of two assignments: Write a brief essay on the fight over the Treaty of Versailles based on the four editorial cartoons in this lesson's Handout or draw an editorial cartoon reflecting why the United States did not enter the League of Nations.

Suggestions for Additional Reading

Foreign Policy Association. *A Cartoon History of United States Foreign Policy, 1776-1976*. New York: Morrow, 1975.

The cartoons used in this lesson can be found in this book.

Bailey, Thomas A. *Woodrow Wilson and the Great Betrayal*. Chicago: Macmillan, 1963. (originally published in 1945).

Students interested in this subject should also be directed to Bailey's study which also makes considerable use of editorial cartoons from that period.

Answers to Review Questions

A. "Getting a Taste of It"

1. Woodrow Wilson is serving a soup representing the League of Nations.

2. Members of Congress.

3. Some don't want any "furrin" (foreign) dishes, "even if it smells good," others find "it's not so bad," and want more.

4. There is a resistance to new ideas such as the "League" until people carefully examine them (or get the taste of it).

5. The cartoon implies that the "League" will become more acceptable the more people are exposed to it, and that Congress will eventually pass the Treaty of Versailles.

B. "The League of Nations Argument in a Nutshell"

6. Congress and Woodrow Wilson as soldiers in WWI.

7. The League of Nations to Prevent Wars.

8. Because there is firing all around and the hole does not seem to be sufficient protection.

9. By saying if they know a better idea (can find a better hole) then try it.

10. The cartoon supports the "League" by suggesting that there isn't a better idea available.

C. "The Prescription That Went Astray"

11. Wilson is a doctor (he had actually earned a doctorate in history and government, but here is presented as a medical doctor); Congress is his delivery boy for prescriptions.

12. The medicine represents "self-determination." The League of Nations was designed to protect nations' right to independence and self-determination.

13. The medicine gives the Senate its own sense of self-determination, drives it wild, and makes it rebel against the doctor.

14. That the Senate would follow an independent course from Wilson's wishes.

15. The cartoonist neither supports nor opposes the "League" in this cartoon, but suggests that Wilson will have a hard time getting it passed.

D. "The One Animal That Wouldn't Go Into the Ark"

16. By comparing the fight over the Treaty of Versailles to Noah building an ark to save living creatures' destruction.

17. As Noah, who built the ark.

18. The treaty compromise is seen as a strange and unruly animal, a combination of Republican elephant trunk and Democratic donkey ears, with an ungainly body, which has broken loose from its supporters.

19. That Wilson will either have to abandon the trip or build a new ark.

20. They have lost control of the compromise and been thrown aside.

21. That the compromise is doomed and that Wilson will have to start all over again.

Failure of the Treaty of Versailles

Background Information

No American President suffered a more serious defeat on a national security issue than Woodrow Wilson did in 1919-1920, when the Senate rejected the Treaty of Versailles, and with it America's participation in the League of Nations.

The issue was Wilson's insistence on peace through collective security. Wilson had won its inclusion in the peace treaty that ended World War I. But many Americans, and their representatives in Congress, were afraid that such an "entangling alliance" would force the United States into future wars against its will. The key provision, for both sides, was Article 10, which read: "The members of the League undertake to respect and preserve as against external aggression the territorial integrity and existing political independence of all members of the League. In case of any such aggression or in case of any threat or danger of such aggression the Council shall advise upon the means by which this obligation shall be fulfilled."

The Senate split into three groups: 1) Those who supported Wilson and the treaty; 2) those "irreconcilables" who opposed the treaty in any form; and 3) those "reservationists" who would accept the treaty with certain reservations. The chief reservations were that the United States would be the sole judge as to whether its obligations to the League had been met, and that it could withdraw from the League when it wished. They also provided that the United States was under no obligation to preserve the territorial integrity or political independence of any other nation; and that the Congress would maintain its constitutional role of declaring war, regardless of any League action.

President Wilson found these reservations unacceptable and advised his supporters to oppose them. As a result, the Senate failed to ratify the Treaty of Versailles, and the United States never entered the League of Nations. Although there was considerable public support for a League at the beginning of the Senate fight, public opinion soon shifted. In 1920, voters overwhelmingly elected candidates opposed to American entry into the League and the issue was dead.

The issue of collective security versus independent action, or isolationism--as it was sometimes called by both its critics and supporters--was fundamental to American national security policy in the period between World War I and World War II. Failure of the Treaty of Versailles significantly influenced public opinion throughout the 1920s and the 1930s. The battle raged through the press as well as in the halls of Congress, and editorial cartoonists helped shape public perceptions.

What follows are four editorial cartoons concerning the Treaty of Versailles and the League of Nations, originally published in newspapers in 1919 and 1920. Study these cartoons carefully to determine who and what they represent, and answer the questions beneath them.

A.

Getting a Taste of It

J. H. Donahey. *The Plain Dealer* (Cleveland), c. 1919.

1. Who is serving the soup, and what does it represent?

2. Who is he serving the soup to?

3. What are the different reactions of those around the table?

4. Explain the differences in their reactions?

5. Does the cartoonist think Congress will pass the Treaty and the League?

B.

The League of Nations Argument in a Nutshell

Jay N. Darling. *The Des Moines Register*, c. 1919.

6. Who are the figures in the foxhole?

7. What does the foxhole represent?

8. Why is Congress complaining?

9. How does the President respond to those complaints?

10. Does this cartoon support or oppose the League? Why?

American History - 20   Handout

C.
The Prescription That Went Astray

Jay N. Darling. *The Des Moines Register*, c. 1919.

11. How are the President and Congress portrayed in this cartoon?

12. What does the medicine represent?

13. What effect does the medicine have on Congress?

14. What message is the cartoonist suggesting?

15. Does this cartoon support or oppose the League?

(c) *American History and National Security*. Mershon Center, The Ohio State University

American History - 20 Handout

D.

The One Animal That Wouldn't Go Into the Ark

Jay N. Darling. *The Des Moines Register*, c. 1920.

16. How does the cartoonist employ a Biblical story in this cartoon?

17. How is President Wilson portrayed?

18. What is the image of the treaty compromise?

19. What does Senator Lodge recommend?

20. What has happened to the treaty's supporters (former President Taft, former Secretary of State Bryan, and Senator Hitchcock)?

21. What does this cartoon suggest about the treaty's fate?

American History - 21   Lesson Plan and Notes for Teachers

National Security Through Air Power: Ideas of Billy Mitchell

by James R. Leutze

Preview of Main Points

This lesson treats the ideas, influence, and controversies associated with Colonel William E. Mitchell's views on air power and national security. Mitchell's ideas were ahead of his time, and they caused a stir among leaders of the military establishment in the 1920s and 1930s. However, subsequent events showed that Mitchell's position on air power was substantially correct.

Connection to Textbooks

This lesson can be linked to textbook content about the military and foreign policies of the United States between the end of World War I and the outbreak of World War II.

Objectives

Students are expected to:

1. know Mitchell's ideas about the use of air power to achieve military preparedness and national security;

2. identify and interpret alternative positions on the controversy that Mitchell generated about the use of air power in national defense and warfare;

3. assess the means and ends of Mitchell and his adversaries;

4. discuss strengths and weaknesses of Mitchell's ideas and their applicability to World War II and to the contemporary world; and

5. evaluate the efforts of Billy Mitchell to change military policy concerning the use of air power.

Suggestions for Teaching the Lesson

Opening the Lesson

o Write the name of Billy Mitchell and the title of his famous book, *Winged Defense: The Development and Possibilities of Modern Air Power*, on the chalkboard. If possible, obtain a copy of Mitchell's book to use as a prop for the opening of this lesson.

o Tell students that Mitchell's ideas on air power, expressed in his book, created a hot controversy. Ask them to speculate about what Mitchell's ideas on air power were and why they were controversial. Ask them also to speculate about the consequences of Mitchell's ideas:

(c) *American History and National Security*. Mershon Center, The Ohio State University

to what extent did they influence the policies of the United States? How did they affect his career?

Developing the Lesson

o Ask students to read the case study in the Handout about Billy Mitchell. Tell them to check their speculations about his ideas, expressed in the opening phase of the Handout, against information in the case study, which is the heart of this lesson.

o Assign the questions at the end of the Handout. Tell students to prepare answers to these questions, which will be discussed in class.

Concluding the Lesson

o Conduct a classroom discussion about the ideas of Billy Mitchell in terms of the questions at the end of the case study in the Handout. These questions require interpretation and evaluation of the ideas and actions of Mitchell and his opponents. Therefore, there is room for variation in students' responses. However, require students to ground their responses in the information of the case study. They should be asked to refer to parts of the case study to explain or support their answers.

o You might want to select two groups of students to represent the positions of Mitchell and his opponents in the military. Have each group present its case on the Mitchell controversy to the rest of the class. Then require each side to the controversy to defend its position in response to questions or criticisms from classmates and from you, the teacher.

Suggestions for Additional Reading

Following is an annotated list of books about the ideas in this lesson. These books are presented as additional sources of information for teachers and for very able students.

Davis, Burke. *The Billy Mitchell Affair.* New York: Random House, 1967.

The majority of this book focuses on the 1919-1926 period when Mitchell devoted himself to developing American airpower. World War I had demonstrated to him the strategic importance of the airplane. Davis supports the notion that Mitchell and his reforms were undermined by conservative superiors.

Hurley, Alfred P. *Billy Mitchell: Crusader for Air Power.* New York: F. Watts, 1964.

Hurley, an Air Force major and history Ph.D., presents a critical assessment of this air strategist. Mitchell emerges from this book not as an original military thinker, but a man dedicated to developing American airpower according to the most modern theories. His effectiveness was undermined by his own pugnacity, vanity, and ambition.

Levine, Isaac Don. *Mitchell, Pioneer of Air Power.* New York: Duell, Sloan, and Pierce, 1958.

Levine presents a sympathetic narrative geared for popular consumption. Mitchell emerges as a military prophet and hero overwhelmed by reactionary forces.

Mitchell, William. *Winged Defense: The Development and Possibilities of Modern Air Power.* New York: G.P. Putnam's Sons, 1925.

This is the book with which Mitchell established his reputation as a pioneering air theorist. It is most interesting as a primary source since lots of the ideas and concepts are now either familiar or obviously outdated.

American History - 21　　　　　　　　　　　　　　　　　　　　　　　　　　　　　　　Handout

National Security Through Air Power: Ideas of Billy Mitchell

Billy Mitchell believed that aircraft would be the dominant military weapons of the future. He held this belief as early as 1915, only twelve years after the historic flight of the Wright brothers, which launched the air age in America.

Mitchell campaigned to build up the air forces as a major arm of the United States military forces. He advised leaders in the military and the federal government that the only way to maintain national security was the development of air power.

Why did Mitchell hold these views? Was Mitchell correct? Did others agree with him? What were the consequences for Mitchell and the United States of his campaign to achieve national security through air power?

Background Information About William E. Mitchell

Colonel William E. "Billy" Mitchell was a very unusual army officer. By 1925, he had spent twenty-seven years in the United States Army.

Born to a prominent, Wisconsin family, Mitchell had joined the Army in 1898 to serve in the Spanish-American War. Although he had not seen combat service in Cuba, he stayed in the Army after the war and had an opportunity to serve in a variety of locations. While at Ft. Leavenworth he had his first experience with airplanes and almost immediately decided that they were the war instrument of the future. At that time, the few available military aircraft were attached to the Army Signal Corps, since their primary role was to facilitate communications; and that was how Mitchell first worked with aviation. However, after this brief experience, he wrote in 1906 that "conflicts no doubt will be carried on in the future in the air, on the surface of the earth, and under the water."

It was not until nine years later (1915), though, that he took his first trip in a plane; it was love at first flight. For the next year and a half he took flying lessons regularly, largely at his own expense. With American participation in the war virtually certain, by early 1917 Mitchell was a logical choice to send to France as an observer of French aviation manufacture and combat techniques. Perhaps not incidentally, it was also a convenient time to get Mitchell out of Washington where he had proved to be a surprisingly outspoken critic of American military preparations.

Mitchell was soon caught up in the excitement of the air war in Europe. His early arrival on the scene, his experience with the French, and his own flying abilities made him a natural to serve as the American Expeditionary Force's Aviation Officer. He filled this post for only a short time before becoming involved in a bitter clash with other air officers sent over from Washington. Mitchell ended up as Chief of the Air Service, First Army, aviation's top combat command. He saw extensive combat experience and commanded large air fleets in both the American attacks at St. Mihiel in September and in the final American offensive on the Meuse-Argonne front in November 1918. By the end of the war, Mitchell was a highly decorated Brigadier General with a dazzling record of air combat achievements. He was the epitome of the daring, dashing air officer, who caught the public's imagination and the loyalty of many of the best young pilots in this the newest of the military services.

New Ideas About Air Power

But Mitchell returned from Europe with more than a chest full of medals and a possibly increased sense of his own importance. Billy Mitchell had become convinced of the future of air

---

(c) *American History and National Security*. Mershon Center, The Ohio State University

power and of the threat it posed to the United States. In his opinion, nations would race to build air fleets that would dominate the battlefield, the seas and the air over civilian capitals. No one was safe from the new weapons, not even the population of the United States, which had always before been able to rest secure, protected as it was by the two oceans that washed its coasts. If he were right, and there was little to indicate in what he wrote and said that there was any doubt, the only recourse was to build a modern air force. Many leaders disagreed with Mitchell and he soon was engaged in public debates about American defense. Mitchell felt very strongly about the issues he was putting forward, and he was not very tolerant of dissenting opinion. It was not only a matter of who was right or wrong, it was also a matter of style. Mitchell knew how to get his ideas into the press, and he played upon his dramatic experiences to try to beat down opposition. Furthermore, he argued with superior officers in the Army and often came close to implying that they did not know what they were talking about when it came to modern war.

Mitchell also was critical of the Navy's view that big ships were invulnerable to air attack. He enthusiastically challenged the Navy to test their theory by holding a series of demonstrations off the coast of Virginia. Mitchell was not only interested in the theory, he was also interested in proving that the aircraft could dominate the ship, and thereby lay claim to a larger share of the nation's defense dollars. The highly publicized tests were held in June-July 1921. In the public mind, Mitchell won, because he succeeded in sinking two battleships, as he said he would. However, for a variety of technical reasons, experts could, and did, disagree about what had actually been proven. There is one thing about which there is no doubt; from this point forward Mitchell and leaders of the Navy became bitter enemies.

Conflict Over Mitchell's Ideas

While that controversy was simmering, Mitchell opened an attack on a new front. It was his view that the air service would never get its just share of funding or authority under the current military command structure. Therefore, he publicly called for the creation of a Department of National Defense in which air would be an equal with land and sea commands. Moreover, he suggested that since the aircraft had proven its superiority over the sea craft, the air service should take over coastal defense up to two hundred miles out to sea. This was a very clever argument intended to justify appropriating money to the air service at a time when the government was willing to think only in defensive terms. It also was an argument intended to see money transferred from the Navy, which had traditionally handled coast defense, to the air service.

Mitchell had embarked on a course almost tailor-made to make him unpopular with a number of powerful people. He was talking about a future war which many people did not want to think would ever come. He was saying that war would be different and consequently that many of the people, weapons, and ideas that had been in control earlier would not, or should not, be in control then. He had taken on the Navy and embarrassed it. Furthermore, he was playing, very obviously, to public opinion by using the press to air his ideas. And finally, his flamboyant, confident, and "slick" manner, offended many senior officers, who believed that arguments about strategy, tactics, weapons, and so on should be handled like gentlemen within the military family. So some of the argument had more to do with the way Mitchell went about making his arguments than with the substance of what Mitchell was saying.

Over the next several years Mitchell studied and perfected his theories about the offensive role of air power--in other words how would planes be used in an attacking role in the war that he was more and more convinced was coming. By 1924, he was prepared to launch another publicity campaign to propose that the U.S. needed a strong bombing force, because strategic bombing was going to play a great role in the next war. Since strategic bombing included bombing civilians, this argument brought Mitchell into contention with a new group of critics, who saw him as proposing an immoral type of warfare.

Mitchell framed and presented his ideas to get the most publicity and stir up the greatest controversy. He was convinced that the country was vulnerable to air attack--particularly in the Pacific area. He had done a study of Pearl Harbor's air defenses and found them woefully inadequate. He also was alarmed, with good reason, about the state of the nation's existing air arm. By his calculation we had only nineteen aircraft fit for combat out of our 1,500 planes (Even Mitchell knew that these figures were somewhat exaggerated. He was trying to capture public attention and, as was not unusual for him, he was willing to bend the truth. More accurate figures were probably presented later by one of his supporters who testified that we had only 59 modern aircraft fit for duty out of 1,830.)

Most of the other aircraft were obsolete at best or at worst threats to the lives of the pilots who attempted to fly them. Maintenance and safety procedures were inadequate and perhaps worst of all the "brass" (high ranking officers) in the War Department knew little and cared less about the Air Service. In this situation, Mitchell portrayed the U.S. as a great big sitting duck at the mercy of any nation that could put together a truly modern air force. The only way to solve the problem and save the nation was to pour money into modernizing the air service and in other ways follow the lead of "Billy" Mitchell.

The Trial of Billy Mitchell

Not surprisingly, the "brass" and the President, Calvin Coolidge, did not appreciate Mitchell saying the things he said, and most of all they did not appreciate his publishing his views in popular national magazines. As a general rule, superior officials do not like junior officials questioning their judgment--especially in public. In the case of the military, this sensitivity is actually covered by military law. "Insubordination" is the name given to openly questioning a superior's judgment; if the superior chooses to charge you with insubordination and bring you before a military court (a "court martial"), the penalty can be very severe.

Mitchell was clearly questioning the judgment of those officers, military as well as civilian, who set U.S. air policy, thereby risking--some would even say inviting--court martial. But his superiors were not ready to haul the popular Mitchell before a court, not yet. Instead Mitchell was removed from his post as Assistant Chief of the Air Service and sent to Texas, where it was assumed that he would be out of the public eye and not so accessible to the press.

The exile to Texas worked for a while, but two air disasters occurred in early September 1925 that gave Mitchell the examples he needed to again charge into print. First, a military aircraft disappeared while trying to fly from the West Coast to Hawaii, and the Navy dirigible *Shenandoah* crashed during a thunderstorm over Ohio. In hindsight, both of these tragedies were avoidable; moreover, both involved bad judgment by the senior military personnel involved. Mitchell, however, was willing to go much further than questioning judgment. He immediately called a news conference, handed out a nine-page statement, and charged that the disasters proved the points he had been trying to make earlier. Furthermore, he said that the crashes were the result of attempts to save money and were examples of "the incompetency, criminal negligence, and almost treasonable administration of the National Defense by the Navy and War Departments."

To no one's surprise, Mitchell's superiors decided the time had come to bring the rebellious officer before a court; President Coolidge shared this view. There were eight charges against Mitchell, but they almost all could be grouped under the heading that Mitchell was guilty of conduct likely to undermine "good order and military discipline [and] . . . conduct of a nature to bring discredit on the military service."

Some observers thought that a trial was just what Mitchell wanted, because it would give him an opportunity to air his ideas before an eager public. But if Mitchell read the charges carefully, and he must have, he should have felt a little uneasy. The question was not whether Mitchell was right about the air disasters, or even about the state of American air power, or most of all about the future of air warfare. Rather, it was whether Mitchell had been insubordinate and brought discredit on the military.

The trial began on October 28, 1925, and ran for more than six weeks. Presumably to avoid charges of unfairness, the court allowed Mitchell to fully state his views whether relevant or not. The trial took on the air of a public forum on the future of air power with the audience applauding or sneering at various witnesses. Many of those witnesses, and apparently most of the audience, was for Mitchell. However, one's feelings about Mitchell were irrelevant. The only legal question before the Court was whether Mitchell had made the inflammatory statement in San Antonio and whether it had the effect noted in the formal charges.

On 17 December the Court found Mitchell guilty. He was sentenced to five years' suspension from active duty without pay or allowances. This penalty was slightly reduced by President Coolidge, but Mitchell preferred to resign from the Army on 1 February 1926. He spent the last ten years of his life writing and speaking on the themes he had popularized during his service career. But other events distracted public and governmental attention from Mitchell's pioneering ideas.

Conclusion

It remained for others to build the modern Air Force that would enter and fight World War II. Mitchell died in February, 1936, well over five years before the U.S. entered the war. He was a pioneer who had seen far more clearly than most the future of air power. He also had been right about the neglect of the nation's air arm by his superiors in the post-World War I period. Mitchell was a man ahead of his time, not a truly original thinker, because he often was building upon the ideas of others, but still a creative, innovative pioneer and prophet.

Reviewing and Interpreting Main Ideas

1. What do you think of Mitchell's methods? Is this how you would have handled a situation such as he found himself in? Can you think of a situation like this where you have had to choose to speak out or be silent?

2. Do we need people like Mitchell in big organizations like the military? Would anything creative or different ever get done if everyone went by the book? (In this case, most officers kept their mouths shut but they were the ones who got the Air Corps ready for World War II.) If you disagree with policy, are you better off inside an organization where you can change things or outside where you can criticize?

3. What is your reaction to the way the military "brass" handled Mitchell? Had you been his boss how would you have reacted? Did they really have a choice after Mitchell's statement in San Antonio? How can big organizations handle people like Mitchell and get the benefit of their ideas?

4. Why does the military tend to be conservative or slow to change? People sometimes say "the generals are always preparing to fight the last war." Why? Does it take someone like Billy Mitchell to shake people up, get people thinking, and get things done?

American History - 22　　　　　　　　　　　　　　　　　　Lesson Plan and Notes for Teachers

Public Opinion and National Security Before World War II

by Donald A. Ritchie

Preview of Main Points

The lesson introduces students to public opinion polls as a means of gauging public sentiment in American history, and raises the issue of what role public opinion should play in determining national security policies. The students are required to examine the polls from a policy-maker's perspective, and to draw conclusions on the political and national security implications of the polls.

Connection to Textbooks

Most textbooks discuss the "great debate" between interventionists and non-interventionists before World War II, and describe the slow steps that America took toward ending its official neutrality and supporting the Allies, in the years before Pearl Harbor. This lesson expands upon textbook treatment of these issues by presenting actual public opinion polls from 1939, showing students the nature of the division, and the shifts in public sentiment.

Objectives

Students are expected to:

1. recognize the importance of public opinion in the shaping of American national security policy;

2. recognize the connection between political considerations and international policy;

3. understand how to read and interpret a public opinion poll; and

4. identify and chart public opinion toward changing American neutrality legislation.

Suggestions for Teaching the Lesson

Opening the Lesson

o Review with the students the key steps in America's entry into World War I: the strong isolationist impulse before the war, Woodrow Wilson's campaign slogan, "He Kept Us Out of War," and the eventual decision to go into the War. Then discuss American disillusionment after the war: the failure of the Senate to ratify the Versailles treaty, the secret treaties that redrew European borders, the harsh treatment of Germany, the rise of isolationism in America and the desire to return to "normalcy" in the 1920s. In the 1930s, a Senate investigation suggested that American munitions manufacturers had influenced the United States' entry into the war to increase their own profits. People came to believe that America should never have fought in World War I, and tried to enact legislation to prevent the nation from making the same mistake a second time.

o There seems to be a natural tendency to try to prevent the last war from happening again. In the 1930s, people passed neutrality acts to keep Americans off of ships of warring nations and to prevent sales of war material to them, acts which might have kept the U.S. out of the First World War. After World War II, leaders frequently promised to avoid another "Munich," an appeasement of an aggressive force. Lyndon Johnson often referred to "Munich," in the early years of the Vietnam War. In recent years, leaders and public opinion have demanded "no more Vietnams."

o The creation of a general, pervasive attitude shapes public opinion and makes it difficult for leaders to change policies to meet new crises. Strong leadership and dramatic world events can change public opinion, but the process is usually gradual. Leaders in a democratic society need to stay carefully attuned to public opinion and not move out too far ahead of it. Thus Franklin Roosevelt's remark in the 1930s: "It's a terrible thing to look over your shoulder when you're trying to lead--and find no one there."

Developing the Lesson

o Have the students read the introduction to the lesson in the Handout. Then have them examine the first poll on the European war found in the Handout. Make sure they understand how to read the poll. (**Note:** All tables in the lesson report responses only for those who expressed an opinion.) Ask the students to comment on the regional nature of opinion. Which regions most strongly believed the U.S. would be drawn into the war? (East Central and West Central) Which section believed it least? (New England) Remind them to compare those regional breakdowns with similar regional breakdowns in other polls. Ask the students if there was a significant difference in the way Republicans and Democrats answered the question (there was not).

o Now have the students examine the remaining polls and do the two exercises, a memorandum to the President and a graph in the Handout. You may wish to assign the memorandum as a take-home project, or in shorter version it can be done in the classroom.

Concluding the Lesson

o Draw the graph on the board, and have a student plot the changes in public opinion on neutrality laws between August and November, 1939.

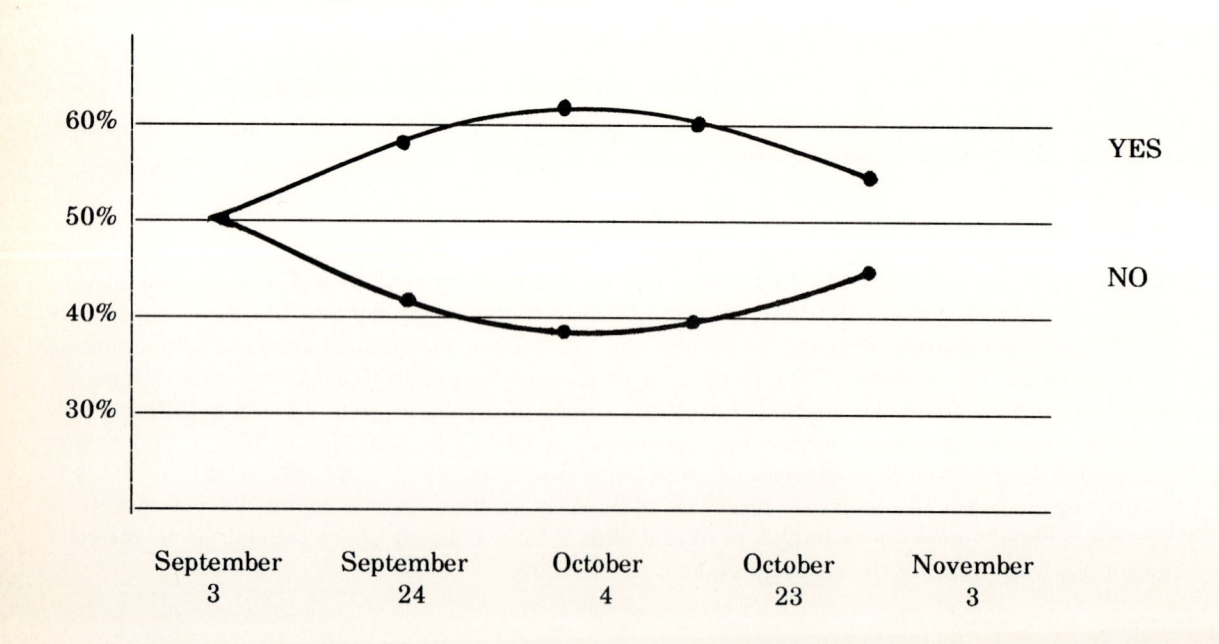

American History - 22

o What trends do you observe? That public opinion, which started out evenly divided before war broke out in Europe (on September 1) at first shifted sharply in favor of repealing the neutrality laws and aiding the Allies, but then began to drift back in favor of keeping the neutrality laws, although the majority still supported repeal.

o What conclusions can you draw from this chart? While sympathetic to the Allies, American public opinion was very fluid in the opening months of the war. It generally supported the Allies, but isolationism held a strong grip in the public's consciousness.

o Ask the students to discuss their memoranda to the President. What major points had they raised? Answers should vary considerably, but ask the students to refer to specific polls wherever possible. These might note that Roosevelt's political support remained strongest in the South and West, regions which took an internationalist position, and weakest in New England, where isolationism was strong. The American people still reacted strongly against anything that seemed to repeat their experience before World War I (September 15: 82% opposed allowing Americans to travel on belligerent ships; November 8, 68% thought it a mistake to have entered WW I, and December 3, 34% thought the U.S. was drawn into WW I as the "victim of propaganda and selfish interests"). Public sentiment was on the side of the Allies and against Germany, but also 84% (September 18) opposed sending American military forces to fight in the war. However, this number fell to 56% if it looked as if England and France might be defeated. Men were more in favor of repealing the neutrality laws than women, 64 to 58% (October 4), and lower incomes more than upper incomes (62 to 59%), and older people more than younger people (63 to 56%). The war in Europe seems to have helped President Roosevelt's voter appeal, (56% on August 23, to almost 65% on October 26).

o Students might conclude that while isolationist impulses were strong, and Americans dearly wanted to stay out of the war, that support for the Allies and opposition to Germany were equally strong, that public opinion supported repealing the neutrality laws to aid the Allies, and that President Roosevelt enjoyed strong public support which he might translate into leadership on these issues. In conclusion, while policy makers might have been ahead of public opinion in support of the Allies (see the poll of people listed in Who's Who, on November 3), public opinion in general was managing to move beyond its preconceptions from World War I and to look at the realities of World War II. Public opinion would support the internationalist program that President Roosevelt would slowly adopt during the next two years before Pearl Harbor.

Suggestions for Additional Readings

Bailey, Thomas A. *The Man in the Street: The Impact of American Public Opinion on Foreign Policy*. New York: Macmillan, 1948.

Bailey offers an entertaining and readable study of this issue.

Gallop, George H. *The Gallop Poll: Public Opinion, 1935-1971*, Vol. I. New York: Random House, 1982.

The polls in this lesson came from this book. Students might also be referred to Gallop's earlier book, *The Pulse of Democracy* (1940).

Public Opinion and National Security Before World War II

Introduction

What role should public opinion play in determining America's national security policies? In a democracy, public opinion expresses itself through votes cast at the polls, letters and petitions to office holders, and public opinion polls. Majority sentiments tend to prevail, but the public rarely speaks with one voice. Political leaders and policy-makers need to be sensitive to the shifts of opinion among the many subgroups of the general public. Effective leadership requires bringing public opinion behind a particular policy, often a very difficult process. As President Franklin Roosevelt remarked during his efforts to alert the nation to Axis aggression, "It's a terrible thing to look over your shoulder when you're trying to lead--and find no one there."

When Europe plunged into the Second World War, following Germany's attack on Poland, on September 1, 1939, most Americans wanted to stay out of the war. But American public opinion was divided between those who favored non-intervention (sometimes called isolationists) and those who favored giving all aid short of war to the British and the French in their struggle against Germany (interventionists, also called internationalists). The Roosevelt Administration moved cautiously in the early months of the European war. President Roosevelt was considering running for a third term in 1940, and gauged his policies on prevailing public opinion.

The following are actual Gallup poll results from 1939. Study these polls from the perspective of a presidential aid, and be prepared to advise the President on the directions of American policy toward the war in Europe.

AUGUST 20
EUROPEAN WAR

If England and France have a war with Germany and Italy, do you think the United States will be drawn in?

Yes	76%
No	24

By Region

	Yes	No
New England	69%	31%
Middle Atlantic	74	26
East Central	78	22
West Central	78	22
South	75	25
West	75	25

By Political Affiliation

Democrats	76%	24%
Republicans	78	22
Others	71	29

AUGUST 23
PRESIDENT ROOSEVELT'S VOTER APPEAL

In general, do you approve or disapprove of Franklin Roosevelt as President?

Favor	56.6%
Oppose	43.4

By Region

	Favor	Oppose
New England	51%	49%
Middle Atlantic	54	46
East Central	51	49
West Central	55	45
South	70	30
West	64	36

(c) *American History and National Security.* Mershon Center, The Ohio State University

SEPTEMBER 3
NEUTRALITY

Should Congress change the present Neutrality Law so that the United States could sell war materials to England and France?

Yes	50%
No	50

By Political Affiliation

	Yes	No
Democrats	56%	44%
Republicans	47	53

By Region

	Yes	No
New England	49%	51%
Middle Atlantic	52	48
East Central	45	55
West Central	49	51
South	60	40
West	51	49

By Sex

	Yes	No
Men	53%	47%
Women	47	53

By age groups, persons 21-29 years old were the least in favor of changing the Neutrality Law.

SEPTEMBER 15
NEUTRALITY

Should the United States allow its citizens to travel on ships of countries which are now at war?

Yes	18%
No	82%

By Region

	Yes	No
New England	16%	84%
Middle Atlantic	19	81
East Central	14	86
West Central	18	82
South	16	84
West	22	78

By Political Affiliation

Democrats	17%	83%
Republicans	19%	81%

SEPTEMBER 18
EUROPEAN WAR

Should we send our army and navy abroad to fight Germany?

Yes	16%
No	84

By Income

	Yes	No
Upper	12%	88%
Middle	15	85
Lower (including reliefers)	20	80
Reliefers only	21	79

By Sex

	Yes	No
Men	19%	81%
Women	12	88

By Political Affiliation

	Yes	No
Democrats	18%	82%
Republicans	13	87

If it looks within the next few months as if England and France might be defeated, should the United States declare war on Germany and send our troops abroad?

Yes	44%
No	56

By Political Affiliation

	Yes	No
Democrats	46%	54%
Republicans	42	58

Which side do you think will win the war?

Allies	82%
Germany	7
Qualified, no opinion	11

American History - 22   Handout

About how long do you think the present war will last?

One year or less	49%
More than one year	51

SEPTEMBER 22
PRESIDENT ROOSEVELT'S VOTER APPEAL

In general, do you approve or disapprove of Franklin Roosevelt as President?

Approve	61%
Disapprove	39

By Region

	Approve	Disapprove
New England	53%	47%
Middle Atlantic	58	42
East Central	59	41
West Central	60	40
South	72	28
West	65	35

How strongly do you feel about this?

Approve strongly	33%
Approve mildly	28
	61%
Disapprove strongly	24%
Disapprove mildly	15
	39%

SEPTEMBER 24
NEUTRALITY

Do you think the Neutrality Law should be changed so that England and France could buy war supplies here?

Yes	57%
No	43

OCTOBER 4
NEUTRALITY

Do you think Congress should change the Neutrality Law so that England and France could buy war supplies here?

Yes	62%
No	38
Strongly in favor	41%
Mildly in favor	21
Strongly opposed	25
Mildly opposed	13

By Region

	Yes	No
New England	56%	44%
Middle Atlantic	65	35
East Central	57	43
West Central	55	45
South	77	23
West	65	35

By Sex

	Yes	No
Men	64%	36%
Women	58	42

By Income

	Yes	No
Upper	59%	41%
Middle	64	36
Lower	62	38

By Age

	Yes	No
21-29 Years	56%	44%
30-49 Years	64	36
50 Years and over	63	37

OCTOBER 23
EUROPEAN WAR

Which side do you want to see win the war?

Allies	84%
Germany	2
No opinion, neutral	14

What should be the policy of the United States in the present European war--Should we declare war on Germany and send our army and navy abroad to fight or should we not send our armed forces overseas?

Should fight 5%
Should not fight 95

Do you think the United States should do everything possible to help England and France win the war, except go to war ourselves?

Yes 62%
No 38

Do you think Congress should make changes in the Neutrality Law so that England and France or any other nation can buy war supplies, including arms and airplanes, in the United States?

Yes 60%
No 40

By Region

	Yes	No
New England	56%	44%
Middle Atlantic	59	41
East Central	57	43
West Central	60	40
South	75	25
West	68	42

Do you think the United States should do everything possible to help England and France win the war, even at the risk of getting into the war ourselves?

Yes 34%
No 66

OCTOBER 26
PRESIDENT ROOSEVELT'S VOTER APPEAL

In general, do you approve or disapprove of Franklin Roosevelt as President?

Approve 64.9%
Disapprove 35.1

By Region

	Approve	Disapprove
New England	59%	41%
Middle Atlantic	65	35
East Central	61	39
West Central	63	37
South	76	24
West	67	33

By Income

	Approve	Disapprove
Upper	46%	54%
Middle	62	38
Lower	78	22

NOVEMBER 3
NEUTRALITY

Do you think Congress should make changes in the Neutrality law so that England and France, or any other nations, can buy war materials, including arms and airplanes, in the United States?

Yes 56%
No 44

Special Survey

Asked of persons listed in *Who's Who in America*: Do you think Congress should make changes in the Neutrality Law so that England and France, or any other nations can buy war materials, including arms and airplanes, in the United States?

Yes 78%
No 22

NOVEMBER 8
WORLD WAR I

Do you think it was a mistake for the United States to enter the World War?

Yes 68%
No 32

American History - 22   Handout

NOVEMBER 12
ARMED FORCES

Do you think the United States should increase the size of the army?

Yes 86%
No. 14

Asked of those who replied in the affirmative: *Would you be willing to pay more money in taxes to support a larger army?*

Yes 64%
No. 36

_____
_____

DECEMBER 3
WORLD WAR I

Why do you think we entered the last war?

America was the victim of propaganda and selfish interests.	34%
America had a just cause	26
America entered for its safety	18
Other reasons	8
No opinion	14

_____

DECEMBER 8
WAR WITH GERMANY

Should the United States declare war on Germany and send her army and navy abroad to fight?

Yes 4%
No. 96

_____
_____

DECEMBER 27
PRESIDENT ROOSEVELT'S VOTER APPEAL

In general, do you approve or disapprove today of Franklin Roosevelt as President?

Approve 63.5%
Disapprove. 36.5

By Income

	Approve	Disapprove
Upper	42%	58%
Middle	61	39
Lower	76	24

_____
_____

Using the information you have gathered from the above polls, write a memorandum to the President, as one of his special advisors. In your memorandum, describe the results and trends of the polls, and give your interpretation of what these polls mean for the conduct and future planning of American national security policy toward the war in Europe.

MEMORANDUM

TO: President Roosevelt
FROM:
RE: Public Opinion and the War in Europe
DATE: December 31, 1939

(c) *American History and National Security.* Mershon Center, The Ohio State University

American History - 22   Handout

NEUTRALITY   (Should Congress change the Neutrality Law so that the United States could sell war material to England and France)

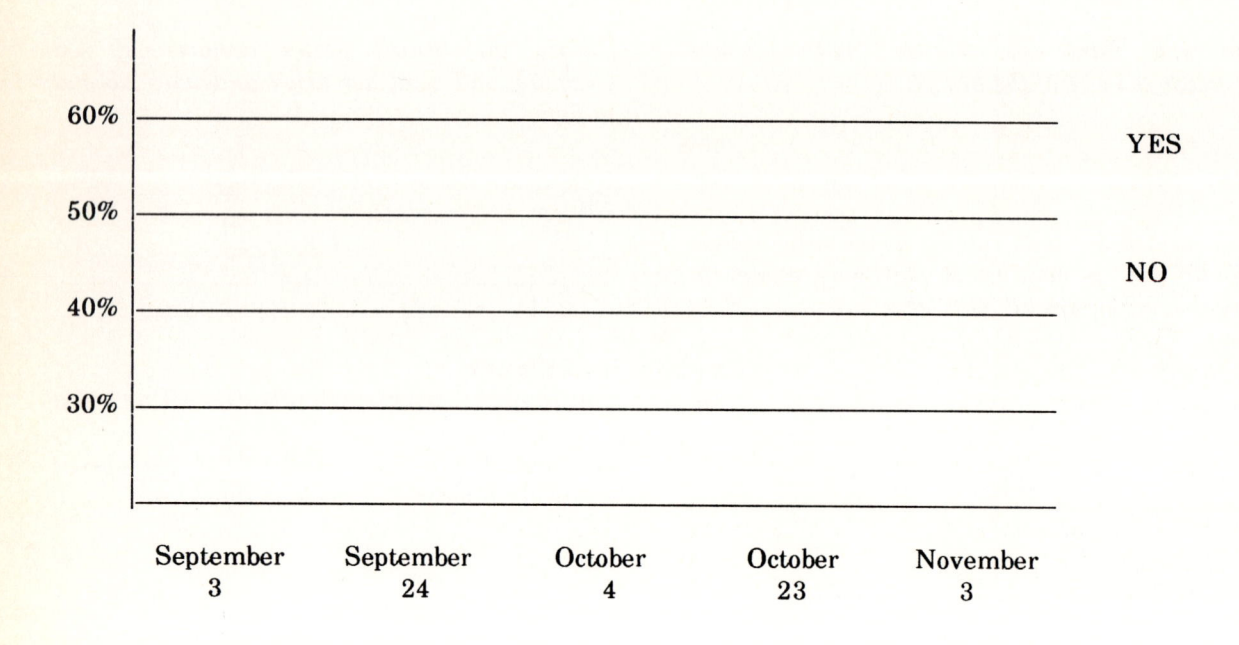

60%					YES
50%					
40%					NO
30%					

September 3   September 24   October 4   October 23   November 3

1. On the above chart, plot the percentages of those who supported and opposed changing the neutrality laws, as recorded between September and November, 1939.

2. What trends do you observe?

3. What conclusions can you draw from this chart?

Discussion Questions

4. What is the relationship of public opinion to foreign policy in a democracy?

5. Should public opinion influence foreign policy? Take a position in response to this question 3 and be prepared to defend it.

(c) *American History and National Security*. Mershon Center, The Ohio State University

American History - 23   Lesson Plan and Notes for Teachers

B-17s: Development and Use of a Weapons System

by James R. Leutze

Preview of Main Points

This lesson deals with the relationship of technology to modern warfare through the example of the development of the Flying Fortress--B-17 by the United States before and during World War II. Furthermore, the moral issue raised by choosing major cities and large civilian populations as targets of strategic bombing is considered. This lesson will have a challenging reading level for many students.

Connection to Textbooks

This lesson can be used with standard textbook chapters on World War II.

Objectives

Students are expected to:

1. know about the development and use of the B-17 (Flying Fortress) by the U.S. before and during World War II;

2. comprehend the relationship of advances in technology and national security;

3. know about the central role of aircraft in modern warfare;

4. understand the moral issue of selecting cities and civilian populations as the targets of air raids; and

5. develop and defend a position about the issue of selecting cities and civilian populations as the targets of air raids.

Suggestions for Teaching the Lesson

Opening the Lesson

o Explain to students that the main point of this lesson is to examine the development and use of the B-17 bomber in World War II.

Developing the Lesson

o Have students read the case study in the Handout on the development and use of the B-17. Ask students to respond to the questions about technology and modern warfare at the end of the case study in the Handout.
o Conduct a classroom discussion about the questions on technology and modern warfare.

Concluding the Lesson

o Ask students to study the last segment of the case study in the Handout, which raises an issue about the selection of cities and civilian populations as targets of air raids in World War II. Ask students to think about the questions and alternative positions presented in response to them in the section titled "A Concluding Moral Issue." Conduct a classroom discussion of the questions at the end of the case study--"Concluding Questions About Targets of Air Raids."

o As an alternative or additional concluding activity, have students complete "A Concluding Exercise" at the very end of the Handout. Divide the class into small groups, from 4-7 persons in a group--depending upon the size of the class. Identify a leader for each group. This person is responsible for making and defending a decision about selection of bombing targets, which is the problem presented in the activity. Other members of each group are to serve as advisors to the leader, who plays the role of commander of 1,000 B-17s in World War II.

o Have students deliberate in their small groups about how to resolve the problem presented in the concluding exercise. Then have each group leader make a decision in response to the problem of the concluding exercise. Finally, have each of the group leaders report and defend his or her decision in front of the class.

Suggestions for Additional Reading

Following is an annotated list of books about the ideas in this lesson. These books are presented as additional sources for teachers. However, very able students might profitably use one or more of these books.

Copp, Dewitt S. *Forged in Fire: Strategy and Decisions in the Air War over Europe, 1940-1945*. Garden City, NY: Doubleday and Co., 1982.

Forged in Fire is a comprehensive overview of Allied bombing in Europe. Whereas Hastings evaluates Britain's Bomber Command, Copp examines the Combined Bomber Offensive, its strategy and implementation.

Craven, Wesley Frank, and Cate, James Lea. *The Army Air Forces in World War II*, 7 vols. Chicago: University of Chicago Press, 1948-1958.

This lengthy publication covers a wide variety of topics. The first five volumes are concerned largely with combat operations. The sixth focuses on the home front while the final volume deals with various subjects including service organizations, women in the AAF, medicine, demobilization, and aviation engineers.

Hansell, Haywood S. *The Air Plan that Defeated Hitler*. Atlanta: MacArthur/Longino & Porter, 1972.

Hansell, an air planner in the World War II period, outlines the development and refinement of the American daylight bombing offensive against Germany. The objective was to cripple Germany and her economy by destroying carefully selected targets.

Hastings, Max. *Bomber Command*. New York: The Dial Press, 1979.

Hastings does not present an exhaustive comprehensive study of Britain's Bomber Command. He does attempt to relate the experiences of the pilots flying missions over Germany, but the book focuses on strategy, the decision-making process behind it, and the effectiveness of its implementation.

MacIsaac, David, ed. *Strategic Bombing in World War II: The Story of the United States Strategic Bombing Survey.* New York: Garland, 1976.

This study traces the evolution of the strategic bombing doctrine as well as the organization and operation of the United States Strategic Bombing Survey.

Overy, R.J. *The Air War*, 1939-45. London: Europa Publications, 1980.

In this ambitious study, Overy examines the impact of airpower on the outcome of the Second World War. Although aircraft played an important role, the Allies' victory was due mostly to their ability to occupy land and supply troops. Allied airpower was more effective than that of the Axis because it was not restricted to a supporting role.

Quester, George H. *Deterrence Before Hiroshima: The Airpower Background of Modern Strategy.* New York: Wiley, 1966.

Quester reviews the history of the ideas and practices of aerial war. The author warns that the post-1945 threat of nuclear destruction does not appear much more terrifying than the prewar perceptions of aerial bombing. Significantly, the latter did not prevent the coming of war or bombing.

Webster, Sir Charles, and Frankland, Noble. *The Strategic Air Offensive Against Germany, 1939-45*, Vols. I-IV. London: His Majesty's Stationery Office, 1961.

These volumes cover a wide variety of topics and material concerning airpower during the Second World War: British planning and operations, Anglo-American cooperation and combined bomber offensives, friction over policy, and types of bombing. The first volume is a collection of appendices, documents, and statistics.

B-17s: Development and Use of a Weapons System

This case study describes the development of the B-17 bomber, the Flying Fortress, and its use for strategic bombing during World War II. The story of the B-17 illustrates the key role technology plays in creating the best weapons systems during wartime. It also illustrates the difficult moral questions raised by choosing major cities and large civilian populations as targets of strategic bombing raids.

Development of the B-17 in the United States

The United States began in the 1930s to build planes for a modern bomber force. The most important of these planes was the B-17. It was a remarkable aircraft. Its four engines would carry it over 2,000 miles while loaded with 4,000 pounds of bombs. It had a crew of ten, some of whom manned its five, .30 caliber machine guns. So powerful was its armament that it was nicknamed the "Flying Fortress." In the B-17, America believed it had found the margin of victory in any war, the proof of the doctrine that the bomber would always get through.

Problems, however, were not long in surfacing. Before the United States entered the war, she provided some B-17s to the British who were eager to get their hands on this war-winning machine. To their distress, the British found that the B-17 was not as fortress-like as its press notices claimed. The most immediate problem was that its .30 caliber machine guns were too light to bring down the fighter aircraft the Germans sent up against it. Furthermore, there were not enough machine guns to adequately protect the B-17 itself. Consequently, a distressing number of B-17s were shot down.

Within a few months after the U.S. entered the war, a new and improved plane, the B-17E ("E" meaning it was the fifth model), entered service. It had increased armor protection, eight .50 caliber machine guns and only one .30 caliber gun. Some 400 of these planes were built, but it was soon recognized that more improvements needed to be made. Higher powered engines were added to the B-17F that was brought into service in 1943; these increased its range and made it possible to carry a maximum load of 13,000 pounds of bombs. Also, three more .50 caliber machine guns were added. A year later the final variation was produced, the B-17G, which could carry as much as 17,600 pounds of bombs for relatively short distances and 6,000 pounds for 3,400 miles. More than 8,000 of these planes were built, and it proved to be the workhorse predicted by its early supporters. But it took long, painful, wartime experience and many lives before a satisfactory design was achieved. By the end of the war, the jet aircraft had been discovered. Before long all bombers with conventional engines were obsolete.

Protecting the B-17s. What has been outlined above was the engineering response to the problems of the B-17; there were many other factors to be considered when thinking about protecting bomber forces. One obvious way to add to their protection would be to send fighter aircraft with them. The problem here was several fold. For one thing, early in the war German fighter aircraft were better than American fighters. Neither the P-39 nor the P-40 were matches for the German ME109. For another, the American fighters did not have the range to fly all the way to the target and back with the bombers. Remember, the range of the B-17 was 2,000 miles; it was 600 miles from London to Berlin or 1,200 miles round trip. Therefore, bombers on long missions would have to fly at least part of the way without fighters to help protect them; the German fighters would wait until the American fighters had turned back and then pounce on the bombers. The longest range for an American fighter in 1942 was 750 miles; by mid-1943 we had the P-47 with a range of just 1,260 miles. Not until early 1944 did the P-51 become operational with a range of 2,080 miles, enough to escort and protect the B-17 to and from the target. The bomber pilots had also by this time learned to fly in formation so that the guns from one plane could protect the other planes in the formation. They flew in a so-called "box" and it helped considerably in cutting their losses.

German Responses to the B-17s. As we improved our bombers and increased the range of our fighters, the Germans countered with changes of their own. They improved their already quite good fighter aircraft increasing its speed, armor, armament and maneuverability. By late 1944 they had brought out nine different models of the basic ME109 as well as the heavily armed FW190. They also had experimented with and actually introduced into combat the first operational jet fighter. Had they been able to bring many of those off the production line, they would have made things even more difficult for the B-17.

The Germans also did other things like increasing the number and the effectiveness of their anti-aircraft guns. By improved anti-aircraft fire, the Germans could not only shoot down more bombers, but they also could force the bombers to fly higher and to take evasive action, thus making it more difficult to hit targets on the ground. By the end of the war, B-17s were flying at 20-25,000 feet which required the air crew to breathe through masks and wear heavy flying suits to protect them from the below zero cold at that altitude. One of the most effective devices the Germans perfected was radar which helped them aim their guns and track the bombers as they approached their targets. In response to the German radar, the bombers began to throw strips of aluminum foil out into the air. These strips showed up on the radar scopes and made it difficult to tell what was a bomber and what was a piece of aluminum. And so it went, move for countermove.

Problems with Finding and Hitting Targets. But protecting the bomber was not the only problem to be solved. Although no one had done a lot of thinking about it before the war, a very simple and basic problem was finding the targets you wished to hit. Even big cities could be difficult to find if you had no navigational aids to help you. Normally, airports send up signals to help planes find them, but in wartime they did not want the enemy to find them. Consequently, they shut down their identifying signals. If you had good aerial maps and good weather you could identify some things visually, but what if it was cloudy? And actually it was often cloudy during fall and winter over northern and central Europe where many of the targets were located. It was a problem finding the target as the British learned early on in the war. In 1941 only one-tenth of their bombers found their way to within five miles of their assigned targets.

The answer was to improve their navigational aids. The first of these was called GEE and was quite helpful if used by a good navigator. The difficulty was that it only had a range of 300 or 400 miles. The system was to have three ground stations sending signals to the plane. The navigator timed these signals and translated them into distance and direction by plotting them on a map. Later we came up with Loran, which was similar to GEE but with a range of 700 miles. Then in March of 1943 a still better system called OBOE was put into operation. By this time it had also been decided to use a Pathfinder system. This meant organizing a special unit of pilots and navigators who would fly in ahead of the main bomber force to mark or identify the target. In this way the Pathfinders would lead the other planes to their objective. The Pathfinders used OBOE and also sometimes H2S which enabled the navigators to differentiate between water and land and builtup areas. H2S emitted a signal which hit the ground and then bounced back to the plane where a fuzzy image of what was below was projected on a screen. It was useful, but the Germans learned to jam it, or worst of all, learned to use it to locate planes so they could be shot down. Despite these difficulties, by the end of the war pilots were much more successful at finding their targets. This should not be interpreted to mean that all planes found their targets, but they did much better than they had at the start of the war.

But protecting the bomber and finding the target were not the end of the problems; there was also the matter of hitting the target once you got there. Early in the war the British did a study of their success in hitting their target and they found that there was a five mile average error. In other words, on average, bombs fell five miles away from where they were aimed. Combined with the fact that the British were losing many bombers in their raids against Germany, this inaccuracy convinced the British that the best solution was to change their tactics and their targeting. They decided to fly at night so as to make it harder for the German fighters to find them and to target what they could hit--cities. From 1942 onward the British dropped a very high percentage of their bombs on cities, making little distinction between military and civilian targets. In 1943-44, 53% of the RAF bombs were targeted on cities and towns. By 1944 they had reduced their average to a three-mile margin of error.

The Americans were more confident of their targeting ability. They had what was considered to be a state-of-the-art bombsight, the Norden. At the beginning of the war American air officers bragged that they could drop a bomb into a barrel from 20,000 feet. The Norden sight was good, but not that good. Furthermore, dropping a bomb when someone was shooting at you and enemy fighters were zooming around was more difficult than practices over the desert in peacetime. The Americans chose to bomb during daylight and tried to hit specific, usually military targets. They lost more men and planes this way, but they slowly improved their equipment, their technique and their accuracy. By 1944 they could boast a two-mile margin of error. Obviously it helped them when their fighter protection improved and aerial photography and experience helped them identify targets more precisely. Furthermore, as Allied bomber and fighter forces increased in numbers and effectiveness, there was a corresponding decrease on the German side. By mid-1944 the Allies had gained command of the air. From this point forward, bombing became more effective.

Strategic Bombing: Making Decisions About Targets

However, once you have protected your bomber, found your target and hit your target, there still remains the issue of which target you select to hit. This was not an easy issue and throughout most of the war debate raged.

Before going into specifics on the various targets, let's make one technical distinction clear. When talking about targeting here we are talking about targeting for "strategic" bombing. The other kind of bombing targets are "tactical" bombing targets. The distinction is between things that are close to or directly connected to the battlefield (tactical) and things that are far from and only indirectly related to the battlefield (strategic). Strategic targets are related to the production of war materiel and to the enemy's ability to conduct war. Objectives for strategic bombing include reducing the enemies' political will to continue the fight. Reducing the enemies' political will is the justification for bombing civilian targets, although some would argue that this is not a justification.

Now, back to the debate about what to bomb. The British and the Americans were working together, but the British were not making much of a pretext of bombing anything other than the cities where manufacturing was going on. The Americans were trying to hit specific factories, roads, bridges, and the like.

From 1942 through mid-1943 the U.S. Eighth Air Force, made up primarily of B-17s, aimed at submarine yards and bases. The submarines were sinking hundreds of ships in the Atlantic and it was vital to try to cripple that industry. Then, in the fall of 1943, the Eighth Air Force targeted ballbearing factories, aircraft production facilities and transportation. The objective was to knock out at least two heavily concentrated industries that were vital to the German war effort. The problem was, both the ball-bearing factories and the aircraft industry were heavily defended. For instance, when the Eighth Air Force went after the ball-bearing factories in Schweinfurt in October 1943, they lost sixty-two out of the 288 bombers sent and 138 others were damaged. Furthermore, the Germans could disperse the factories to other areas and even heavy damage was quickly repaired. As for bombing transportation, it was difficult to put out of operation because it was so spread out. Railroad tracks damaged by bombs could be repaired or trains routed around the damage. Bridges were hard to hit. In any case, measuring the effect of raids was difficult, so the Eighth Air Force decided to concentrate on aircraft production and this they did throughout the winter and spring of 1944. Then from May to September, they were ordered, somewhat to their distress, to shift back to transportation systems to make it more difficult to move equipment and men to France to oppose the Allied landings which took place in June. This bombing was more tactical than the advocates of strategic bombing liked although many of the raids were conducted deep inside Germany.

Then in September they were ordered to bomb German oil production facilities. By September 1944, oil production facilities looked to many like the German Achilles heel. But the oil refineries were very well protected and located a long way from Allied bases. Usually they were located outside of cities and had to be hit very accurately in order to be knocked out of production. But by now the Germans' problems were multiplying. They could not defend everything and the German planes that rose to defend vital targets were now encountering better American aircraft manned by more experienced pilots. The more planes the Germans sent up to be shot down, the more they played into Allied hands. By late 1944 the Germans were playing a losing game, almost everything they did contributed to Allied air superiority which was the ultimate objective.

Then in the spring of 1945 the Eighth Air Force went back to attacking transportation, especially railroads. Allied armies were now inside Germany so the distinction between tactical and strategic bombing hardly applied. Moreover, planners had learned of more effective ways to attack railroads; concentrate on the routes leading into and out of marshalling yards. If trains could not switch from one track to the next, and if spare cars and engines in the yards were knocked out, the system would grind to a halt. Without fuel, plants could not operate, planes could not fly, and tanks could not roll.

Despite these successes in bombing various industries, there continued to be large raids on cities. Between January and May 1945 the RAF dropped 36.6% of their bombs on cities and towns versus 26.2% on transportation targets.

The most famous, and in some ways most questionable, raid was in February 1945 against the beautiful old university city of Dresden. Previously Dresden had been left off the list of appropriate targets, but in the winter of 1945, for reasons still not fully known, it was decided that Dresden would be bombed. The raid was a continuous one, the British bombed during the night of 13-14 February and Americans during the day of 14 February. By this time the Allies had learned how to bomb so that a fire storm was started. These storms generated intense heat and hurricane force winds thus increasing destructiveness. Almost 800 British bombers and over 300 American bombers participated in the raid. The fires burned for four days and the raid was so destructive that no one knows how many people were killed--probably more than 100,000. Some 60% of the built-up area was destroyed with 85% of the inner city leveled. Yet within 48 hours the railroad, the primary military objective in the city, was running. So poorly defended was the city that only five British planes were lost. Many people in Europe thought that the Dresden raid was more morally questionable than the dropping of the atomic bombs on Hiroshima and Nagasaki.

A Concluding Moral Issue

Now, it seems appropriate to raise a moral issue. Are civilians appropriate targets in modern war? Those who favor bombing cities say that civilians work in war-related industries and in other ways actually contribute to a nation's ability to wage war; therefore, killing them, or otherwise taking them out of action is just as helpful in gaining victory as is targeting soldiers. In modern war the **will** to fight is an appropriate target; if the people in a nation lose their will to fight the war will end. In practical terms, cities are relatively easy targets to hit; they also are often not as well protected as industries like oil, so your risk of losing your own men and planes is lower.

Those who argue against bombing cities say that the rules of war have always made a distinction between civilian and military targets. Women, children and non-combatants are not appropriate targets for a civilized nation to aim at. In totalitarian states what the public wants is of very little concern, so attacking the public will is ineffective. Experience has shown, that although cities are easy to hit, they are hard to destroy, rebuilding takes place quickly, people put out of work in service industries (restaurants, theaters, etc.) are quickly put to work in the war industry. Firebombing raids, or massive, continuous raids can destroy a city, but the industries located there can be relocated.

What do you think about the alternative responses, presented above, to the moral issue about civilians as targets of bombing raids in a war?

Concluding Questions About Technology and Modern Warfare

1. What was the B-17?

2. Why did the United States develop the B-17?

3. What technological responses did the Germans make to development of the B-17?

4. How did responses of the enemy influence further development of the B-17 and its use as a weapon of war?

5. What is the relationship between technological advances and national security?

Concluding Questions About Targets of Air Raids

6. Should German cities and their civilian residents have been targets of American air raids in World War II?

7. In general, is it ever justified for a nation to use aircraft to bomb cities of the enemy and the civilians who live in them?

A Concluding Exercise

Assume that you are the commander of 1,000 B-17s, which are based in England. It is October 1943. Based on information in this lesson, what places would you select as your main targets and why? Would your main targets be major cities of the enemy and their civilian populations? Or would your main targets be military airfields, naval bases and other military targets? Or would your main targets be industries producing weapons of war or resources used in war, such as oil and steel? Or would you use your aircraft mainly to bomb enemy troops or naval craft engaged in battle? You may, if you wish, target anything under control of the enemy, not just what is listed above. Consider the alternatives and consequences of your decision about selection of main targets. What is your decision and why?

American History - 24   Lesson Plan and Notes for Teachers

Deciding to Use the Atomic Bomb, 1945

by James R. Leutze

Preview of Main Points

In this lesson, students have an opportunity to examine factors involved in President Truman's decision to use the atomic bomb against Japan in 1945. The lesson shows that the decision making process is very complex and that there are limits upon the choices of a President, including the ideas and actions of advisors and predecessors. This lesson has a challenging reading level.

Connection to Textbooks

This lesson can be used with standard textbook chapters on World War II. All of the textbooks mention Truman's decision. None of them, however, treat the decision making process in detail, as this lesson does.

Objectives

Students are expected to:

1. know when and where the United States used an atomic bomb in World War II;

2. discuss major factors that influenced President Truman's decision to use the atomic bomb to end World War II;

3. explain why President Truman decided to use the atomic bomb in preference to other options open to him in concluding the war with Japan; and

4. make defensible judgments about President Truman's decision to use the atomic bomb against Japan.

Suggestions for Teaching the Lesson

Opening the Lesson

o Inform students about the objectives of this lesson. Next, ask them to read the case study in the Handout on Truman's decision to drop the Atomic bomb.

Developing the Lesson

o After students read the case study, have them answer the questions at the end of the Handout in preparation for classroom discussion.

Concluding the Lesson

o Conduct a classroom discussion on the questions at the end of the lesson. Emphasize that answers to questions 1-4 in the Handout can be checked directly against information in the case study. Answers to question 5 might vary. However, students should be required to ground their answers to question 5 on information in this lesson and to provide sound reasons for their judgments.

Background Information For Teachers

o It is useful to keep two issues regarding the use of the atomic bomb against Japan in perspective. These issues are (1) the question of whether the Japanese were attempting to surrender **before** the bombs were used, and (2) the question of whether Truman's prime motivation in using the bombs was to scare the Soviets and inhibit Soviet adventurism in Europe and Asia.

o As to the first issue, it has become common now to see authors saying that the Japanese government was trying to surrender during the spring and summer of 1945. In fact, this is not correct. **Some** members of the Japanese government, particularly within the diplomatic corps, were very eager to find out whether surrender was possible. They did not approach the United States directly, instead going to governments, most notably the Soviets with whom they were not at war. We knew of these efforts, though, because we were reading the Japanese codes. But knowing was not the issue. The issue was that the Japanese **never** signaled a willingness to surrender unconditionally which was a vital precondition for the Americans. It is ironic, and sad, that eventually the Japanese were allowed to retain the Emperor as a figurehead acting under the supervision of the American commander. Had we been willing to accept that condition in the spring of 1945, who knows what might have happened. But the point is that no one, on either side, thought of the solution until **after** the bombs were dropped. Furthermore, it is important to recognize that there were powerful elements inside the Japanese government who did not want to surrender before--or after-- the bombs were dropped. There was an attempted military takeover of the government when it was learned in Tokyo that surrender was being considered. Thus it is incorrect to say that the Japanese government was trying to surrender but that the U.S. ignored these efforts.

o As to the second issue, the point has often been made that the U.S. dropped the bomb not to end the war, but instead because of our relationship with the Soviets. This is a complicated issue. First, decisions are seldom made for a single reason, there are usually lots of reasons and sometimes it is even difficult to tell which is the most important out of the agreed upon list of whys. In this case it does not seem that difficult. Far and away the most logical, most often stated reason was to end the war quickly and spare American lives. At the same time it is true that some Americans wanted to end the war quickly so that the Soviets, who were beginning to be troublesome in Europe, would not have an opportunity to get deeply involved in Asia and gain thereby an opportunity to be troublesome there. This does not mean that those same people did not have as their highest priority the saving of American lives.

Students should realize two additional things about this argument between historians (those who emphasize the Soviets and those who do not). First, there is an argument between historians about who is responsible for starting the Cold War. The first people to suggest the U.S. dropped the bomb to warn or impress the Soviets were those historians who were trying to prove that the U.S. had started or significantly accelerated the Cold War. Second, because the issue of U.S.-Soviet relations came to dominate the world after the war, there is a very natural tendency to look at things in the U.S.-Soviet context even in 1945. Some historians would point out that this overlooks the fact that in 1945, rightly or wrongly, the U.S. had to be more concerned with U.S.-Japanese relations than with U.S.-Soviet relations.

Suggestions for Additional Readings

Following is an annotated list of books that might be used as additional survey information about this lesson.

Alperovitz, Gar. *Atomic Diplomacy: Hiroshima and Potsdam*. New York: Vintage, 1967.

    Alperovitz challenges the traditional view that the atomic bomb was dropped in order to bring a speedy conclusion to World War II. The Soviet Union, not Japan, was the focus of Harry Truman's decision. The President resorted to intimidation, "atomic diplomacy," to gain Russian compliance with American plans for postwar Europe.

Bernstein, Barton J., ed. *The Atomic Bomb: The Critical Issues*. Boston: Little, Brown, 1976.

    Since the use of the atomic bomb in 1945, scholars have offered a wide range of explanations for the decision. Bernstein presents selections from the major works on the atomic bomb and American foreign policy.

Bernstein, Barton J. "Roosevelt, Truman, and Atomic Bomb, 1941-1945: A Reinterpretation." *Political Science Quarterly* 90 (1975): 23-69.

    Bernstein argues that the United States contributed to the onset of the Cold War. Truman, inheriting Roosevelt's foreign policy, accepted the bomb as a legitimate weapon and realized its potential for influencing postwar negotiations. Possession of this devastating weapon reduced flexibility and incentives for compromise.

Giovannitti, Len, and Freed, Fred. *The Decision to Drop the Bomb*. New York: Coward-McCann, 1965.

    Considering the reasons and alternatives for dropping the bomb, Giovannitti and Freed conclude that the decision to use the atomic bomb was well calculated and designed to end the war quickly.

Schoenberger, Walter S. *Decision of Destiny*. Athens: University of Ohio Press, 1969.

    Schoenberger traces the development of the atomic bomb and the policy concerning its use. Truman's decision to drop the bomb was a logical culmination of the earliest assumptions concerning its purpose.

Deciding to Use the Atomic Bomb, 1945

In the summer of 1945, President Harry Truman faced a difficult decision: whether or not to drop an atomic bomb on a target in Japan. What was the occasion for decision? How was the decision made? What factors influenced the President's choice? To what extent and how was the President limited in his alternatives in making this critical decision?

Background to a Difficult Decision

The war in Europe was moving toward its close and ended on May 9, 1945. By allied agreement, the war in Europe had been the primary activity--Germany first, Japan second had been the priority list. This list reflected the fact that for the United States Europe was more important than Asia. Now, with the war over in Europe, there was the tremendous problem of rebuilding a war-torn continent. This was not a simple problem, there were many issues to be decided and the consequences of failure to act quickly and effectively were very serious. Not only would millions of people suffer terribly from hunger and lack of housing, but also out of war might grow revolution and even new war. There was reasonable concern that communists might seize power in France, Italy and Greece and it seemed possible that the Soviets might help them. Policy-makers believed the best way to deal with these problems would be to bring the war in the Pacific to a close as quickly as possible so that attention could be turned to rebuilding Europe.

At the same time there was growing awareness that the wartime cooperation with the Soviets would not last long after the end of actual hostilities. There were already disturbing indications that the Soviets would be difficult to deal with in Eastern Europe and that they interpreted some agreements entered into with the allies differently than the allies interpreted them. The Cold War had not really begun yet, but a chill was already in the air.

One agreement the Americans believed the Soviets would honor was the agreement entered into at Teheran and confirmed in writing in Yalta. This "Yalta Agreement" stated that the Soviets would enter the war against Japan within 90 days after the war ended in Europe. At the time the agreement was made, U.S. military authorities had wanted all the help they could get in defeating the Japanese. The problem was the larger the role the Soviets played in defeating Japan, the larger the role they would claim in settling the future of Asia. Since they were proving difficult to deal with in Europe, would it not be wise to limit their role in Asia? In the summer of 1945 the invitation to enter the war in the Pacific could not be withdrawn since that would stir Soviet suspicions and make them even more difficult to deal with. The best solution was to end the war against Japan as quickly as possible.

Basic to dealing with all of these issues was the military course of the war. By the summer of 1945, the U.S. had been fighting for three and one-half years. There has already been more than one million casualties and significant losses of materiel. During recent fighting in the Pacific there had been some disturbing developments. When the Marines had assaulted Iwo Jima in February of 1945, only 212 Japanese soldiers chose surrender over death. In April, the Japanese had begun their suicidal Kamikaze attacks on American naval ships. At Okinawa they had again put up fanatic resistance, fighting virtually to the last man before finally being overrun. What this meant to many American planners was that the planned assault on the Japanese home islands would be an extremely bloody affair. There were hundreds of thousands of Japanese soldiers on the main islands and if they fought as the soldiers had fought on Iwo Jima and Okinawa, an invasion of those islands would probably result in a million U.S. casualties as well as untold military and civilian casualties on the Japanese side.

As always, there were personality and experience factors at play as well. Harry Truman had become President in April 1945 when Franklin Roosevelt died. Roosevelt, the only president in U.S. history to be elected to the highest office four times, had left very big shoes to fill. FDR had been a hero to many for seeming to cope successfully with the Depression; then he had taken on the war against the Axis Powers and by spring 1945 seemed to be winning that as well. Truman, on the other hand, was a virtual unknown. Roosevelt had surprised most of the party regulars, and large numbers of voters, when he had picked the obscure Senator from Missouri to be his Vice-Presidential running mate in 1944. Although Truman had served in World War I and later became a judge, what many people remembered about him was that he had gone bankrupt as the owner of a hat store. Whereas Roosevelt had looked presidential, Truman with his bow ties and glasses looked like a schoolmaster; while Roosevelt had socialized with kings and queens, generals and princes, Truman seemed most comfortable in the presence of his World War I buddies and the plain folks of Independence, Missouri. In the spring of 1945, as Truman was getting used to the complexities of leading the nation and its allies toward the conclusion of the greatest war in history, the American public was getting used to a new kind of leader. In this situation, the wisest thing for Truman to do if he intended to lead successfully was to deviate as little as possible from the course set by FDR.

Roosevelt had left Truman with at least two important legacies. First was an atomic bomb program that by 1945 had spent the almost unheard of sum of one billion dollars. As Vice President, Truman had not even known of this program and it was not until weeks after he became President that his Secretary of War filled him in on the details. Building the weapon had been a great scientific challenge with the U.S. racing to beat German scientists to be the first to have the weapon. During its development stages the clear intent had been to use the bomb either against Germany or Japan once it was developed. With Germany out of the war, Japan remained the sole target. No one knew precisely when the bomb would be ready, but Roosevelt had apparently left Truman with a weapon that might end the war--if it were used properly.

The other thing FDR had left his successor was a policy regarding how countries could surrender. At the Casablanca Conference in 1943, Roosevelt had announced that the only kind of acceptable surrender was "unconditional surrender." In other words, a surrender in which the enemy could set no terms: they simply laid down their arms. Germany had surrendered under those terms so there was already evidence that even fanatical enemies could be forced to accept these very harsh terms.

The problem was that by summer 1945 the U.S. knew that some powerful elements within the Japanese government were considering surrender, but they had terms that they insisted upon. By means of reading secret Japanese codes, the U.S. knew that some Japanese wanted to surrender but only if they could retain the Emperor. To some Americans, the Emperor was seen as the cause of the war and hence that term was particularly unacceptable; to others, probably most, any terms were unacceptable. In this case, had Truman accepted any terms he would have been going directly against the policy set by FDR, and seeming to ignore the success gained against Germany.

Disagreement Among the President's Advisors

The foregoing were all major factors in the developing situation, but there are still other influences to be considered. Governments are made up of many individuals with many points of view. This multitude of opinions was certainly true in this case. The senior Japanese expert in the Department of State was former Ambassador to Japan Joseph Grew; during part of the spring he was Acting Secretary of State. Grew believed that it would be wise to allow the Japanese to retain the Emperor because he would bring much needed stability to a defeated Japan. Differing with Grew was Truman's personal advisor who would become Secretary of State in July, James

Byrnes. Byrnes believed that the Emperor represented much that was wrong with the Japanese government and definitely should go.

If the Japanese were going to surrender unconditionally, the next question was how to end the war. An obvious option was to drop the bomb, but even among the scientists who had worked on the weapon there were differences of opinion. One group, the so-called Chicago scientists, urged that the bomb not be used or that at a minimum it only be used against a military target after a demonstration. Another group, the so-called Los Alamos scientists, believed that the bomb should be used first against a military target. The issue of a demonstration also caused heated debates. Some feared that if we announced where we were going to demonstrate the bomb, the Japanese would move U.S. POW's there, thus making it impossible to drop the bomb. Others argued that we did not have enough bombs to waste them in demonstrations. Since it was estimated that by August we would have only two bombs, that was a pretty good argument.

The deciding argument against a demonstration, and one that has a bearing on other parts of the story, seems to have been that no one really knew if a bomb could actually be dropped successfully on a target. Furthermore, there was uncertainty about how much damage the bomb would do. If we held a highly publicized demonstration and the bomb either did not go off or did comparatively little damage, the U.S. would end up looking ridiculous and it might even increase Japanese will to resist. Since the primary objective in using the bomb was to bring the war to a speedy conclusion, doing anything that might undermine that purpose was a fundamental question under consideration.

Finally, there were differences of opinion among the President's senior military advisors. Admiral William Leahy, who had been FDR's and was now Truman's personal military advisor and chairman of the U.S. Joint Chiefs of Staff, was opposed to using the bomb on moral grounds. General George C. Marshall, the Army Chief of Staff and in some ways the most influential military voice in Washington, was in favor of using the bomb because he believed that in the long run it would save lives. Some naval officers, knowing that the U.S. was now sinking Japanese shipping virtually at will, believed the bomb was unnecessary because soon Japan would be starved into submission. Some air corps officers like Curtis LeMay believed that conventional fire bombing raids such as the one in March against Tokyo which burned out fifteen square miles and killed 83,000 people, would be sufficient to bring Japan to its knees.

Deciding to Use the Atomic Bomb

What should a President do when experts disagree? Truman did what many decision-makers do in such a situation: he appointed a committee. The Interim Committee, as it was called, was made up of some of the wisest and most experienced men in American government. Chairing it was Secretary of War Henry Stimson who had first come into prominence in 1911 as Secretary of War under William Howard Taft. Since that time he had served various Republican and Democratic Presidents, most notably as Secretary of State from 1929-1933. Included as advisors to the committee were some of America's most brilliant scientists. This was a group of very important men.

On June 1, 1945, the Interim Committee made its recommendation to President Truman. They recommended that the bomb be used against the Japanese as soon as possible. Furthermore, they noted that "we can propose no technical demonstration likely to bring an end to the war; we see no acceptable alternative to direct military use."

There was yet a final decision for Truman to make: when and where to drop the bomb. But as for actually using it, Truman said: "[I] never had any doubt that it should be used." Recent evidence suggests that there was more soul searching than this comment would imply; however, by early summer the basic decision had been made. Soon thereafter Truman decided **where** it should be used, against "a war production center of prime military importance."

Two additional factors influenced Truman's decision-making. After 1 June 1945, the only way to keep the bombs from dropping would have been by Truman deciding **not to act on a decision that had already been made.** In other words, he would have had to stop a process in motion. That is a quite different thing than deciding to put a process in motion. One could agree that from the very day the process of building the bomb was started, the logical and likely thing to do was to go forward, not to stop. In any case, by June the decision had been made and from that point forward things happened more or less automatically. It would have taken an act of tremendous political courage for the new President to have overruled his advisory committee, even if he had disagreed with them, and to run the risk of more American deaths. Can you see the headline: "President Spares Japanese: A Million G.I.'s Die." The alternative became very clear to him on 18 June when the Joint Chiefs of Staff forwarded him the plan for the invasion of Japan. He approved it. Invasion would occur unless the war could be ended quickly.

Decisions are like stones rolling downhill. The further they roll the more difficult they are to stop. They pick up speed or, in this case, involve more and more people. At some point they become almost impossible to stop. Only in movies or novels does a character step in at the last moment and stop the landslide. In real life, the fact that money has been spent becomes an argument for spending more money, that one group has decided something becomes an argument for others to go along, that one plan has been made leads to the next plan being made. That is how it was in the summer of 1945.

Another factor was chronology or the quick pace of events in 1945. Things happened fast in the summer of 1945. Truman had become President on 12 April: less than a month later, 9 May, Germany surrendered. Three weeks later, 1 June, the Interim Committee made its recommendation. Truman had been President less than nine weeks. On 6 July Truman left Washington for the first meeting he would have with our wartime allies, Churchill and Stalin. The meeting was at Potsdam outside Berlin. Truman would cross the Atlantic by ship. The conference began on 16 July. The same day Truman received a message that the test explosion at Alamogordo had been a success. Truman and Churchill immediately set to work on a document that came to be known as the Potsdam Proclamation which called on the Japanese to surrender--unconditionally--or face complete destruction. The possession of a new weapon was hinted at but not spelled out. On 24 July, orders were sent to the Air Corps Commander in the Pacific to drop the bomb on one of four Japanese cities as soon after 3 August as weather would permit. **When** had now been decided. On 28 July, the Japanese broadcast what was interpreted to be a rejection of the Potsdam Proclamation. On 1 August, the Potsdam Conference ended and Truman began the trip home. He was on board the cruiser *Augusta* when, on 6 August, the first bomb was dropped on Hiroshima; Truman had been President for four months.

Several other chronological points: the President had been out of the country and consequently somewhat out of touch for the month preceding the dropping of the bomb; only three weeks separated the first test explosion and the actual dropping of the bomb from a plane. (There was absolutely no assurance that an air drop would work; the test had been a bomb fixed to the top of a tower, set off by remote control. Estimates were that if it did work there would be far fewer casualties than there were. Finally, during most of the two months between the time the original decision was made (1 June) and the actual drop (6 August), Truman's mind was fully occupied preparing for and participating in a conference that would decide the fate of post-war Europe--an issue that probably seemed more important than the issue of whether you killed Japanese by dropping firebombs or by dropping this new atomic bomb.

Who Was Responsible?

In conclusion, let us turn to the matter of who, in the final analysis, was responsible for the dropping of the bomb. Obviously, Truman was in part responsible, because as the famous sign on his desk said, "The Buck Stops Here." But Truman was in many ways a prisoner of events and time. He was influenced by advisors and by decisions made by others. Although easy for us to forget, the ghost of Franklin Roosevelt must have haunted Truman. Roosevelt had made many of the decisions that propelled Truman down the road he followed. Very significantly, FDR had made the decision not to inform his Vice-President about the work on the bomb, thus insuring that Truman's decision-making would take place without preparation in the first hectic weeks of his presidency. Finally, Truman's decision to drop the bomb was a decision to try not to do something else, in this case invade the Japanese Home Islands. This points up the important fact that decisions are often choices between unpleasant alternatives.

But there was another group who might be charged with at least some responsibility for dropping of the bomb. The Japanese governmental leaders also made decisions that bore on this event. In the first place, the Japanese made a positive decision in the winter of 1941. They **chose** to attack the United States. Had there been no Pearl Harbor, there would have been no Hiroshima. The Japanese also made a negative decision in the summer of 1945. They chose **not** to surrender unconditionally. Leaving aside the good reasons for why they did not want to do this, and there were some, the fact remains that they had the opportunity to surrender and they chose not to. By the summer of 1945, the Japanese were, in the words of an American general, being "bombed back into the stone age." Their ships could not defend their harbors or bring in the raw materials necessary for survival. The war was lost, but the leadership would not give up. They made a decision not to do something and that brought about Truman's decision to do something. Let us hope that other leaders at another time will not find themselves so trapped by events and previously made decisions.

Reviewing and Interpreting Main Ideas

1. When did President Truman decide to use the atomic bomb as a weapon in war?

2. Where was the first atomic bomb dropped?

3. How did each of the following factors affect President Truman's decision to use the atomic bomb against Japan?

   a. actions of Truman's predecessor, President Roosevelt

   b. the end of the war against Germany

   c. the Soviet Union's agreement with the U.S. to declare war on Japan

   d. the response of the Japanese government to the U.S. demand for unconditional surrender

   e. the fighting abilities and resources of the Japanese army

   f. the number of atomic bombs available to the U.S.

   g. the fact that the atomic bomb had neither been used in warfare nor dropped from an aircraft

   h. advice from top-level advisors

American History - 24   Handout

4. Why did Truman decide against the following alternatives?

   a. Demonstrating the power of the atomic bomb, and thereby influencing the Japanese to surrender, by dropping it on an uninhabited island

   b. using conventional weapons in an invasion of Japan

   c. dropping the demand for unconditional surrender and negotiating a peace settlement with the Japanese

5. What is your judgment of Truman's decision to drop an atomic bomb against Japan? Was it a good decision? Why?

SECTION VI
AMERICA IS CHALLENGED BY THE COLD WAR

List of Lessons

This section contains six lessons about national security policies of the United States after World War II. These lessons treat American policies associated with the "Cold War" conflict between the United States and the communist nations led by the Soviet Union. The lessons are

25. Mr. X and Containment

26. The Vandenberg Resolution and NATO

27. A Network of Alliances

28. The Domino Theory

29. Ex Comm and the Cuban Missile Crisis

30. Why Was the Salt II Treaty Never Ratified?

Overview for Teachers

World War II marked an important transition for U.S. security policy. Both the events leading up to it and the redistribution of power that followed it convinced American leaders that the United States must assume new responsibilities in the world. It could no longer protect and promote its interests by following the isolationist principles that had guided the nation in the inter-war security environment.

From this evaluation two conclusions emerged that would form the basis of U.S. conduct in the evolving post-war order. The first was that it was imperative for democratic nations to resist aggression firmly and immediately or else it would lead to wider conflict. This view was known as the "Munich syndrome" because of the conviction that French and British appeasement at Munich in 1938 by granting Hitler his territorial demands on Czechoslovakia, had emboldened him to go to war.

The second conclusion was that the League of Nations had been a clearly inadequate mechanism. There were two parts to this view. First, the League had been incapable of acting decisively against aggression (it "had no teeth"). Second, the United States itself had failed in not taking part. Thus, American policy makers began as early as 1939 to design a new "international security organization," the United Nations, intended both to overcome the flaws of its predecessor and to provide an effective leadership role for the United States.

The security problems of the post-war environment proved to be no less difficult than those that had come before. World War II had unalterably changed the nature of security requirements. Nations had engaged in "total war," using strategic bombing to attack both the economic capacity and the "will to fight" of the enemy. There were profound changes in the scope, tempo and destructive potential of conflict culminating with the onset of the "nuclear age" at Hiroshima and Nagasaki.

The post-war era was also marked by the emergence of "bi-polarity." By war's end the former pattern of the European balance of power was replaced by the presence of only two powers, the United States and the Soviet Union. These two nations with opposing value systems, great military potential and competitive global interests became the core of a new international system. Other nations were left to cluster around one or the other pole of power. For the United States, Soviet power was a major challenge and definitive presence in the development of its post-war security policy. Because of the growing fear of Soviet expansion and the immediacy of war introduced by advancements in weapons technology, U.S. security policy adopted a posture equivalent to wartime preparedness. America's new involvement in international affairs was thus defined by a "cold war" with the Soviet Union.

One of the first tasks of the "cold war" for the U.S. was to provide a coherent framework for policy. American leaders feared continuing Soviet expansion. To

187

counter that prospect, the United States sought to provide assistance to nations threatened by communist aggression. Such assistance required a rationale that could attract political support in Washington. As presented in **Lesson 25**, the rationale came from an analytical article on the nature of the Soviet system by American diplomat George Kennan. In his article Kennan recommended "the adroit and vigilant application of counterforce" in order to "contain" the Soviet Union, giving rise to the prevailing post-war U.S. doctrine of the "containment" of communism.

One of the first tests in the implementation of this new doctrine came in 1949 with the establishment of the North Atlantic Treaty Organization (NATO). NATO was designed to present a unified front against the threat of Soviet expansion in Europe. Having committed itself already to the defense of Europe, the United States was an essential element in the development of this alliance system. However, U.S. participation in a peacetime alliance was unprecedented. Since Washington's warning against "entangling alliances," the United States had remained clear of such commitments. **Lesson 26** traces how President Truman worked through the Senate leadership to lay the groundwork for American participation in the NATO Alliance, a successful though often challenging political and military alliance that continues today as a fundamental part of American security. And, as **Lesson 27** shows, NATO became the model for an effort to extend containment around the periphery of the Soviet Union through a system of alliances, interlinked through the overlap of U.S. participation (as well as that of other countries).

The U.S. commitment to preventing communist aggression was affected by yet another post-war development, the end of the colonial period in international affairs. The former colonial powers were either vanquished or so weakened by the war that they could no longer maintain their colonial rule. The 1940s and 1950s witnessed the emergence of more and more new nations, often becoming independent in the midst of internal turmoil.

For the United States these circumstances created grave concern about the potential for communist expansion. Many of the revolutionary forces seeking independence were communist and often Soviet-backed. **Lesson 28** discusses the "domino theory," one of the consequences of this uneasy atmosphere. The domino theory, held by some U.S. leaders, predicted that the fall of any state to communism would lead to the fall of others in the same region, thus heightening American concerns.

It was the nuclear age, however, that provided the greatest level of concern for the United States. Although the United States enjoyed a brief period of nuclear monopoly followed by a longer period of nuclear superiority, the Soviet Union moved quickly to catch up. The 1960s and 1970s were characterized by increasing arms competition. The most dramatic incident in this period was the Cuban Missile Crisis of 1962. The crisis began when the United States discovered that the Soviet Union had started placing offensive medium and intermediate range ballistic missiles in Cuba, ninety miles off the American shore. **Lesson 29** chronicles how President Kennedy and his advisors responded to this threat.

The nuclear confrontation of the Cuban Missile Crisis illustrated the risk contained in the prevailing nuclear environment. It also brought increased impetus to efforts by the superpowers to define and stabilize their security relationship through direct negotiations for arms control. By the 1970s, the Soviet Union had acquired nuclear capability at least equivalent to that of the United States ("parity") adding further impetus to this effort. In a series of continuing negotiations called Strategic Arms Limitation Talks (SALT), the United States and the Soviet Union pursued agreement on the quantity and quality of nuclear arms. SALT I was negotiated from 1969-72 and SALT II was negotiated from 1972-79. However, as **Lesson 30** shows, the SALT II Treaty was never ratified.

American History - 25　　　　　　　　　　　　　　　　Lesson Plan and Notes for Teachers

Mr. X and Containment

by Donald A. Ritchie

Preview of Main Points

This lesson deals with the policy of containment of Soviet expansion by focusing on one of its chief authors, George F. Kennan. Specifically, it deals with Kennan's frustration over what he believed were the misperception and misapplication of the theory with which his name was associated. The lesson deals with his famous "X" article, with criticisms of that article, and with Kennan's own admissions of the article's deficiencies which led people to misuse it.

Connection to Textbooks

This lesson should be taught in connection with the Truman Administration and the origins of the containment doctrine. It can also be used in connection with the Vietnam war, where containment was cited as a reason for American intervention, and where George Kennan believed it was being misapplied.

Objectives

Students are expected to:

1. identify and explain the policy of containment;
2. understand the different reactions to the policy;
3. recognize the problems with imprecision in national security policy; and
4. analyze the effects of changing situations on established policy.

Suggestions for Teaching the Lesson

Opening the Lesson

o Ask the students if they have ever found themselves unable to get a point across to someone else, or have ever been frustrated over their inability to make themselves understood. Suggest the magnification of such problems when national policy issues are at stake.

o Preview the main parts of the lesson for the students.

Developing the Lesson

o Have the students read the Handout. Then ask them to respond to the review questions at the end of the lesson.

o Conduct a discussion of the review questions to be sure they have understood the main points of the lesson.

o Discuss the dialogue between Kennan and Senator Lauche at the end of the Handout. Point out why people, like the Senator, might be puzzled why Kennan seemed to have changed his mind; reinforce why Kennan felt so frustrated.

(c) *American History and National Security*. Mershon Center, The Ohio State University

Concluding the Lesson

o Read to students the following quote from George C. Herring's *America's Longest War: The United States and Vietnam, 1950-1975* (New York, 1979), pp. 270-271:

> Vietnam made clear the inherent unworkability of a policy of global containment. In the 1940s the world seemed dangerous but manageable. The United States enjoyed a position of unprecedented power and influence, and achieved some notable early successes in Europe. Much of America's power derived from the weakness of other nations rather than from its own intrinsic strength, however, and Vietnam demonstrated conclusively that its power, however great, had limits. The development of significant military capabilities by the Soviet Union and China made it too risky for the United States to use its military power in Vietnam on a scale necessary to achieve the desired results. Conditions in Vietnam itself and the constraints imposed by domestic opinion made it impossible to reach these goals with limited means. Vietnam makes clear that the United States cannot uphold its own concept of world order in the face of a stubborn and resolute, although much weaker, foe. The war did not bring about the decline of American power, as some have suggested, but was rather symptomatic of the limits of national power in an age of international diversity and nuclear weaponry.

o Ask the students to discuss this statement in light of the lesson they have just read. Ask them to speculate about how the United States might view the concept of containment in the future.

o Conclude with the discussion question at the end of the Handout. Ask them to speculate about ways that ideas and policies might get out of control and tumble wildly away from their originators.

Answers to Handout Questions

1. Because of his official position in the State Department.

2. Because it offered a reason and a solution for a major problem facing the United States, and because of the mysterious nature of its author "X."

3. That the United States should follow a policy of containing Soviet expansionism "at a series of constantly shifting geographical and political points."

4. Lippmann believed the United States by itself could not contain the Soviet Union everywhere in the world.

5. Because of his official position in the State Department.

6. That he did not make clear the difference between political and military containment; and that he had not distinguished between geographic areas, limiting containment to those areas that most directly influenced the security of the United States.

7. That the United States should not make unilateral concessions to the Soviet Union, but should inspire and support resistance efforts to Soviet expanionism.

8. After Stalin's death and the division between China and the Soviet Union, world communism was no longer monolithic, which he believed invalidated the containment policy.

9. For the popularity of the containment policy in the United States.

10. No, the situation had changed.

11. Answers will vary.

Mr. X and Containment

The creation and implementation of national security policies are highly complex matters, and so is the communication of the intentions behind those policies. There are grave risks involved in imprecision. One of the most distinguished architects of America's Cold War policies, former Ambassador George F. Kennan, suffered much frustration over what he considered the misunderstanding--and the misapplication--of his recommendations for "containment" of Soviet expansion.

An Article by X

In July, 1947, the magazine *Foreign Affairs* published an article on "The Sources of Soviet Conduct," which was signed only by "X." Within a very short time, it became widely known that X was really George F. Kennan. Kennan was head of the State Department's Policy Planning Staff and one of the nation's top Soviet specialists. Because of his position, Kennan had not signed his name to the article. But in the long-run his attempt to remain anonymous had only drawn more notoriety to himself and his ideas.

Kennan's X-article appeared at a time when U.S.-Soviet relations had reached a breaking-point. The wartime alliance between the two nations had turned into a postwar rift, and they now confronted each other at trouble spots around the world. The X-article drew much interest because it offered both a reason and a solution for this problem. The Soviet Union had not moved into Eastern Europe just to build a buffer zone to protect its security, Kennan argued. Stalin's policies, and the Soviet Union's Marxist-Leninist ideology, called for an aggressive, expansionist program. The United States must meet Soviet expanionism by vigilantly applying "counter-force at a series of constantly shifting geographical and political points." This policy, known as containment, became the mainstay of the Truman Administration's programs to deal with events in Europe and the Middle East during the late 1940s.

Criticism of the X-Article

Kennan's X-article was widely read and highly influential, but it also came in for strong criticism. The newspaper columnist Walter Lippmann devoted a series of columns (later printed in a book called *The Cold War*) to attacking Kennan's article. Lippman did not believe that the United States by itself could contain the Soviet Union everywhere in the world. Such a policy would require sending troops everywhere to every trouble spot. Instead, Lippman advocated concentrating on the situation in Europe. He urged both the United States and Soviet Union to withdraw their troops from European nations, to make that continent a demilitarized zone.

Kennan did not see a sharp difference of opinion between Lippman and himself. Rather, he thought Lippman had misread or misunderstood the article. But Kennan felt he could not respond publicly to these criticisms because of his official position in the State Department.

Kennan's Self-Criticism of the X-Article

The controversy over his article in *Foreign Affairs* caused George Kennan to reevaluate what he had written. In his memoirs he admitted to a number of deficiencies in the article. The most serious of these was: "The failure to make clear that what I was talking about when I mentioned the containment of Soviet power was not the containment by military means of a military threat, but the political containment of a political theat." Some of the words used by

Kennan were ambiguous--such as "a long-term, patient but firm and vigilant containment of Russian expansive tendencies" or "the adroit and vigilant application of counterforce at a series of constantly shifting geographical and political points." Some readers misinterpreted these words.

Kennan also regretted that he had not distinguished between the various geographic areas of the world, "and to make clear that the 'containment' of which I was speaking was not something that I thought we could, necessarily, do everywhere successfully, or even needed to do everywhere successfully, in order to serve the purpose I had in mind." Kennan believed that the United States must distinguish between those areas that were vital to its security and those that were not.

Kennan's chief point in writing the article had been to urge the United States not to make unilateral concessions to the Soviet Union, but to inspire and support resistance efforts and to "wait for the internal weaknesses of Soviet power" to moderate their ambitions and behavior. "The Soviet leaders, formidable as they were, were not supermen," wrote Kennan, looking back twenty years later. "Like all rulers of all great countries, they had their internal contradictions to deal with. Stand up to them, I urged, manfully but not aggressively, and give the hand of time a chance to work."

The Situation Changed but the Policy Did Not

To Kennan's dismay, the policy of containment that he advocated in 1947 continued in effect long after the situation had changed. When he wrote about "Soviet Power" in the X-article, Kennan had meant the monolithic power structure created by Joseph Stalin. But Stalin had died, and China had broken from Soviet leadership. Although the monolithic structure had come apart, people were still trying to apply the doctrine of containment against some vague notion of "Communism," without specifying what country and system they meant. "If then, I was the author in 1947 of a "doctrine of containment," Kennan declared, "it was a doctrine that lost much of its rationale with the death of Stalin and with the development of the Soviet-Chinese conflict."

Despite Kennan's efforts to disassociate himself from containment and to encourage Americans to examine new situations realistically, he could not escape from his association with the popular doctrine. A striking example of this was his testimony in February, 1966, before the Senate Foreign Relations Committee. Kennan testified in opposition to the U.S. war in Vietnam. Senator Frank Lausche, an Ohio Democrat who supported the war, then questioned him.

Senator Lauche: Ambassador Kennan, it has been said frequently that you were the designer and architect of the policy of the United States that we cannot suffer the expansion of Communism, and, therefore, there must be adopted a plan of containment. Were you a participant in the design of that plan?

Mr. Kennan: Senator Lausche, I bear a certain amount of guilt for the currency this word--"containment"--has acquired in the country. I wrote an article, an anonymous article, in 1947 . . . in which this word was used, and the article got much more publicity than I thought it would get, and it is true in this sense I am the author, at least of this word with regard to our policy toward the Soviet Union.

Senator Lausche: Right. Now, then, isn't it a fact that when this policy was announced, it was [based] upon the belief that the security of the nation required that there be a stoppage of the aggressive advancement of Communism into different areas of the world than those in which it was then prevalent?

American History - 25   Handout

Mr. Kennan: Yes, sir. At that time . . .

Senator Lausche: Now, then, if that is so, has your view changed?

Mr. Kennan: No, the situation has changed.

No wonder that George Kennan, in his *Memoirs*, described his reaction to the effect of the X-article as "Feeling like one who has inadvertently loosened a large boulder from the top of a cliff and now helplessly witnessed its path of destruction in the valley below, shuddering and wincing at each successive glimpse of disaster." [From *Memoirs*, Vol. I, pg. 356]

Questions for Review and Interpretation

1. Why did George Kennan publish his article anonymously?

2. Why did the article draw so much attention?

3. What did the article advocate?

4. In what ways did Walter Lippman disagree with the X-article?

5. Why didn't Kennan respond to Lippman's criticisms?

6. What deficiencies did Kennan see in his X-article?

7. What did Kennan say was the chief point he was trying to make?

8. How had changes in the world situation affected Kennan's views on containment?

9. For what did Kennan accept "a certain amount of guilt"?

10. According to Kennan, had he changed his mind about containment?

11. Why might George Kennan compare his publication of the X-article to "inadvertently loosening a large boulder from the top of a cliff"? What does this analogy suggest about the dangers or risks of decision-making?

(c) *American History and National Security*. Mershon Center, The Ohio State University

American History - 26   Lesson Plan and Notes for Teachers

The Vandenberg Resolution and NATO

by Donald A. Ritchie

Preview of Main Points

This lesson tells how Senator Vandenberg worked to achieve a consensus in the Senate Foreign Relations Committee, the United States Senate, and the American nation, to overcome historic suspicion against "entangling alliances" and clear the way for American participation in NATO. It uses a primary document--excerpts from the transcript of a closed-door session of the Foreign Relations Committee--to show the students how this consensus was achieved. It also demonstrates the role of Congress in national security decision-making.

Connection to Textbooks

This lesson can be used with standard textbook chapters on the Cold War. All textbook accounts discuss NATO, and many give credit to the Vandenberg Resolution for enabling American participation in NATO. This lesson highlights the legislative branch's role in the formulation of American national security policy, as well as the bipartisanship of the Truman Administration (Democratic) and the 80th Congress (Republican majority) on foreign policy and national security issues. Unlike most textbooks, this lesson emphasizes how decisions are made and consensus is reached, rather than only discussing the outcome.

Objectives

Students are expected to:

1. explain the purpose of the Vandenberg Resolution;

2. identify the concerns Americans had about peacetime mutual security agreements, as expressed by members of the Foreign Relations Committee;

3. identify the arguments used in defense of such alliances; and

4. understand how consensus is reached on important national issues.

Suggestions for Teaching the Lesson

Opening the Lesson

o   Begin by asking the students to recall earlier discussions of America's entry into World War I and World War II. Remind them of the isolationist impulse in the United States, the fears of "entangling alliances," and the desire to remain outside of European wars, which delayed America's entry into both global conflicts. Ask: What suspicions of the United States would these actions have created in the minds of Europeans? Ask: How did the start of the Cold War raise these suspicions once again in both the United States and in Europe?

(c) *American History and National Security.* Mershon Center, The Ohio State University

o Raise an open-ended question about how policy-makers might go about changing American attitudes on issues where there has been longstanding hostility and suspicion. Define the term "consensus" (reaching a collective agreement on an issue) and ask for ways consensus might be reached: perception of a common threat; presenting information on an issue; finding prominent sponsors for one's side; patient answering of questions from those with concerns; construction of a logical alternative to older policies, etc.

Developing the Lesson

o Have the students read the introduction in the Handout. Remind them of the larger setting, drawing from the Cold War chapter in their textbook: the U.S.-Soviet break after World War II; the Republican majorities in Congress from 1947-1948 during the Democratic Truman Administration; the "Iron Curtain" across Europe; the rebuilding of Western Europe; containment; etc.

o Explain to the students that not all business of government is conducted in public, that much of it goes on in secret. Explain that the document they will read was a secret, closed-door session of the Senate Foreign Relations Committee, which was conducted in 1948, but was not released to the public until 1973. Explain that they will be reading excerpts from a much longer transcript, but that these excerpts present a sampling of the questions raised and the answers given. Have the students read the document as presented in the Handout.

Concluding the Lesson

o Have the students answer the review questions, and then move on to the interpretation questions. The last question--"How would you describe Senator Vandenberg's style of reaching a consensus?"--represents a summary of the lesson and the previous questions. Discuss with them the importance of achieving consensus, and ask if they can suggest types of national security issues where consensus was especially difficult--or impossible--to reach (e.g., American involvement in Vietnam; the nuclear freeze movement; the SALT II treaty; etc.).

o Bring the students into a discussion of the arguments for and against bipartisanship in foreign affairs. What might we sacrifice as a democracy (and a three-branch government with competing parties) to agree that politics stops at the water's edge?

Suggestions for Additional Reading

Vandenberg, Arthur H. Jr., ed. Chapter 31, "The Vandenberg Resolution." *The Private Papers of Senator Vandenberg* Boston: 1952.

Students wishing to pursue this issue may find this chapter useful.

Vandenberg, Arthur H. Jr. *The Vandenberg Resolution and the North Atlantic Treaty, Executive Session Hearings of the Committee on Foreign Relations, Historical Series.* Washington: 1973.

This volume can be found in the government documents section of most larger libraries, and is also available in a reprint by Garland Press, New York, 1979.

Answers to Reviewing the Facts

1. Because of historic opposition to "entangling alliances," dating back to George Washington's farewell address and the terminating of the Alliance with France.

2. Because of Western European concerns that the United States would not come to its aid in case of a Soviet invasion.

3. As part of the collective self-defense provisions of article 51.

4. Because they were afraid such agreements would drag the United States into war against its wishes.

5. By using his resolution to calm fears, build a consensus, and demonstrate that the Senate would vote to ratify a mutual security treaty.

Answers to Interpreting the Document

6. By meeting for 3 to 4 weeks to draft the resolution as a starting point for committee discussion.

7. By answering other senators' questions, sometimes separately and sometimes together, to ease their concerns.

8. That they were trying to avoid arbitrary or automatic commitments; that the United States' involvement in such mutual security agreements would only be to promote its own national security interests; that the arrangements could be done under article 51 of the U.N. charter, "which is outside the [Soviet] veto."

9. That any mutual security pact would be a treaty, requiring Senate approval, and not an executive agreement.

10. That the United States did not necessarily have to become a member of any regional collective security pact, and that membership in such a pact would not automatically involve the United States in warfare.

11. By assuring him there would be no "open-ended obligations" that would involve the United States unless it were in the interests of U.S. national security, and that the United States would maintain its own right of "self-determination."

12. He was concerned that the House would feel that the Senate was trying to exclude it and "assume a prerogative."

13. By assuring Smith that he was willing to have the House join in the resolution.

14. By pointing out that the United Nations was referred to in an earlier part of the resolution.

15. He wanted as many of the members as possible to be present to hear individual members' concerns and questions and the answers they received.

16. Patient answering of individual questions until all concerns had been satisfied, assuring members that the resolution and the mutual security agreements would be in the national interest, and assuring them that the United States would not lose its independence of action by joining such collective security pacts.

American History - 26   Handout

The Vandenberg Resolution and NATO

Introduction

Recalling George Washington's words in his Farewell Address, Americans had long avoided any "entangling alliances." After the Treaty of Alliance with France was terminated in 1800, a century and a half would pass before the United States entered into another peacetime military alliance: NATO. (In 1947, the United States signed the Rio Pact with Latin American nations, but this was generally accepted as an extension of the Monroe Doctrine.)

The Truman Administration became convinced that a mutual security agreement with Western Europe was essential to American national security. The Soviet Union was putting pressure on West Berlin and the Western European nations needed assurances that the United States would stand with them in case of a Soviet invasion. The United Nations was not answering the problem either since Soviet vetoes were blocking Security Council decisions.

Article 51 of the United Nations Charter permitted nations to use "collective self defense if an armed attack occurs." The Rio Pact had been created under this provision, and Western Europeans wanted a similar military pact. But before such a treaty could be negotiated and signed, both the Truman Administration and the Western allies needed some assurance that the United States Senate would ratify it. Many Senators disapproved of peacetime alliances and feared that they would drag the United States into future wars against its will.

Senator Arthur H. Vandenberg, Republican of Michigan, was chairman of the Senate Foreign Relations Committee during the 80th Congress from 1947 to 1949. A leading isolationist before World War II, Vandenberg had made a dramatic conversion to internationalism and collective security during the war. Now he took the lead in encouraging a mutual security arrangement with Western Europe. In 1948, Vandenberg sponsored a resolution by which the Senate could endorse participation in military alliances. Its passage was far from certain.

Vandenberg needed to calm senatorial fears and build a consensus of support in favor of his resolution. In the following excerpts from an executive session transcript (that is a meeting held in secret, behind closed-doors), Chairman Vandenberg and Undersecretary of State Robert A. Lovett, work to convince other members of the Foreign Relations Committee to support the Vandenberg Resolution:

EXECUTIVE SESSION
Tuesday, May 11, 1948

United States Senate,
Committee on Foreign Relations,
Washington, D.C.

The committee met at 10 a.m. in the committee hearing room, U.S. Capitol, Senator Arthur H. Vandenberg, chairman, presiding.

Present: Chairman Vandenberg and Senators Arthur Capper, Wallace White, Alexander Wiley, H. Alexander Smith, Henry Cabot Lodge, Jr., Tom Connally, Walter George, Elbert Thomas and Carl Hatch.

The Chairman. . . . You are all familiar with the fact that we have a large number of resolutions pending proposing one formula after another for dealing with our United Nations attitude, and you are also familiar with the fact that there is constant

(c) *American History and National Security.* Mershon Center, The Ohio State University

current discussion as to what our security relationships are to be with Western Europe, and it seemed desirable, if possible, to bring both of these subjects to a focus. . . .

In order to attempt to facilitate the work of the committee in that connection I sat with Mr. Lovett off and on during the last 3 or 4 weeks attempting to put a position on paper to which we at least could subscribe as a starter in the direction of committee consideration. . . .

In connection with Defense for Western Europe, we were seeking most emphatically to avoid any arbitrary or automatic commitments, and to largely proceed on the same theory, that upon which we built the European recovery program [the Marshall Plan]. Namely, that anything contemplated by us should be at our option as a result of the activities of these beneficiary countries in Europe which might integrate their own security efforts in a fashion which would invite some sort of cooperation on our part in our own interest. . . .

All we have really done . . . is to remind ourselves and the world that there is a means of using the United Nations Charter [Article 51] . . . [as] a means of immediately proceeding to integrate international security in those areas which involve our national security, and having emphasized the possibility of this character, we are leaving it to others to initiate any such movements if they desire, and we are simply saying that we are prepared to consider associating ourselves with such efforts if we find that our national security is enhanced thereby.

Secretary Lovett. That is absolutely correct, Mr. Chairman, and . . . any pacts discussed within the terms of this formal proposal would, of course, require congressional action [ratification]. . . .

Senator Wiley. There is no intention of bypassing, then, the constitutional provision or enlarging the scope of the executive agreements [agreements reached with other nations by the president which do not require congressional approval].

Secretary Lovett. There is none whatsoever, Senator Wiley. . . .

Senator Connally. . . . You say, "Association of the United States with such regional and other collective arrangements." That does not necessarily imply that we are to become members of it.

Secretary Lovett. No, sir.

Senator Conally. But that we are sympathetic onlookers and we reserve the right to support them if we decide to do so at the moment.

Secretary Lovett. It would also permit, if it was in the national interest and supported our national security aims, for this country, together with others, for example, to join in a collective arrangement by, we will say, mutual agreement. In other words, or to take an extravagant case, it would not be impossible for the associates of the Rio Treaty to find themselves in a situation sometime in the future where they would wish to make a common cause with, we will say, a Western European region.

Senator Connally. They have an escape clause, of course, in the Rio Treaty.

What I am getting at is, I don't think we ought to go this far . . . to the extent that we become a member of the regional association, that we would have to go in whether we wanted to or not if the other nations so voted.

Secretary Lovett. That is clear, Senator Connally. Our position has been throughout that we would take no engagement which automatically involved the entrance of this country into war or into the giving of assistance. Second, that we would not undertake obligations on the occurrence of a series of circumstances except as we determined whether or not those circumstances constituted a threat to our national security.

Senator Connally. Otherwise we know how anxious they are to put us in the front ranks. A lot of little weak countries might, if we did not have those provisions, vote, "Yes, we are going to war," and if we were to be drawn in as a result of that action we would have the bag to hold.

Senator Lovett. Senator Connally . . . in this approach we most certainly would not leave an open-ended obligation out which anyone could grasp as they walked by. Nor would we accept the responsibility for engaging in any form of assistance, whether it be supplied or otherwise except as we might determine that it would be in the interest of our national security.

The Chairman. May I interrupt, Senator Connally, to say that . . . I have persistently and relentlessly stood on the precise proposition you are talking about, that there can be no open-ended obligation of any sort whatsoever in respect to military assistance to Western Europe; that we must maintain our right of self-determination even as we grant it to others. . . .

Senator Smith. Why [does the resolution] say that "the Senate reaffirms"?

The Chairman. Because it is written on the theory that this is under the advice section of the Constitution. [Article 2, section 2]

Senator Smith. The House [of Representatives] will take that up and say we are trying to assume a prerogative [an exclusive right].

The Chairman. If the House is willing to join in this resolution we will be glad to have them do so. . . .

Senator Thomas. I would like to ask a question . . . Would it be desirable to add, "and in accordance with the [United Nations] Covenant," so that we are not in any sense trying to work outside the United Nations scheme?

Secretary Lovett. We say in the early part of this the equivalent, I think: ". . . to achieve international peace and security through the United Nations, and that the President be advised of the sense of the Senate that this Government should particularly pursue the following objectives within the United Nations Charter". . . .

The Chairman. . . . Suppose we call this off for today and meet at 10 o'clock tomorrow morning. . . . unless you prefer to continue.

Senator Lodge. I have a number of questions.

The Chairman. I would . . . rather have more of the committee here when you ask them, because, for any questions that anybody has, I want the full committee to have the benefit of them. . . . [Whereupon a recess was taken, to reconvene at 10: a.m. of the following day, Wednesday, May 12, 1948.]

After several more meetings, the Foreign Relations Committee voted unanimously in favor of the Vandenberg Resolution. On June 11, 1948, the Senate voted 64 to 6 in support of the resolution, far more than the two-thirds majority needed to pass a treaty. The Truman Administration immediately set to work creating the North Atlantic Treaty Organization (NATO).

Reviewing the Facts and Main Ideas

1. Why were Americans hesitant about entering military alliances?

2. Why did the Truman Administration feel it was necessary to enter into a peacetime mutual security pact?

3. How would such a pact be consistent with membership in the United Nations?

4. Why were many Senators skeptical of such a pact?

5. How did Senator Vandenberg hope to aid the formation of a mutual security arrangement with Western Europe?

Interpreting the Primary Document

6. How did Senator Vandenberg collaborate with Secretary Lovett before the Committee met?

7. How did Vandenberg and Lovett work together during the hearing?

8. What points did Senator Vandenberg want to assure members about in his opening statement?

9. What constitutional issues concerned Senator Wiley?

10. What issue troubled Senator Connally?

11. How did Secretary Lovett and Senator Vandenberg try to assure Senator Conally?

12. Why was Senator Smith concerned about the House of Representatives?

13. How did Senator Vandenberg answer Smith's concerns?

14. How was Secretary Lovett able to satisfy Senator Thomas' difficulty with the resolution?

15. Why did Senator Vandenberg recess the hearing?

16. How would you describe Senator Vandenberg's style of reaching a consensus?

American History - 27   Lesson Plan and Notes for Teachers

A Network of Alliances

by Donald A. Ritchie

Preview of Main Points

This lesson describes the network of alliances into which the United States entered in the decade after World War II, aimed at containing Communist expansion. Students use a map to study this network graphically. The map exercise is then followed by a discussion of the strengths and weaknesses of the alliance system.

Connection to Textbooks

This lesson corresponds to standard textbook chapters on Truman, Eisenhower and the Cold War. NATO and SEATO are mentioned in all books, and some also deal with ANZUS and CENTO. This lesson is designed to give the students a more visual image of the strategies of the Truman and Eisenhower Administrations.

Objectives

Students are expected to:

1. understand the basic motivations behind America's network of alliances in the post-World War II era;

2. locate and identify those alliances on the map; and

3. interpret the strengths and weaknesses of the alliance system.

Suggestions for Teaching the Lesson

Opening the Lesson

o   Have the students open to the map in the Handout. Have them identify and then shade in the Soviet Union. Then ask them to name, locate and shade in the Eastern European satellite nations (East Germany, Poland, Czechoslovakia, Hungary, Rumania, Bulgaria, Albania and Yugoslavia--although the latter two nations maintain a more independent stance than the others). With the exception of Yugoslavia and Albania, these nations were occupied by Soviet troops immediately after World War II. Have the students similarly shade in China, where Chinese Communist forces took power in 1949. Have the students draw upon their reading of the Cold War chapter in their textbooks to discuss Western fears of Soviet expansion in the period after World War II. Make sure that they recall correctly and understand the strategy of containment. Ask them to speculate, again looking at the map, which areas of the world American strategists might be most concerned about potential aggression by the Soviet Union and its allies.

Developing the Lesson

o   Have the students read the introduction to the lesson in the Handout. Be sure they understand the material covered in the introduction and the instructions for working on the map.

(c) *American History and National Security*. Mershon Center, The Ohio State University

Then have them locate the various networks of alliance as instructed. Have the students answer the questions following the map, and review their answers in class:

1. NATO and CENTO

2. SEATO and ANZUS

3. United States, Great Britain, France, Turkey, Pakistan, Australia and New Zealand

4. United States and Great Britain (3 each)

5. CENTO

6. Latin America (although most nations there were part of the Rio Pact), Africa, where many countries were still held as colonies, and much of South Asia

7. Finland, Sweden, Ireland, Switzerland, and Austria

8. In South Asia, where Afghanistan, India, and Burma maintained their neutrality between East and West.

Concluding the Lesson

o So far, the class has been talking about the 1940s and '50s. Ask the students, based on current events, which of the American alliances are still the strongest (NATO and ANZUS, although both have had recent disagreements with the U.S.), and which are the weakest, or no longer in existence (CENTO's effectiveness was demolished by Arab nationalism after 1958, SEATO's by Communist victories in Vietnam, Cambodia and Laos). Why did so much of the network of alliances prove illusory?

o Point out that the strongest alliances were with countries that were economically and militarily strongest. Alliances with weaker nations were not equal partnerships, but made the weaker nations clients of the stronger nations. The alliance system also caused the United States to align itself with autocratic and undemocratic governments, as in Iran and South Korea, a source of potential friction and weakness. In addition, U.S. relations with China changed dramatically following President Nixon's visit in 1972 and eventual normalization of relations between the two nations, an act which put new and different pressure on the Soviet Union.

The network of alliances, therefore, did not work as the policymakers of the Truman and Eisenhower Administrations hoped and expected. American and Soviet tensions have shifted beyond the chain of alliances to other areas such as Latin America, Africa and the Middle East.

Suggestions for Additional Reading

Ambrose, Stephen E. *Eisenhower: The President.* New York: Simon and Schuster, 1984.

Ambrose provides a solidly written account of this topic.

Donovan, Robert. *Conflict and Crisis: The Presidency of Harry S. Truman, 1945-1948.* New York: Norton, 1977, and *Tumultuous Years: The Presidency of Harry S. Truman, 1949-1953.* New York: Norton, 1982.

The rationale of the Truman and Eisenhower Administrations for their network of alliances are explored in these two lively volumes.

TEACHER'S MAP

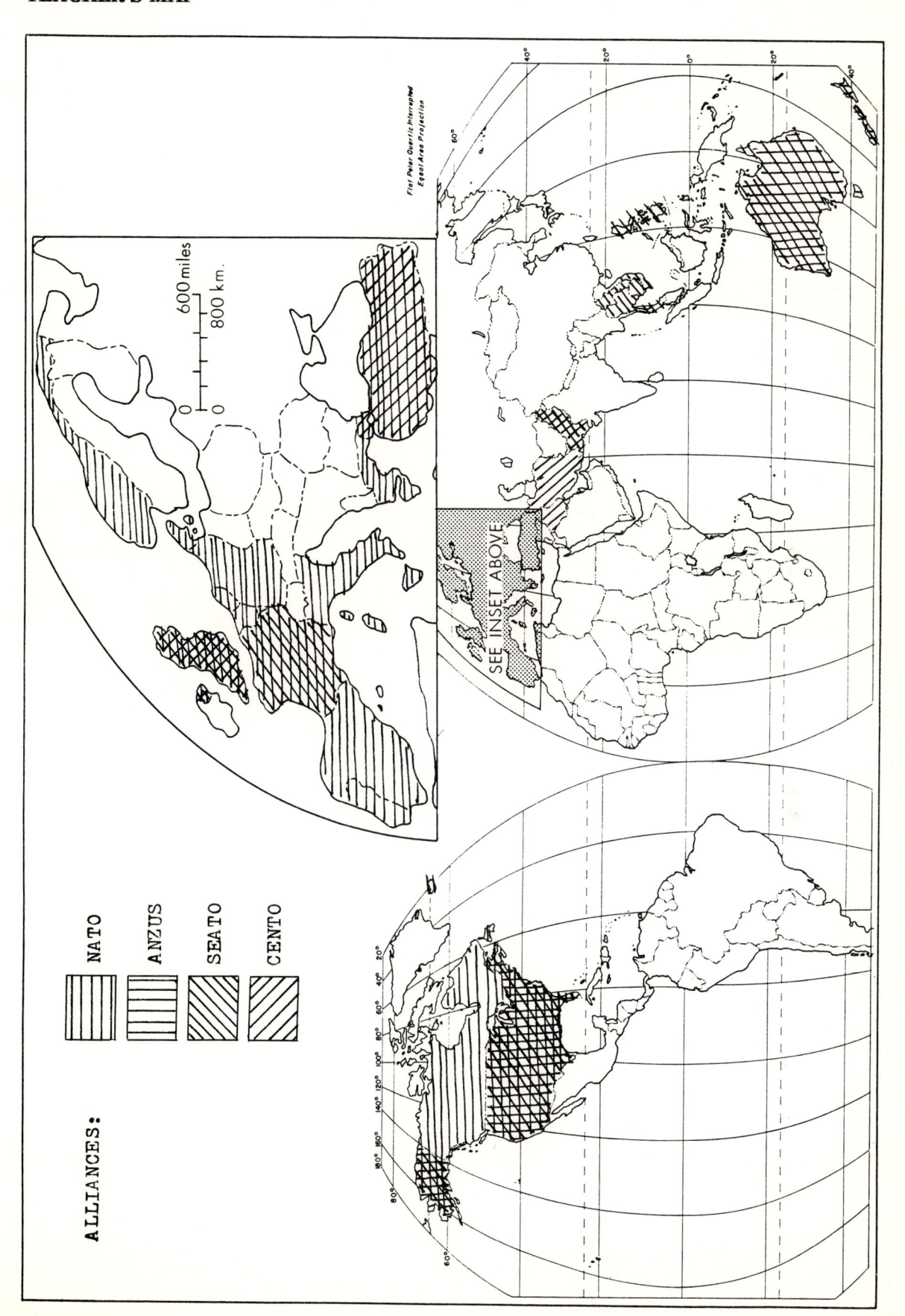

ALLIANCES:
- NATO
- ANZUS
- SEATO
- CENTO

American History - 27

205

A Network of Alliances

After World War II, in reaction to Soviet expansion in Eastern Europe and threats of aggression elsewhere, the United States adopted a policy of "containment." Containment was designed to hold the Soviet Union and its satellites in place and to check their further spread. With bipartisan support, the Truman Administration abandoned the traditional American policy of avoiding "entangling alliances" and began to negotiate collective security agreements, that is, treaties promising mutual support to groups of nations, usually in one region.

The United States reached its first collective security agreement with the nations of Latin America in 1947. This was the Inter-American Treaty of Reciprocal Assistance, better known as the "Rio Pact," for the city where it was signed. Although the Rio Pact set the precedent for other collective security agreements that would follow, it was different in that the Latin American nations were geographically isolated from the Soviet Union. Afterwards, America's collective security agreements were with the nations that ringed Eastern Europe, the Soviet Union, and China.

The most important collective security agreement was the North Atlantic Treaty Organization, which was created in 1949. NATO included most of the Western European nations and the United States. They agreed that "an armed attack against one or more of them in Europe or North America shall be considered an attack against all of them." In 1951, the Truman Administration also signed the ANZUS pact, a collective security agreement with Australia and New Zealand. Bilateral (or two-country) agreements were signed with Japan, the Philippines, South Korea, and Taiwan.

President Eisenhower and Secretary of State John Foster Dulles worked to complete the chain of collective security agreements started by NATO. In 1954 they promoted the negotiations that led to creation of the South East Asia Treaty Organization, or SEATO. And in 1955 the United States gave its blessing to (although it did not join) the "Baghdad Pact," later known as the Central Treaty Organization, CENTO, in the Middle East.

On the following page are the countries that made up NATO, ANZUS, SEATO and CENTO. Locate and identify these nations on the attached map. Identify NATO nations with horizontal lines (= = =), ANZUS nations with vertical lines (| | |), SEATO nations with right slashes (/ / /), and CENTO nations with left slashes (\ \ \ ).

NATO	CENTO	SEATO
Belgium	Iran	Australia
Canada	Pakistan	France
Denmark	Turkey	Great Britain
France**	Great Britain	New Zealand
Iceland	Iraq*	Pakistan
Italy	(*Member of Baghdad Pact, but not of CENTO)	Philippines
Luxembourg		Thailand
Netherlands		United States
Norway	**ANZUS**	Laos*
Portugal	Australia	Cambodia*
United States	New Zealand	South Vietnam*
Greece*	United States	(*Not members, but treaty extended protection to)
Turkey*		
West Germany*		
Spain*		

(*not original members; joined in later years)

(**later withdrew from military membership)

Map Interpretation

1. Which alliances were aimed primarily against the Soviet Union?
2. Which were aimed against China?
3. Which nations belonged to more than one alliance?
4. Which nations belonged to the most alliances?
5. Of which alliances was the United States not a member?
6. What regions of the world were not included in these alliances?
7. Which Western European nations were not members of NATO?
8. Which were the largest gaps in the chain of alliances?

American History - 27 Handout

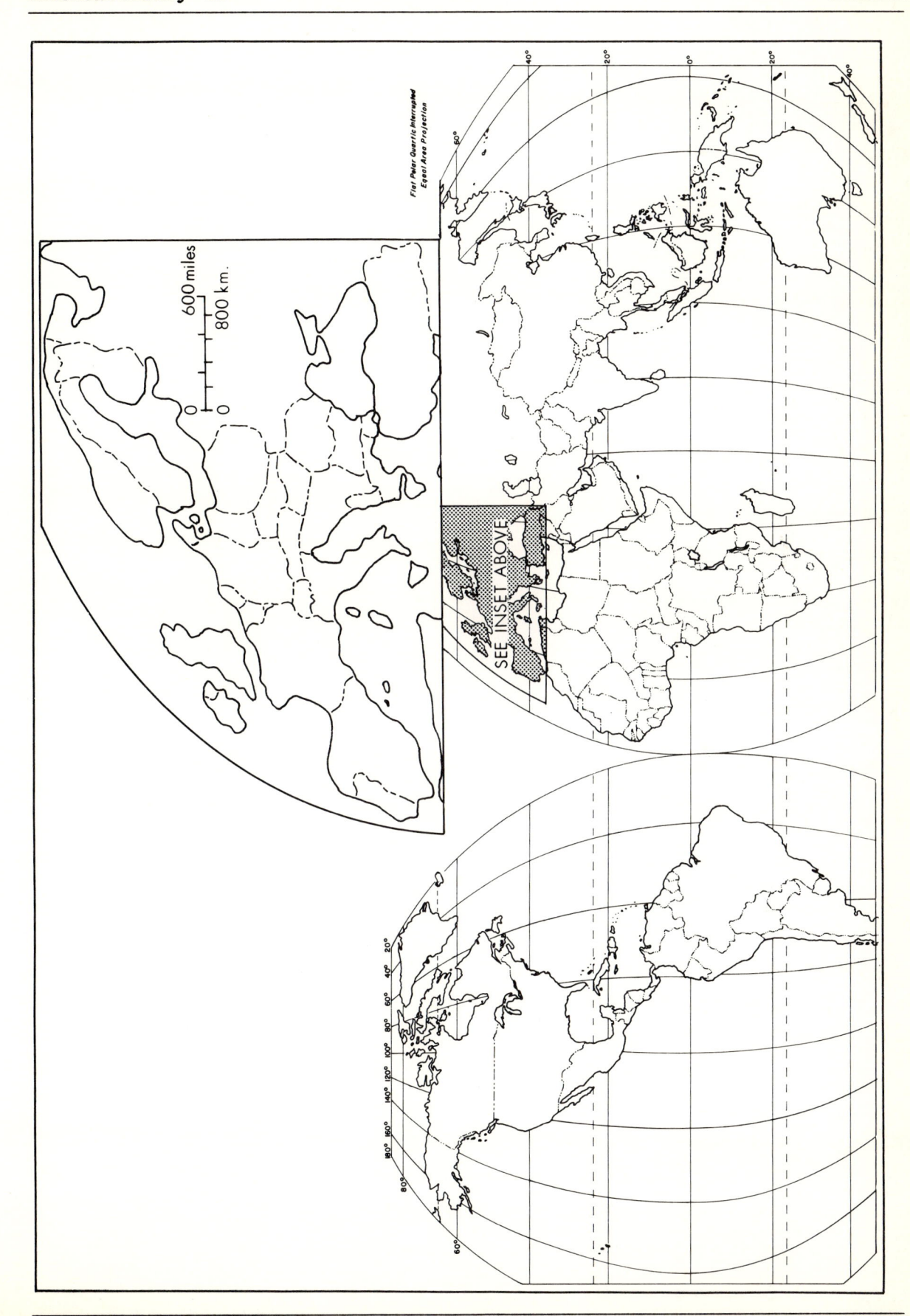

(c) *American History and National Security.* Mershon Center, The Ohio State University 209

American History - 28   Lesson Plan and Notes for Teachers

The Domino Theory

by Donald A. Ritchie

Preview of Main Points

This lesson focuses on how abstractions or slogans, specifically the "domino theory," either illuminate or obscure national security problems. It presents, through a series of quotations from primary sources the different ways in which the domino theory was perceived, applied and evaluated from 1950 to the present. By presenting differing sides, it raises questions whether the theory was a valid one, or whether it limited American options in Vietnam.

Connection to Textbooks

The Vietnam war is a major part of the textbook accounts of the 1960s and '70s. This lesson helps tie together the policies of the Truman, Eisenhower, Kennedy, Johnson and Nixon Administrations, showing the continuities of events that are usually divided into several textbook chapters. It also gives the students the first-person arguments for and against a major element of American policy in Vietnam.

Objectives

Students are expected to:

1. identify and understand the domino theory;

2. recognize changes in the theory as it evolved;

3. distinguish between the different views of the theory; and

4. draw conclusions as to the validity and effectiveness of the domino theory.

Suggestions for Teaching the Lesson

Opening the Lesson

o This lesson can be taught in connection with the Vietnam war in either the 1960s or '70s, and students should have read relevant portions of their textbooks in advance of the discussion.

o Begin by citing some of the more familiar slogans and fighting phrases of American national security history: "Millions for defense but not one cent for tribute;" "Fifty-four forty or fight;" "Remember the Maine," "Neutral in mind as well as in deed;" "America First;" "No More Munichs;" "Who Lost China?" In each of these cases, a few words captured much larger and more complex issues. Ask the students to explain what they think the image of "falling dominoes" suggests. You might perhaps set up a row of dominoes to demonstrate. Why was this simple, graphic phrase so effective in capturing the imagination of the public and the policy-makers?

(c) *American History and National Security.* Mershon Center, The Ohio State University

Developing the Lesson

o   Have the students read the Handout. (You might choose students to "role play" the speakers by reading a selection out loud to the class or students can work individually.) Have the students complete questions 1-10; question 11, an essay question, can be completed either in class or at home.

o   Discuss the selections and answers to the questions with the students. Point out the different perceptions of which country poses the chief threat: the Soviet Union (Dulles) or China (the Truman Administration, Kennedy, etc.). Note the differences in the extent of the theory to different people, those who confine the domino theory to Indochina, those who expand it to all of Southeast Asia, and President Johnson who cited a global threat. Note how each President considered that he was carrying out an inherited pledge, and how each accepted the domino theory.

o   Contrasts can be made between Schlesinger's view that whether or not the domino theory was valid in 1954, it had become valid by the 1960s because other nations had staked their futures on America's ability to live up to its commitments, and Nixon and Kissinger's views that the domino theory meant most to the domino nations, to Clark Clifford's observations that other Asian leaders did not accept the theory; and to the Post's conclusions on why the dominoes did not fall.

Concluding the Lesson

o   Review the last selection in the Handout on the post-Vietnam period to be sure the students understand it. The Reagan Administration official cited notes the strong nationalist differences between the nations of Southeast Asia that the domino theory overlooked. The official also sees the Indochina struggle limited to Indochina, without implications for Southeast Asia or the rest of the world. Point out how greatly events had changed, especially with the Sino-Soviet split, American recognition of China, and the strained and even hostile relations between Vietnam and China. Finally, note that ten years after the Vietnam war, other nations of Southeast Asia have become more economically prosperous and politically stable-- with some exceptions--and have grown more self-reliant.

Answers to Handout Questions

1. President Eisenhower.

2. Nos. 1, 2, 3, 4, 5, 6, 8, 10, 11.

3. Nos. 7, 12.

4. John Foster Dulles.

5. China.

6. That the appetite of aggressive nations is never satisfied.

7. The "domino" nations, Japan, Thailand, and other Southeast Asian nations.

8. Schlesinger belived that the other nations of Southeast Asia had staked their futures on the domino theory; Clifford found that the leaders of these nations did not seem to believe in the domino theory.

9. That it would dim the prospects of freedom and national independence in Southeast Asia and encourage China and the Soviet Union to pursue aggressive policies.

10. Recognizing the limits of American military power, they were forced to deal with their own internal security problems, and to become more self-reliant and therefore more self-confident.

11. a. Depending on whether this question is answered in class or as a take-home, in which case, answers would be more extensive and inclusive. The answer should cite the arguments of the Truman and Eisenhower Administration that Communist aggression seemed imminent (following the Chinese Revolution and the Korean war) and needed to be contained. Indochina was the one area where armed conflict was underway, originally involving French forces. Senator Gruening, however warns against allowing the "dead hand of past mistakes" to continue to determine policy. Clark Clifford and the Washington Post both cast doubts on the continued validity of the domino theory and indicate that it masked the real situation. Students might also take the opposite point of view, that the domino theory might not have been valid from the start, but that it gained validity over the passage of time, by citing Schlesinger, Johnson, Nixon and Kissinger.

    b. This question requires more imagination and thought to answer. Essentially, it raises the point that if the domino theory was true, then there seemed no way for the United States to disengage from Vietnam without causing the rest of Southeast Asia to topple. Therefore, it limited American options. John Foster Dulles tried to qualify this in selection #4, and for different reasons Senator Gruening (#7) also opposed the idea that there was no choice involved. Others accepted the inevitability of the domino theory.

Citations for Selections and Suggestions for Additional Reading

1. Pratt, John Clark. *Vietnam Voices: Perspectives on the War Years, 1942-1982*. New York: Viking, 1984, pp. 6-8.

2. cited in *Congressional Record*, March 10, 1964.

3. cited in Ross Gregory, "The Domino Theory," in *Encyclopedia of American Foreign Policy*, Alexander De Conte, ed. New York: Scribner, 1978, vol. I, p. 275.

4. cited in *Congressional Record*, March 10, 1964.

5. *Public Papers of President John F. Kennedy*. Washington, 1964), pp. 657.

6. Schlesinger, Arthur Jr., *A Thousand Days: John F. Kennedy in the White House*. Boston: Houghton Mifflin, 1965, pp. 537-8.

7. cited in *Congressional Record*, March 10, 1964.

8. Pratt, *Vietnam Voices*, pp. 210-2.

9. Clifford interview in Herbert Y. Schandler, *The Unmaking of a President: Lyndon Johnson and Vietnam*. Princeton: Princeton University Press, 1977, pp. 129-130.

10. Gregory, "The Domino Theory," p. 279.

11. Henry Kissinger, *Years of Upheaval*. Boston: Little, Brown, 1982.

12. Lena H. Sun, "The 'Dominoes' Are Standing Tall," *Washington Post*, April 26, 1985.

Also see Herring, George C. *America's Longest War: The United States and Vietnam, 1950-1975*. New York: Wiley, 1979.

The Domino Theory

Background

Complex national security issues are sometimes reduced to an abstraction or slogan to make them understandable to the public. Policy-makers also use abstractions as a form of verbal shorthand for long and involved policy consideration. Although useful tools, such abstractions and slogans can often obscure changing realities and divert attention from what is actually taking place. Slogans designed to rally public support and unity can themselves become symbols of public disagreement and debate.

The "domino theory" was the slogan most closely identified with American policy toward Vietnam, from the 1950s to the 1970s. President Eisenhower first used the concept at a press conference in 1954, when he warned that a Communist victory in Indochina (the French colony which included Vietnam, Cambodia and Laos) could set off a chain reaction of Communist take-overs throughout Southeast Asia, like one domino knocking down another and causing a whole row to fall. This theory actually had its origins in the Truman Administration, and continued to be cited by Presidents Kennedy, Johnson and Nixon.

As American involvement in Vietnam increased, many critics questioned the validity of the domino theory. They argued that America should determine the best policy toward Vietnam alone, and that Communist control of Vietnam would not inevitably lead to Communist victories elsewhere in Southeast Asia. What follows are selections from both sides of the debate over the domino theory and Vietnam.

Different Expressions of the Domino Theory

1. This secret National Security Council document established the Truman Administration's policy toward Vietnam, on February 27, 1950:

   > It is recognized that the threat of communist aggression against Indochina is only one phase of anticipated communist plans to seize all of Southeast Asia. . . . [Indochina is] the only area adjacent to communist China which contains a large European army, which along with native troops is now in armed conflict with the forces of communist aggression. A decision to contain communist expansion at the border of Indochina must be considered as a part of a wider study to prevent communist aggression into other parts of Southeast Asia. . . . The neighboring countries of Thailand and Burma could be expected to fall under Communist domination if Indochina were controlled by a Communist-dominated government. . . .

2. Secretary of State John Foster Dulles explained his views in a press conference on January 27, 1953, just a few days after the Eisenhower Administration took office:

   > Now the Soviet Russians are making a drive to get Japan, not only through what they are doing in the northern areas of the islands and in Korea, but also through what they are doing in Indochina. If they could get this peninsula of Indochina, Siam, Thailand, Burma, Malaya, they would have what is called the rice bowl of Asia. That's the area from which the great people of Asia, great countries of Asia, such as Japan and India, get in large measures, their food. And you can see that if the Soviet Union had control of the rice bowl of Asia, that would be another weapon which would tend to expand their control into Japan and into India. . . .

3. President Eisenhower responded to a question at a news conference about why Indochina should not be permitted to fall to the Communists; April 7, 1954:

> First of all, you have the specific value of a locality in the production of materials that the world needs. Then you have the possibility that many human beings pass under a dictatorship that is inimical to the free world. . . .
>
> Finally you have broader considerations that might follow what you would call the "falling domino" principle. You have a row of dominoes set up, you knock over the first one, and what will happen to the last one is the certainty that it will go very quickly. So you have a beginning of a disintegration that would have the most profound influences. . . .

4. The domino theory stuck in the public imagination, but a month later, Secretary of State Dulles tried to qualify the theory. At a news conference on May 11, 1954, he was asked whether a collective security arrangement could succeed in Southeast Asia if any part of that region was lost to the Communists. Dulles responded:

> The situation in that area, as we found it, was that it was subject to the so-called domino theory. You mean that if one went, another would go? We are trying to change it so that would not be the case. That is the whole theory of collective security. . . . What we are trying to do is create a situation in southeast Asia where the domino situation will not apply. And while I see it has been said that I felt that southeast Asia could be secured even without perhaps Vietnam, Laos, and Cambodia, I do not want for a minute to underestimate the importance of those countries nor do I want for a minute to give the impression that we believe that they are going to be lost or that we have given up trying to prevent their being lost. On the contrary, we recognize that they are extremely important and that the problem of saving southeast Asia is far more difficult if they are lost. But I do not want to give the impression, either, that if events that we could not control and which we do not anticipate should lead to their being lost, that we would consider the whole situation hopeless, and we would give up in despair. We do not give up; in despair. Also, we do not give up Vietnam, Laos, or Cambodia. . . .

5. Eisenhower's successor, John Kennedy, both accepted and intensified America's commitment to Vietnam. On September 9, 1963, he was questioned about the domino theory in a televised interview:

> **David Brinkley:** Mr. President, have you had any reason to doubt this so-called 'domino theory,' that if South Vietnam falls, the rest of southeast Asia will go behind it? **The President:** No, I believe it. I believe it. I think that the struggle is close enough. China is so large, looms so high just beyond the frontiers, that if South Viet-Nam went, it would not only give them an improved geographic position for a guerilla assault on Malaya, but would also give the impression that the wave of the future in southeast Asia was China and the Communists. So I believe it. . . .

6. After Kennedy's death in 1963, one of his aides, historian Arthur Schlesinger, Jr., gave this account of the domino theory in his book, *A Thousand Days*:

> Whether we were right in 1961 to make this commitment [to South Vietnam] will long be a matter of interest to historians, but it had ceased by 1961 to be of

interest to policy-makers. Whether we had vital interests in South Vietnam before 1954, the Eisenhower letter [pledging American support to Vietnam] created those interests. Whether we should have drawn the line where we did, once it was drawn we became every succeeding year more imprisoned by it. Whether the domino theory was valid in 1954, it had acquired validity seven years later, after neighboring governments had staked their own security on the ability of the United States to live up to its pledges to Saigon. Kennedy himself . . . who as President used to mutter from time to time about our 'overcommitment' in Southeast Asia, had no choice now but to work within the situation he had inherited. . . .

7. Senator Ernest Gruening of Alaska disagreed that there was no choice. In a speech in the Senate on March 10, 1964, Gruening urged the United States to get out of Vietnam. Later that summer, Gruening was one of only two Senators to vote against the Gulf of Tonkin Resolution:

> The theory has been advanced that the United States has no alternative but to remain in South Vietnam regardless of the course of action followed by the people and the government of South Vietnam. This theory follows the line that if we pulled our support out of South Vietnam now, it would quickly be taken over by the Vietcong who in turn would be controlled by North Vietnam which in turn would be controlled by Red China. The theory then continues that if this happens then Cambodia and Laos would also fall 'like a row of dominoes' to Red China. . . .
>
> Recent actions on the part of Cambodia in seeking its own neutralization cast considerable doubt on this theory. Cambodia, the middle domino, fell out of its own accord. The $300 million we have spent there was totally wasted. . . .
>
> The United States should no longer permit the dead hand of past mistakes to guide the course of our future actions in South Vietnam. . . .

8. President Johnson, who campaigned in 1964 against widening the war in Vietnam, soon after became deeply embroiled in a vastly widened war there. In this speech at Johns Hopkins University, on April 26, 1965, President Johnson explained why the United States was in Vietnam:

> We are there because we have a promise to keep. Since 1954 every American President has offered support to the people of South Vietnam. We have helped to build, and we have helped to defend. Thus, over many years, we have made a national pledge to help South Vietnam defend its independence. And I intend to keep that promise . . . . We are also there to strengthen world order. Around the globe, from Berlin to Thailand, are people whose well-being rests in part of the belief that they can count on us if they are attacked. To leave Vietnam to its fare would shake the confidence of all these people in the value of an American commitment and in the value of America's word. The result would be increased unrest and instability, and even wider war. . . .

9. Clark Clifford supported President Johnson in Vietnam, but as Johnson's Secretary of Defense in 1967-69, he developed doubts about the war and urged its de-escalation. In this interview, given in the 1970s, he told about the beginning of his doubts:

I supported President Johnson on Vietnam. I believe in our policy. I accepted the original domino theory--that is a simple way to describe it--and felt we had to oppose [Communist aggression in Vietnam]. [Then in the summer of 1967, Clifford visited Asian leaders at President Johnson's request, to ask them to increase their troops in Vietnam.] I came back with doubts. It bothered me that, as I discussed the domino theory, I found a unanimous attitude on the part of the leaders in the countries we visited that they just didn't accept it. This created doubts, but these doubts were not sufficient to change my mind [at the time]. . . .

10. President Nixon, who succeeded Johnson, sought new ways to solve American problems in Asia, both by opening communications with the People's Republic of China and by "Vietnamization" of the war, but he still defended the domino theory, in these remarks in 1970:

Now I know there are those who say the domino theory is obsolete. They haven't talked to the dominoes. They should talk to the Thais, to the Indonesians, to the Singaporans, to the Japanese, and the rest, and if the United States leaves Vietnam in a way that we are humiliated or defeated . . . this will be immensely discouraging to the 300 million people from Japan clear around to Thailand in free Asia; and even more important, it will be ominously encouraging to the leaders of Communist China and the Soviet Union who are supporting the North Vietnamese. . . .

11. Nixon's National Security Advisor and Secretary of State, Henry Kissinger, agreed that the original theories had been correct, despite the frustrations of the war in Vietnam:

The rulers of Hanoi were anything but the benign nationalists so often portrayed by gullible sympathizers: they were cold, brutal revolutionaries determined to dominate all of Indochina. The impact of a North Vietnamese victory on the prospects of freedom and national independence in Southeast Asia was certain to be grave, especially on governments much less firmly established than was the case a decade later: the much-maligned domino theory--shared by **all** the Non-Communist governments in the area--turned out to be correct. . . .

12. Ten years after Communist take-overs in South Vietnam, Cambodia, and Laos, the rest of the "dominoes" in Southeast Asia had not only failed to fall to communism, but were more economically strong and politically stable than ever before. The United States had established relations with China, and Vietnam was at odds with China. *The Washington Post* made this report on April 26, 1985:

The Vietnamese revolution was confined to Indochina, said one high level [Reagan] administration official. 'There is little evidence that Vietnam was supporting insurgents outside Indochina.'

The domino theory was not credible, in this view, because it was based on an idea of an irreversible communist expansion. 'Nations with strong nationalistic backgrounds don't commit suicide,' the official said.

As for Laos and Cambodia, he said, 'Laos was never a country and Cambodia was part of the Indochina war.' The Vietnamese long have regarded Indochina, including Laos and Cambodia, as their bailiwick. . . .

There is recognition, however, that the wartime failure of U.S. policy in Indochina dramatically demonstrated the limitations of American military power in local Asian conflicts and, according to Tommy Koh, Singapore's ambassador to Washington, galvanized the economics of the noncommunist countries. It also forced them to deal with their internal security problems, resulting in greater Asian self-reliance and self-confidence. . . .

Questions Concerning the Different Views of the Domino Theory

From your reading of the above selections, you have probably noticed that the domino theory did not mean exactly the same thing to all people who cited it, and that they disagreed over if and when it was ever valid. As a means of reviewing and understanding these selections, answer the following questions:

1. Who first stated the domino theory?

2. Which selections supported the domino theory?

3. Which selections cast doubt on the theory?

4. Which Secretary of State considered the Soviet Union as a grave threat to the "rice bowl" of Indochina?

5. Which nation did John Kennedy see as the greatest threat to Southeast Asia?

6. What did Lyndon Johnson think was the central lesson of our time?

7. Who did President Nixon cite as believers in the domino theory?

8. How did Clark Clifford's observations about the domino theory differ from Arthur Schlesinger's?

9. What effects of an American defeat in Vietnam did President Nixon and Henry Kissinger fear?

10. In what ways did Singapore's ambassador see the situation in Indochina strengthening other nations of Southeast Asia?

11. Looking back on all these selections, write an essay on one of the following questions, citing specific selections in your answer. Do not hesitate to give your own opinions.

    a. Was the domino theory a case of a once-sound argument that lost its validity over a period of time?

    b. Did the domino theory limit America's options in Vietnam?

American History - 29   Lesson Plan and Notes for Teachers

Ex Comm and the Cuban Missile Crisis

by Donald A. Ritchie

Preview of Main Points

This lesson follows the decision making process that led to a peaceful settlement of the Cuban Missile Crisis, averting the greatest threat of nuclear war the U.S. had ever faced. It outlines the way President Kennedy used Ex Comm (Executive Committee of the National Security Council), a group of government officials, and former officials, who met for a free and open discussion of the problem and the options, and how Ex Comm helped the President to decide in favor of a blockade of Cuba.

Connection to Textbooks

All textbooks cover the Cuban Missile Crisis in their accounts of the Kennedy Administration, but few have the space to explain how decisions were made during this momentous event. This lesson can be used in connection with the Cold War, the 1960s, or to contrast with the ways in which other presidents made major decisions affecting national security policy.

Objectives

Students are expected to:

1. identify the nature of the Cuban Missile Crisis;

2. identify and explain the various options facing the President;

3. analyze the way in which the President made his decision; and

4. evaluate the decision making process in this crisis.

Suggestions for Teaching the Lesson

Opening the Lesson

o Present the class with the following scenario. You are President of the United States. The Director of the CIA brings word that an aggressive nation has been placing offensive weapons in a small country near your borders. These offensive weapons are not yet in place or operational, but within a matter of weeks they may be. The purpose of the aggressive nation is not clear, but it could plan to use these weapons as a threat to the United States, or as some form of blackmail: to make the United States back down somewhere else in the globe. So far, the existence of these weapons is a secret. The aggressive nation denies that they exist. What should you do?

o Ask the students to respond, and note their suggested actions on the blackboard. After gathering all the possible ways they might respond, ask them: How, as President, would you reach your decision on what to do? Discuss with them the ways in which they think a President does, or should make decisions.

o Finally, point out that the above scenario is not far-fetched, but actually faced President Kennedy in October 1962.

(c) *American History and National Security*. Mershon Center, The Ohio State University

Developing the Lesson

o Have the students read the Handout. Focus their attention not only on the options, but on the ways they were debated, and the way the decision was reached.

o Have the students complete the Decision Tree and respond to the questions at the end of the Handout.

Concluding the Lesson

o Compare the students' initial suggestions for action to the actual events of the Cuban Missile Crisis. Ask them to note the differences, both in the actions they would have taken and the ways they would have made their decisions. Ask them to speculate on the consequences of their actions.

o Remind the students that even after Ex Comm presented the options and the President made his decision, diplomatic negotiations had to take place with the Soviet Union, and that the crisis was settled when **both** sides could agree to terms.

Suggestions for Additional Reading

Kennedy, Robert F. *Thirteen Days: A Memoir of the Cuban Missile Crisis*. New York: W.W. Norton Co., 1969.

The book is written in a simple and direct manner that most students should be able to grasp, and it expands upon the issues raised in the lesson. Kennedy's book served as the basis for this lesson.

Neustadt, Richard E. and May, Ernesst R. *Thinking in Time: The Use of History for Decision Making*. New York: The Free Press, 1986.

See also Neustadt and May for a study on decision making.

Answers to Questions

1. Soviet offensive missiles were being placed in Cuba.
2. Air strikes to destroy the missile bases, or a blockade to stop new missiles and equipment from being delivered to Cuba.
3. Neither option could guarantee the destruction or removal of missiles already in Cuba; air strikes might require a full-scale military invasion of Cuba; the Soviet Union might respond militarily; Soviet ships might challenge a blockade.
4. To blockade Cuba.
5. Decision left to the class; answers will vary.
6. A variety of government officials were invited to express their candid opinions, criticize others' suggestions, and raise all possible objections to proposals.
7. Members of Ex Comm settled on two likely options, prepared full reports, drafts of the President's speech, and responses to situations that might follow. Members also warned the President what the consequences might be of either decision.
8. Diplomatic negotiations with the Soviets.
9. When the President chose to respond to an earlier proposal by the Soviet Union, in which they removed their missiles in return for a pledge by the U.S. not to invade Cuba, **and** when the Soviets accepted that agreement and turned their ships around.

American History - 29   Handout

Ex Comm and the Cuban Missile Crisis

Background to the Crisis

In October 1962, the world came very close to nuclear war when the United States discovered Soviet offensive missile bases on Cuba and demanded they be dismantled. For thirteen days, between October 16 and 29, tensions mounted until the Soviets agreed to remove the missiles and the crisis ended peacefully. During those tense days, President Kennedy made use of a special group of advisors, known as Ex Comm (Executive Committee of the National Security Council) to present, explore and debate all of the possible options open to the President.

Ex Comm included the Secretaries of State and Defense and their top staff, the director of the CIA, the National Security Advisor, the chairman of the Joint Chiefs of Staff, and on some occasions the Vice President, the Ambassador to the United Nations, and Congressional leaders. This group met almost continuously during the crisis and was encouraged by the President to speak out openly and to argue forcefully for their differing proposals and opinions. From their deliberations, the President was able to grasp fully all of the alternative courses of action open to him, and their possible risks.

This lesson will examine some of the arguments made in the Ex Comm, and how the President used this mechanism to help solve the gravest challenge of his administration.

The Cuban Missile Crisis

On October 16, CIA officials presented the President and Ex Comm with high-altitude photographs taken by U-2 planes flying over Cuba. These photographs demonstrated conclusively that the Soviets were placing missiles in Cuba, capable of firing atomic weapons at the United States. It seemed clear that the Soviets had lied when they promised not to place such missiles in Cuba.

Alternatives Presented to the President

1. A small minority of Ex Comm felt that the missiles did not change America's defense capacity and that the U.S. should take no action against them.

2. Most members initially favored a surprise air strike to destroy the missile bases before they could launch missiles against the United States.

3. Defense Secretary Robert McNamara disagreed that air strikes could knock out all of the bases, and believed that a full-scale military invasion would be necessary to complete the job. Instead, he recommended that the U.S. conduct a naval blockade of Cuba to prevent further missiles and equipment from reaching the island.

Debate Over the Alternatives

Those who wanted an air strike responded that a blockade would neither stop work on the bases or remove the missiles already in Cuba. Members of the Joint Chiefs of Staff unanimously favored immediate military action.

President Kennedy was skeptical of military views that the Soviets would not respond to a military attack on Cuba. He believed that if the Soviets did not act in Cuba, they would retaliate by blockading Berlin.

(c) *American History and National Security.* Mershon Center, The Ohio State University

Former Secretary of State Dean Acheson argued that the President must protect the security of the United States by destroying the missiles in Cuba.

Attorney General Robert Kennedy, the President's brother, supported the idea of a blockade. He argued that America's history and traditions ran against launching a surprise attack on a smaller nation. Such an action would weaken America's moral position at home and abroad.

Ex Comm was now deeply divided between those favoring an air strike and those favoring a blockade. Feeling the pressure that a wrong decision could trigger a nuclear war and destroy all humanity, the members continued their deliberation. They divided into groups to write out their recommendations to the President, and draft his speech to the nation. They were also asked to anticipate all conceivable consequences that might result from the action and recommend how to deal with them. After writing their papers, the groups exchanged and criticized each other's work.

Those advocating a blockade had outlined the legal reasons for a blockade, called for meetings of the Organization of American States and the United Nations to deal with the crisis, and outlined procedures for stopping Soviet ships and responding to any military force that might be used. Those advocating air strikes listed their targets, outlined the way they would defend their actions to the world, and suggested a letter to the Soviet leadership warning against any retaliation against Berlin or any other trouble spot in the world.

The decision was now up to the President.

President Kennedy's Decision

On Saturday, October 20, both sides made their presentations to President Kennedy. After considerable discussion, the President decided in favor of a blockade.

The President was convinced of the wisdom of his decision after further military advice that the Air Force could not be certain of destroying all missile sites in Cuba with a surprise attack. If a blockade would not remove the missiles, neither would an air attack.

On Monday, the President met with Congressional leaders. They also favored air strikes, but the President remained committed to a blockade, and announced his decision on national television that evening.

Diplomatic negotiations continued during the tense days as the blockade went into effect. The world watched as Soviet ships steamed toward the American blockade around Cuba, wondering if they would turn back, or if there would be a confrontation.

On October 26, Soviet Premier Khrushchev sent President Kennedy a long, rambling, secret letter in which he warned of the danger of nuclear war. "What good would a war do you?" Khrushchev wrote. "You threaten us with war. But you well know that the very least you would get in response would be what you had given us; you would suffer the same consequences." Then Khrushchev made an offer: "I propose: we, for our part, will declare that our ships bound for Cuba are not carrying any armaments [missiles]. You will declare that the United States will not invade Cuba with its troops and will not support any other forces which might intend to invade Cuba. Then the necessity for the presence of our military specialists in Cuba will be obviated [made unnecessary]." Then, the next day, Khrushchev sent a second, more formal letter with an added demand: that the United States must also remove its missiles from Turkey. President Kennedy felt that to accept this second demand would weaken NATO. He decided to accept Khrushchev's first offer and to ignore the Turkish missile demand.

The gamble worked. At the last moment, the director of the CIA brought word that Soviet ships had stopped dead in the water. They would not confront the American blockade. The Soviet Union accepted the American pledge against invading Cuba, and turned their ships around. The missile bases were dismantled and the crisis ended. As Robert Kennedy wrote, "For a moment the world had stood still, and now it was going around again."

Evaluating Decision Making During the Cuban Missile Crisis

Use the Decision Tree to help you answer the following questions:

1. What was the occasion for the decision facing President Kennedy?

2. What alternatives did Ex Comm recommend?

3. What were negative consequences of these alternatives?

4. Which alternative did President Kennedy choose?

5. What is your judgment of President Kennedy's decision? Why?

Now, consider the ways in which decisions were reached during the Cuban Missile Crisis:

6. In what ways did Ex Comm permit full discussion of the problem and the options to solve it?

7. How did Ex Comm help the President reach his decision?

8. What steps were necessary to solve the crisis **after** the President had reached his decision?

9. How was the Cuban Missile Crisis finally solved?

DECISION TREE

GOALS/VALUES

CONSEQUENCES

GOOD

BAD

ALTERNATIVES

OCCASION FOR DECISION

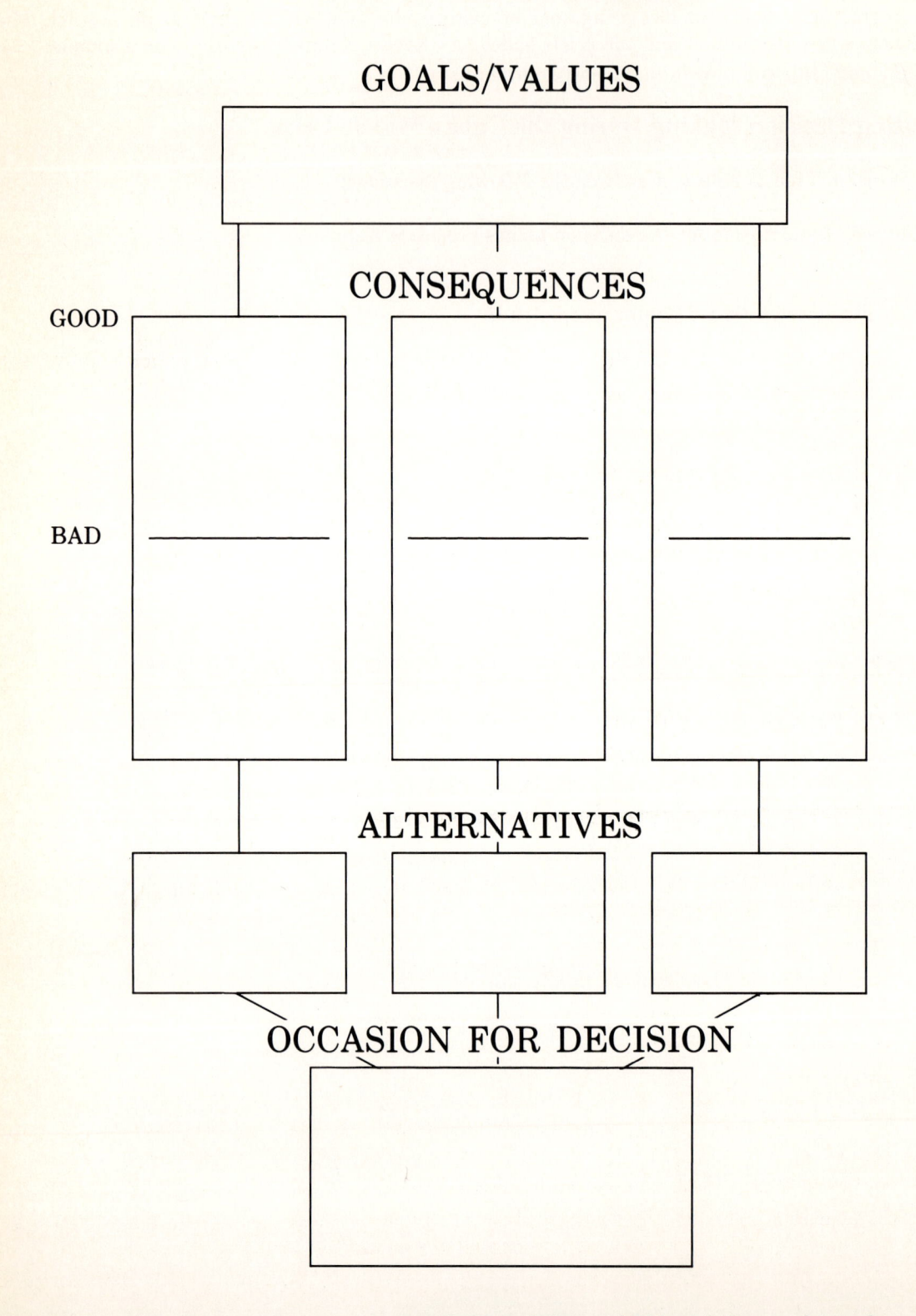

The decision-tree device was developed by Roger LaRaus and Richard C. Remy and is used with their permission.

American History - 30   Lesson Plan and Notes for Teachers

Why Was the SALT II Treaty Never Ratified?

by Donald A. Ritchie

Preview of Main Points

The purpose of this lesson is to increase students' awareness of the chronology of Salt II and to demonstrate the effect of the sequence of events, both planned and unexpected, on national security policy.

Connection to Textbooks

This lesson corresponds to textbook chapters on the Carter Administration, and supplements them with greater detail on the events which led to the withdrawal of the SALT II treaty from Senate consideration.

Objectives

Students are expected to:

1. recognize direct and indirect influences on national security policy;

2. understand the development of a political climate that favors or undermines a policy; and

3. demonstrate an awareness of the interconnection of world events and American policies.

Suggestions for Teaching the Lesson

Opening the Lesson

o Open the lesson by explaining that even the most careful plans regarding national security and foreign policy can be upset by unexpected events. Note that the SALT II treaty provides a good example. Inform students that in this lesson they will use a timeline to study events which affected approval of the SALT II treaty.

Developing the Lesson

o Have the students read the introduction to the chronology in the Handout. Then assign them to read through the chronology and answer the questions in the Handout, either individually or in small groups.

Concluding the Lesson

o Poll the students for their responses to the questions.

o Conclude the lesson by asking what events contributed to a spirit of cooperation that led to the signing of SALT II, and what events undermined its ratification.

o Explain that although unratified, the terms of the SALT II treaty were honored by the United States and the Soviet Union until 1986. The effort to seek cooperation in arms control continues.

Suggestions for Additional Reading

Students who wish to investigate these subjects more can be referred to the following readings:

Carter, Jimmy. *Keeping Faith: Memoirs of a President*. New York, 1982, especially the chapter entitled "Shadow Over the Earth: The Nuclear Threat."

Congressional Quarterly. *U.S. Defense Policy*. Washington, 1983.

Garthoff, Raymond. *Detente and Confusion*. Washington, 1985.

Answers to Handout Questions

1. The Soviet invasion of Afghanistan.

2. Those who favored increased defense spending, and who distrusted the Soviet Union; including Alexander Haig, Senator Howard Baker and presidential candidate Ronald Reagan.

3. They feared the treaty would leave the Soviet Union in a stronger military position than the United States, that the United States was not spending enough for defense, and that the treaty could not be easily verified.

4. By arguing that the world would be more dangerous without it; and that the treaty would strengthen the U.S. military position and the cause of world peace.

5. The slow growth of the U.S. military budget in comparison to the larger growth of the Soviet military budget suggested that the Soviets were surpassing the United States militarily.

6. By warning that rejection or amendment of the treaty would mean an end to negotiations.

7. The Iranian revolution, the suspected Soviet brigade in Cuba and the Soviet invasion of Afghanistan unsettled international relations, increased suspicion of the Soviet Union, and made the United States feel more vulnerable.

8. The election of a candidate hostile to SALT II made its ratification all the more unlikely.

9. It created a perception of U.S. weakness and Soviet aggression.

10. Planning and negotiations of the SALT II treaty took years to accomplish. The campaign for its ratification, however, was upset by unanticipated events in Cuba and Afghanistan and by public concerns over America's defenses.

11. Discussion should consider the importance of consensus in foreign policy, versus the danger of delay and inaction on important issues.

Why Was the SALT II Treaty Never Ratified?

On June 18, 1979, President Jimmy Carter met Soviet General Secretary Leonid Brezhnev in Vienna, Austria, to sign the SALT II treaty. SALT stood for Strategic Arms Limitation Talks. SALT I (limiting antiballistic missile systems) had been signed by President Nixon in 1972 and quickly ratified by the Senate. The purpose of SALT II was to limit the numbers of American and Soviet intercontinental missiles, nuclear warheads, missile launchers and heavy bombers.

From July to October 1979, the Senate Foreign Relations Committee held hearings on SALT II, taking testimony from ninety-four witnesses for and against the treaty. On November 9, the committee voted 9 to 6 in its favor (with seven Democrats and two Republicans supporting the treaty, and two Democrats and four Republicans opposing it). Despite the committee's endorsement, the Senate did not ratify SALT II. Instead, in December, President Carter withdrew the treaty from consideration.

Why was SALT II never ratified? Examine the following chronology and consider which events worked for and against the treaty:

1977, January 27, President Carter, a week after his inauguration, announces his desire for an early resumption of the SALT negotiations.

March 30, Soviet leaders reject President Carter's initial SALT II proposals, which called for a freeze on all new weapons, and dramatic reductions in strategic nuclear arsenals.

May 18, NATO agrees to increase defense spending.

June 30, President Carter decides to cancel production of the B-1 bomber.

September 27, President Carter and Soviet Foreign Minister Andrei Gromyko reach agreement on framework for SALT talks.

December 16, SALT II negotiations recess.

1978, February 2, citing increases in Soviet strength, Defense Secretary Harold Brown calls for buildup of U.S. defenses.

February 22, Congress agrees to halt spending for B-1 bomber.

October 22, SALT II talks resume.

December 15, United States gives formal diplomatic recognition to the People's Republic of China.

1979, January 16, the Shah flees Iran, an Islamic Republic is proclaimed.

January 22, President Carter sends "lean" budget to Congress, holding back social spending and limiting defense to a three percent increase.

January 23, President Carter promises not to sign a treaty with the Soviets unless it is verifiable and the United States retains an overwhelming deterrent force.

February 1, the Soviet Union tests a cruise missile, launched from a "Backfire" bomber, which the Soviets wanted exempt from SALT II.

March 1, the Republican National Committee denounces Carter's defense policies as weak.

April 4, although the SALT II treaty is still being negotiated, the Carter Administration launches its campaign to win ratification.

April 16, newspapers report that CIA Director Stansfield Turner had told the Senate that the revolution in Iran had closed U.S. listening posts in Iran, which would hinder U.S. monitoring of Soviet missile tests, and hence verification of Soviet compliance to the SALT treaties.

April 25, President Carter says that "the choice we face is between an imperfect world with SALT II and an imperfect and more dangerous, world without it."

May 16, NATO leaders endorse draft of the SALT II treaty.

June 7, President Carter approves development of the MX missile.

June 15, President Carter and General Secretary Brezhnev open meetings in Vienna. Brezhnev agrees to limit production of the Backfire bomber.

June 18, Carter and Brezhnev sign the SALT II treaty. Carter returns to Washington to address a joint session of Congress where he describes the treaty as being in the self-interest of the United States "--a move that happens to serve the goals both of security and of survival, that strengthens both the military position of the United States and the cause of world peace."

June 19, the Joint Chiefs of Staff agree to support SALT II.

June 25, Soviet Foreign Minister Gromyko warns that Senate rejection or amendment of SALT II would mean "the end of negotiations."

June 26, former NATO commander Alexander Haig urges delay in ratification until the treaty is amended and improved.

June 27, Senate Republican Leader Howard Baker says he could not support SALT II without amendments.

July 31, former Secretary of State Henry Kissinger says SALT II should be ratified only if U.S. defense spending is increased.

August 31, State Department announces that the U.S. had discovered 2,000 to 3,000 Soviet combat troops stationed in Cuba.

September 4, Senator Frank Church, chairman of the Foreign Relations Committee, postpones SALT hearings to deal with reports of a Soviet brigade in Cuba.

September 11, President Carter rejects a five percent defense increase and decides in favor of a three percent increase. Newspapers report that the Soviet Union's military budget was 43 percent higher than the U.S. military budget.

September 16, Moslem rebellion in Afghanistan and turmoil in the government leads to the overthrow of the Afghan President, a Soviet supporter.

October 1, President Carter announces increased surveillance of Cuba and military exercises in Guantanamo Bay naval base.

November 4, Iranians take over U.S. embassy and seize American hostages.

November 9, Senate Foreign Relations Committee approves SALT II by a vote of 9 to 6. Republican Leader Howard Baker votes against it.

December 12, NATO agrees to deploy U.S. nuclear weapons and missiles in Western Europe.

December 13, Congress approves President Carter's defense budget with funds for the MX missile.

December 27, the Soviet Union invades Afghanistan.

1980, **January 3**, President Carter asks the Senate to postpone consideration of SALT II, following Soviet invasion of Afghanistan.

February 20, Carter asks U.S. athletes not to participate in Summer Olympics in Moscow.

April 24, U.S. mission to rescue hostages in Iran fails; Secretary of State Cyrus Vance resigns in protest of the mission.

July 16, Republicans nominate Ronald Reagan, who is publicly critical of the SALT II treaty, calling it "fatally flawed."

August 13, Democrats renominate Jimmy Carter, who supports the treaty.

November 4, Reagan overwhelmingly defeats Carter for the Presidency.

Reviewing and Interpreting Main Ideas and Facts

1. What was the immediate reason for President Carter's request that the Senate postpone action on the SALT II treaty?
2. Who were the leading opponents of the SALT II treaty?
3. What reasons did they have for opposing the treaty?
4. How did the Carter Administration attempt to defend the treaty?
5. In what ways did the issue of defense spending relate to the debate over SALT II?
6. In what way did Soviet Foreign Minister Gromyko attempt to influence Senate ratification of SALT II?
7. How did events outside of the United States and the Soviet Union influence the SALT II debate?
8. What impact did the 1980 election have on SALT II?
9. In what ways did the political climate of the time become unfavorable to the SALT treaty?
10. How would you assess the importance of unexpected events in the shaping of national security policy?
11. President Carter did not believe SALT II could get a two-thirds vote in the Senate (65 votes as compared to 35 opposed). Is ratification by a two-thirds vote a good way to conduct foreign policy?